Linguistic borrowing in bilingual contexts

Studies in Language Companion Series (SLCS)

The SLCS series has been established as a companion series to *Studies in Language*, International Journal, sponsored by the Foundation "Foundations of Language".

Series Editors

Werner Abraham
University of Vienna

Michael Noonan
University of Wisconsin-Milwaukee
USA

Editorial Board

Joan Bybee
University of New Mexico

Ulrike Claudi
University of Cologne

Bernard Comrie
Max Planck Institute For Evolutionary Anthropology, Leipzig

William Croft
University Manchester

Östen Dahl
University of Stockholm

Gerrit Dimmendaal
University of Leiden

Martin Haspelmath
Max Planck Institute For Evolutionary Anthropology, Leipzig

Ekkehard König
Free University of Berlin

Christian Lehmann
University of Erfurt

Robert Longacre
University of Texas, Arlington

Brian MacWhinney
Carnegie-Mellon University

Marianne Mithun
University of California, Santa Barbara

Edith Moravcsik
University of Wisconsin, Milwaukee

Masayoshi Shibatani
Rice University and Kobe University

Russell Tomlin
University of Oregon

† John Verhaar
The Hague

Volume 62
Linguistic borrowing in bilingual contexts
by Fredric W. Field

Linguistic borrowing in bilingual contexts

Fredric W. Field
California State University, Northridge

Foreword by Bernard Comrie
Max Planck Institute for Evolutionary Anthropology

John Benjamins Publishing Company
Amsterdam/Philadelphia

The paper used in this publication meets the minimum requirements of American National Standard for Information Sciences – Permanence of Paper for Printed Library Materials, ANSI z39.48-1984.

Library of Congress Cataloging-in-Publication Data

Field, Fredric W.
 Linguistic borrowing in bilingual contexts / Fredric W. Field; Foreword by Bernard Comrie.
  p. cm. (Studies in Language Companion Series, ISSN 0165–7763 ; v. 62)
 Includes examples in Nahuatl and Spanish, with additional Nahuatl text in the appendix.
 Includes bibliographical references and indexes.
  1. Language and languages--Foreign elements. 2. Languages in contact. 3. Grammar, Comparative and general--Morphology. 4. Semantics. I. Title. II. Series.

 P324 .F54 2002
 404'.2-dc21   2002074680
 ISBN 90 272 3065 X (Eur.) / 1 58811 285 3 (US) (Hb; alk. paper)

© 2002 – John Benjamins B.V.
No part of this book may be reproduced in any form, by print, photoprint, microfilm, or any other means, without written permission from the publisher.

John Benjamins Publishing Co. · P.O. Box 36224 · 1020 ME Amsterdam · The Netherlands
John Benjamins North America · P.O. Box 27519 · Philadelphia PA 19118-0519 · USA

Table of contents

Foreword   XI

Preface   XIII

List of figures   XVII

List of tables   XIX

CHAPTER 1
Introduction   1
- 1.0.1 Social factors   4
- 1.0.2 Linguistic factors   5
- 1.1 Borrowing as bilingual performance   8
- 1.2 Mixed languages — Language intertwining or extensive borrowing?   11
  - 1.2.1 Defining mixed language   13
  - 1.2.2 From product to process   15
  - 1.2.3 The concept of matrix language   16
  - 1.2.4 The correlation of transfer, substrate, and matrix   18
- 1.3 The plan of this book   22

CHAPTER 2
Morphological structuring and system compatibility   25
- 2.1 Scales, indices, hierarchies, and clines: Continua of forms and meanings   27
  - 2.1.1 The indices of synthesis and fusion   27
  - 2.1.2 The cline of grammaticality   29
  - 2.1.3 The cline of lexicality   32
  - 2.1.4 A scale (or continuum) of morpheme types   33

2.2 Hierarchies of borrowability 34
    2.2.1 Borrowing hierarchies: Lexical items 36
    2.2.2 Borrowing hierarchies: Grammatical items 37
    2.2.3 Summary of hierarchies 37
2.3 The Principle of System Incompatibility 40
    2.3.1 Predictions within general classes 42
    2.3.2 The occurrence of anomalies: Reanalysis 44
    2.3.3 Predictions within subclasses 45
    2.3.4 The relative timing of borrowed elements 46

CHAPTER 3
Form classes and semantic types 49
    3.0.1 The relationship of word class and semantic type 50
    3.0.2 Form–meaning sets and semantic types 52
    3.0.3 Organization of this chapter 53
3.1 Notions of word and word class 53
3.2 Contrasting points on a continuum 57
    3.2.1 Formal characteristics: Grammatical affixes versus content items 57
    3.2.2 Semantic characteristics: Grammatical affixes versus content items 59
    3.2.3 Function words: Formal and semantic characteristics 62
    3.2.4 Function words versus content words 65
    3.2.5 Function words versus inflectional affixes and elements in between 66
    3.2.6 Derivational affixes: Between content and inflection 67
3.3 Semantic types: Groupings of morphemes according to meanings 70
    3.3.1 Semantic types and subtypes of N, V, and Adj 73
    3.3.2 Person 75
    3.3.3 Object 76
    3.3.4 Activity 77
    3.3.5 Space 78
    3.3.6 Time 78
    3.3.7 Quality 79
3.4 Summary and comments 81

CHAPTER 4
The identification of form–meaning sets   83
    4.0.1   The spread and integration of borrowed form–meaning sets   84
    4.0.2   Identifying clusters of properties   86
4.1   Form identification characteristics: The role of salience   88
    4.1.1   Transparency versus opacity   89
    4.1.2   The opacity of fusional affixes   94
    4.1.3   Borrowing continua of forms   98
4.2   Semantic characteristics   100
    4.2.1   Inflectional meanings   102
    4.2.2   Borrowing continua of meanings   105
    4.2.3   Linking form and meaning   111
4.3   Issues of semantic complexity   113
4.4   Summary and general predictions   116

CHAPTER 5
Borrowing patterns in modern Mexicano   123
    5.0.1   Bilingual phenomena   126
    5.0.2   The corpus   128
    5.0.3   Organization of this chapter   130
5.1   Overview of the participants: Mexicano and Spanish   132
    5.1.1   Morphological structuring: The words of each language   134
    5.1.2   The borrowing hierarchy of Mexicano   141
5.2   The role of form–meaning interpretation characteristics (FMICs)   144
    5.2.1   FMICs pertaining to form   146
    5.2.2   FMICs pertaining to meaning   148
5.3   The effects of borrowing   154
    5.3.1   A chronology of borrowing   154
    5.3.2   Phrasal and clausal organization   158
5.4   Discussion: The roles of form and meaning in borrowing   159
    5.4.1   Issues of form   161
    5.4.2   Issues of meaning   162

CHAPTER 6
Discussion   165
    6.0.1   The relevance of form–meaning interpretation characteristics (FMICs)   166
    6.0.2   The organization of this chapter   168
   6.1   The PSI, FMICs, and other contact situations   169
    6.1.1   Typologically similar languages   171
    6.1.2   Along the index of fusion: Agglutinating versus fusional types   172
    6.1.3   Along the index of synthesis: Isolating-analytical versus synthetic types   173
   6.2   The analysis of apparent exceptions   174
    6.2.1   Ma'a   174
    6.2.2   Mednyj (Copper Island) Aleut   176
    6.2.3   Wutun   178
    6.2.4   Family trees with crooked branches   179
   6.3   Connecting borrowing and various contact phenomena   180
    6.3.1   Distinguishing code-switching and borrowing   183
    6.3.2   Convergence and a composite matrix   187
   6.4   The borrowability of inflectional categories   190
    6.4.1   The emergence of category values   191
    6.4.2   The inheritance of categories and category values   192
    6.4.3   Limits on types of borrowable meanings/concepts   194
   6.5   Conclusions   197

Appendix A: Additional Mexicano text   201

Appendix B: Spanish borrowings in the data   205

References   229

Name index   243

Subject index   245

Foreword

The question of whether there are constraints on what can be borrowed from one language into another, and if so what these constraints are, is one that is at the forefront of current research on language contact. The issue is important not only for our understanding of borrowing as a phenomenon in its own right, but also because of its broader implications for studies in the general area of language contact. For instance, if there is a controversial claim about whether similarities between two languages could be the result of language contact, rather than, for instance, of inheritance from a common ancestor, then knowing what the constraints on borrowability might be could help us to resolve the controversy.

Answers that have been given traditionally to the question of constraints on borrowability, once it is observed that at least some borrowing is possible, range from the positing of absolute constraints — certain things would be simply unborrowable under whatever circumstances — to the opposite extreme that anything can be borrowed under any circumstances. There are also intermediate positions, for instance that there is a hierarchy of borrowability, such that certain elements can only be borrowed if certain other elements are also borrowed, for example that verbs can only be borrowed if there is also borrowing of nouns. Another intermediate position would argue that certain kinds of borrowing are permitted, facilitated, impeded, or prevented by particular properties of the borrowing language. A persistent problem with the last mentioned kind of constraint has been the difficulty of pinning down just exactly what the constraint is meant to be: While statements might seem empirically testable that claim, for instance, that is quite generally impossible for a language to borrow features that are incompatible with its own nature, it has proven almost impossible to pin down, with any degree of reliability, exactly what constitutes a violation of the "nature" of a borrowing language.

In the present work, Fredric W. Field not only examines critically a number of claims that have been made about hierarchies of borrowability, but also proposes — and this I see as the major contribution to the ongoing debate —

a particular constraint on borrowability that relates to an empirically ascertainable property of the borrowing language. Field argues that the borrowing language's morphological typology — whether it is isolating, agglutinating, or fusional — will constrain the possibility of borrowing features from another language. An isolating language can borrow neither agglutinating nor fusional morphology. An agglutinating language can borrow agglutinating, but not fusional morphology. A fusional language can borrow both agglutinating and fusional morphology. And of course, all languages can borrow "instances of isolating morphology", since this simply amounts to the absence of morphology. The hypothesis is formulated in Section 2.3 as the complementary Principles of System Compatibility and of System Incompatibility (PSC/PSI).

The PSC/PSI hypothesis is investigated in detail against the material of Modern Mexicano, the result of language contact between the indigenous Nahuatl language of central Mexico and Spanish, whereby Nahuatl has borrowed substantially from Spanish. Nahuatl is an agglutinating language, while Spanish is a fusional language, so according to the PSC/PSI hypothesis Nahuatl should be able to borrow agglutinating morphology from Spanish, but not fusional morphology, and this is exactly what is observed: The Spanish agglutinating plural suffix -*s* has been borrowed into Mexicano, but not any of the fusional morphology of Spanish (for instance, in the verb system).

Field goes on to discuss a number of other cases where the PSC/PSI hypothesis seems to bear fruit, and also cases where, at least on one interpretation of the data, it might seem to be counter-exemplified. In all cases of the latter type there are competing historical interpretations of the data, some consistent with the PSC/PSI hypothesis, others inconsistent with it. Further research will be needed to ascertain whether, in such cases, it is possible to decide on independent grounds which of the competing interpretations is correct. If no counterexamples to the PSC/PSI hypothesis are found, then this would suggest that the PSC/PSI hypothesis is empirically robust and can in turn be used to decide among competing accounts, selecting the one that is compatible with the PSC/PSI hypothesis.

Like all good hypotheses, the PSC/PSI both provides solutions to existing problems and opens up a vast area of research that will follow up on testing the hypothesis. It has been my great pleasure to accompany the author on some of the initial stages of this journey of discovery.

Bernard Comrie
Leipzig/Los Angeles, January 2002

Preface

When I first traveled through Europe, I could not help noticing how people seemed to learn all sorts of languages with relative ease and how they cleverly moved from one to another in the course of normal conversation. It was very impressive. Raised in Southern California, I was used to a different sort of multilingualism (jokes about the American's lack of linguistic prowess notwithstanding), and the contrast was rather stark. My interest was definitely piqued. Even today, in many parts of California, the use of anything other than (standard) English is discouraged, and those who speak "foreign" languages are even looked down upon to a certain extent. Clearly, there are social and linguistic consequences to asymmetrical multilingual situations of this type, not all of them good, particularly as they play out in such areas of society as education. As I have continued to reflect on my own individual community over the years, its interlocking parts and the ways it interfaces with others, my attention has been increasingly drawn to how very ordinary people appear to snatch words from each others' languages. In fact, speakers of many different language varieties, from Spanish to Vietnamese and beyond, constantly seem to be weaving English words and expressions into their conversations, that is, when they are not switching from one complete system to another. Needless to say, this kind of linguistic phenomenon — borrowing — is not restricted to Los Angeles or other parts of the U.S.

So began a sincere and growing interest in language contact and what happens to languages (and their speakers) when cultures collide. The content of this particular book has been influenced to a great extent by many similar experiences and the actual work that was to follow. As it took shape, a number of friends and colleagues have taken part, offering input in the form of dialogue, data (apparent examples and counterexamples), correction, encouragement, and occasional agreement. As a result, I am indebted to a growing number of people for help and continuous support, but especially to John Hawkins and Bernard Comrie, without whose help this book would not have been completed. I am especially grateful for Hawkins' vision and his faith in me as his student.

For his constant input and encouragement, special thanks go to Comrie; he has been a friend, teacher, editor, proofreader, and at times anchor. The obligatory disclaimer is appropriate here: all mistakes, errors of commission and omission, and all instances of wrong-headed thinking are solely mine.

For their kindness, I would like to express special gratitude to Kenneth and Jan Hill of the University of Arizona for their inspiration and for making available their extensive corpus of Modern Mexicano. The Hills also made themselves continuously available as sounding boards for my thoughts and observations. *Their* work on Modern Mexicano continues to stand as a bench mark in the study of the links among society, culture, and language. I know that I am not alone in my appreciation; their contributions to the field cannot be understated. Of course, it should go without saying that no work such as this could be done without the pioneering efforts of such scholars as Edward Sapir, Einar Haugen, and Uriel Weinreich, and the current contributions of authors such as Sarah Grey Thomason.

As the ideas underlying this book were developing, I got into numerous stimulating and rewarding discussions. The context for much of this was the atmosphere that surrounds the various conferences available for specialists and students of language. For me, one of the best examples is the annual joint meetings of the Linguistic Society of American and Society of Pidgin and Creole Linguistics. The ongoing debate among the various schools of thought on the emergence of new language varieties and the constant evolution of older, perhaps more established ones provides much more than background information on such fields as contact linguistics (including such diverse areas as bilingual phenomena, creolistics, and language change), language acquisition (native and non-native), and so on. Open and honest interaction among peers undoubtedly leads to new ways of viewing our uniquely human capacity for language. In this regard, I thank Peter Bakker, now of the University of Aarhus, who from the very beginning of my studies freely offered his comments and continual support; Salikoko Mufwene for his candid responses to my work; Armin Schwegler for his unflagging friendship and sharing of ideas and data; Pieter Muysken for the example he sets as a scholar; Ad Backus for constant encouragement from the time of our first meeting in San Diego, California; and particularly, Carol Myers-Scotton for her tremendous example of commitment to the field and tireless giving of her time and self. I would be remiss if I didn't mention John Lumsden, whose prodding often got me back into motion in my work.

I would also like to acknowledge Bill Rutherford, Masha Polinsky, Joseph Aoun, Jean-Roger Vergnaud, Ed Finegan and the other teachers with whom I had the privilege of studying during my graduate days at the University of Southern California. I will always remember each one vividly and the unique ways they had of challenging me to grow and expand my linguistic horizons. Others made contributions in perhaps slightly different ways, so I send thanks also to Laura Alvarez for her input; to John Singler, John Holm, and John Rickford, all past presidents of the Society of Pidgin and Creole Linguistics; Tom Klammer, Angela Della Volpe, Bob Noreen, and especially Sharon Klein for their encouragement and support in teaching; to Linda Williams-Culver for her kindness and willingness to listen on those days when it was especially needed; to David Kwak for his technical expertise on the computer; to Scott Kleinman for both his collegiality and computer smarts; and to Linda McCullum, Cindy Togami, Dee Polk, Tameika Hall, Janaki Bowerman, and Marjorie "Marjie" Seagoe — friends and colleagues on the administrative front. Also, special thanks go to my friends at John Benjamins, Bernadette "Bernie" Martinez-Keck and Paul Peranteau in Philadelphia, and to Anke de Looper and Kees Vaes in Amsterdam.

Last and most, a very special note of appreciation goes to my wife, Cathy and the boys, who had to put up with me during my studies and in preparation of this manuscript. To all those I may have unintentionally neglected in this preface: Thanks.

List of figures

Chapter 2
Figure 2.1. Language types and allowable morphemes   40
Figure 2.2. Compatibility and incompatibility   41

Chapter 4
Figure 4.1. Mapping patterns of grammatical affixes   96
Figure 4.2. The mappings of Spanish verbal -o   97
Figure 4.3. Calculating mapping possibilities (present tense) 97

List of tables

Chapter 4
Table 4.1.	Form–meaning interpretation characteristics (FMIC): Forms	93
Table 4.2.	Inflectional categories associated with verbs	103
Table 4.3.	Form–meaning interpretation characteristics (FMICs): Meaning	104
Table 4.4.	Content items according to semantic and syntactic complexity	115
Table 4.5.	Compatibility versus incompatibility	118
Table 4.6.	FMICs: form–meaning sets	119
Table 4.7.	Summary of predictions regarding FMICs	120

Chapter 5
Table 5.1.	The occurrence of Spanish content items	141
Table 5.2.	The occurrence of Spanish function items	141
Table 5.3.	The occurrence of Spanish form–meaning sets in Mexicano	142
Table 5.4.	The occurrence of Spanish form types based on selection	147
Table 5.5.	The occurrence of Spanish concept types	149
Table 5.6.	Borrowed Spanish nouns	151
Table 5.7.	Borrowed nouns: semantic (sub)types	152
Table 5.8.	Borrowed nouns: ratios of hyperonyms to hyponyms	153
Table 5.9.	Spanish content items according to Karttunen and Lockhart (1976)	156

CHAPTER 1

Introduction

A number of attempts have been made to establish systematic approaches to the studies of lexical borrowing, code-switching, contact-induced language change, language attrition and convergence, and so on, with some proposing various links among these seemingly disparate phenomena. Recent developments have focused attention on the social and linguistic factors they hold in common and apparent similarities found in underlying processes. Examples of this growing trend are Thomason and Kaufman (1988) — more recently Thomason 2001 — who stress that the transmission of languages within differing social contexts by other than normal (i.e., "parental") means shapes their fundamental characters (hence, their distinction between genetic and non-genetic origins), and Myers-Scotton (1995, 1993a, 1993b), who consistently advances the argument that the similar characteristics found in contact phenomena are traceable to similar underlying cognitive processes operating in the heads of individual (bilingual) speakers that collaborate to form what appears to be a matrix or base language system in performance, which, in turn, determines the nature of these phenomena (cf. Myers-Scotton 1995: 239). She also suggests correspondences between language transfer (and the development of interlanguages) in second/subsequent language acquisition and substrate influence in the emergence of new speech varieties (e.g., pidgin and creole varieties), especially with respect to those evincing degrees and types of language mixing.[1] These works have generated much discussion in the growing field of contact linguistics.

In many of these studies, one can find a number of common linguistic threads, especially regarding the roles of the languages involved. Specifically,

---

1. Some linguists include pidgins, creoles, and other mixed languages under a general heading of "mixed languages" (Thomason and Kaufman 1988:3). Lines between these types may appear blurry owing to the particular and varied circumstances of their origins. Nevertheless, to avoid the obvious terminological confusion, in the present work, the term "*mixed language*" will refer specifically to a variety that clearly and overtly shows relationships to two (or more) distinct languages and does not include pidgins or creoles. The inclusive term "*contact language*" will be used to refer to all language varieties arising in contact situations.

when speakers of two distinct languages (representing two individual cultures) come into intense, day-to-day contact with each other, degrees of bilingualism are to be expected. Their respective languages, then, are said to be in contact when they are both spoken (alternately) by the same persons (Weinreich 1953:1), that is, at the same time in the same place (Thomason 2001:1). Languages in this kind of intimate contact often undergo a number of resultant changes, and these changes are generally concentrated in a single direction. In cases where one language is clearly dominant in a number of social domains, the dominant (or superordinate) will usually exert greater influence on the recessive (or subordinate) than the recessive does on the dominant (Thomason and Kaufman 1988:67–68; Thomason 2001:10–13). The dynamic relationships established among speakers and between linguistic systems have the potential to induce (perhaps, precipitate) a number of possible outcomes. For instance, the dominant language may assume the role of lexical donor, providing certain kinds of words or morphemes to be selected by speakers of the recessive language for adoption while the recessive language system becomes the recipient of the "donated" words and morphemes, acting as a kind of morphosyntactic matrix into which these elements are grafted. In the most extreme cases, borrowed elements have replaced native ones to such an extent that a new and distinct variety emerges (Thomason and Kaufman 1988:48, 76ff; Thomason 2001:85–91).

The present study is primarily concerned with the processes by which forms (i.e., form–meaning sets) from a lexical donor language, language Y, are imported and integrated into a recipient language, X — X being the original language spoken by a speech community. It is assumed that speakers of X initially attempt to reproduce in their own speech (perhaps by some sort of imitation) forms that previously existed only in Y (Haugen 1950:212). These forms may or may not be fully accepted by speakers of X as subsequently belonging to X. Consequently, the term *borrowing* will be used primarily to refer to the integration of forms into a recipient language. As discussed in later sections of this work, the importation of foreign words or morphemes into one's native language typically include various degrees of phonological adaptation; another possibility is the direct borrowing of foreign phonemes (or close approximations). However, to point out the obvious, phonological processes which may have applied to a particular phoneme in its source language are not normally borrowed along with the morpheme (or phonetic string) in which it appears. Borrowed morphemes, including those with non-native sound segments, generally become subject to the phonological processes of the new linguistic environment. In fact, as evidence of an underlying matrix structure, reanalysis of some kind, at various levels of grammar, is to be expected. While it is possible that a borrowing language will adopt certain phonological and structural characteristics from another independently of lexical borrowing, extensive borrowing from an individual source may gradually lead to phonological and other structural changes in the recipient in a kind of domino effect (Haugen 1950:225). It is also safe to say that a significant amount of lexical borrowing is to be expected *before* one finds evidence of other "interferences", i.e., actual structural borrowings (Thomason and Kaufman 1988:20–21; Thomason 2001:69). Regarding morphology, it has been proposed that free morphemes are more easily borrowed than bound, and that the more highly bound the morpheme (e.g., inflectional affixes versus function words), the less likely it will be borrowed (Weinreich 1953:29–37). Generally speaking, the more closely associated elements are to the particular grammar (morphosyntax) of the potential donor, the more difficult they will be to borrow (Haugen 1950:224–225; cf. Thomason 2001:60). Consequently, syntactic characteristics are often considered to be the least easily diffused aspects of language (Romaine 1995:64) and the very last to be borrowed.[2]

On the one hand, when there is casual contact between languages, i.e., among their speakers, lexical items may be borrowed where there is little or no extensive bilingualism. For instance, American English has borrowed many cultural items from immigrant groups, e.g. *kosher* from Yiddish, *pizza* from Italian, *sauerkraut* from German, *tortilla* from Mexican Spanish, *sushi* from Japanese, and so on. On the other hand, many studies of extensive borrowing, the result of intensive contact, assume that the requisite starting point is a subset of the total number of native speakers of the recipient variety who are also relatively proficient and perhaps equally skilled in the donor,[3] who act as a kind of conduit for the diffusion of lexical items and other properties of the

---

2. This is with the likely exception of word order (Thomason and Kaufman 1988:54f; cf. Thomason 2001:69). Contact induced word order changes have been observed in a number of instances, for example, in U.S. versions of Spanish (Sánchez 1982:34ff) and Low German (Thomason and Kaufman 1988:81–83), Asia Minor Greek (Thomason and Kaufman 1988:18, 220–222), and so on.

3. In many respects, degrees and types of bilingualism are always relative and difficult to assess, especially regarding competence and patterns of usage in each language (Hoffmann 1991:17–32, Grosjean 1982:230ff). As a consequence, many scholars posit the existence of proficiency continua in all varieties represented in a particular community (e.g., Silva-Corvalán 1994:11; Campbell and Muntzel 1988:185).

donor language (Thomason and Kaufman 1988:66). In this respect, Grosjean (1982), among others, distinguishes between (a) when an individual speaker spontaneously uses a form from another language within an utterance (perhaps adapting it phonologically and morphologically to varying degrees), what he terms *speech borrowing*, and (b) when words from one language have been borrowed by another and used by monolingual speakers of that recipient language, termed *language borrowing*. The connection between the two is obvious: languages borrow words because individual speakers have at one time borrowed them.

1.0.1 Social factors

A number of social factors have been discussed to account for the amount and types of borrowing. Thomason and Kaufman (1988:65ff), for example, discuss (a) the intensity and length of contact; (b) the relative number of speakers of each variety; (c) cultural and political (therefore, economic) dominance of one group of speakers, and so on. In situations where these factors conflict, e.g., when a politically dominant group is numerically inferior to the subordinate group, patterns of borrowing may differ. The cultural pressure of a politically and numerically dominant group on a subordinate population is also offered as an explanation for why speakers of a minority language often learn a majority, prestige variety, while members of the dominant group do not, as a rule, seek to become bilingual by mastering the minority language.

Below is a brief list summarizing reasons for borrowing that have been posited by researchers in recent years:

a. as a result of the cultural dominance of the donor language (Watson 1989:49–51; Mougeon and Beniak 1989:303–307; Hill and Hill 1986:4; cf. Gal 1989:318);
b. to be associated with speakers of the dominant language (and gain socially from its prestige) (Mertz 1989:112; Hill and Hill 1986:103ff; Thomason and Kaufman 1988:44ff; Grosjean 1982:336–337);
c. to fill lexical gaps in a recessive language well along in the process of shift (Myers-Scotton 1993a:167; Huffines 1989:212; Bavin 1989:270ff; Haugen 1989:65; Grosjean 1982:336; Karttunen and Lockhart 1976:16ff);
d. to facilitate understanding with younger speakers who are no longer familiar with original forms of the recessive language (Bavin 1989:277; Haugen 1989:67);
e. for affect or convenience (Hoffmann, 1991, pp. 102–103; Grosjean 1982: 311–313).

Grosjean (1982) also points out that borrowing of specific words may occur because only one language has the desired word, or because an individual is not equally familiar with the words of both languages and chooses the most available word (311). Whatever the actual reasons may be, patterns of borrowing remain nonetheless fairly predictable with respect to the formal characteristics of borrowed elements.

1.0.2 Linguistic factors

Two linguistic factors often cited as playing promoting and inhibiting roles in borrowing are frequency and (formal) equivalence (Van Hout and Muysken 1994: 42; Weinreich 1953: 61). The first, frequency, refers to how often specific items occur in a *donor* language. Frequently occurring items may have a pushing effect on a borrowing language: on the one hand, the more frequent an item is in the donor, the better it is as a candidate for borrowing; on the other, the more frequent an item is in the recipient language, the more of an inhibiting affect it will exert, thereby resisting or blocking the borrowing and subsequent usage of a corresponding lexical item from the donor. The second of these factors, equivalence, pertains to word classes, i.e., whether or not a particular form finds a structural or formal equivalent (usually defined as an equivalent form class such as N, V, Adj, and so on), which will either facilitate (if the answer is in the affirmative) or inhibit its inherent borrowability.

There are three points of caution when considering frequency as a cause. One, if frequency has a significant statistical impact on borrowing, its effects appear primarily with respect to certain morpheme types, i.e., those constituting content items such as nouns, verbs, and adjectives, whether free-standing or bound roots or bases. For example, content morphemes in the Romance languages normally occur with obligatory inflections for gender, number, and so on. Nevertheless, when a particular lexical item is borrowed, only the content morpheme, as perceived by speakers of the borrowing language, is incorporated into that language.[4] Grammatical morphemes, which may consist of independent

---

4. This implies morphological reanalysis. For example, there are a number of Spanish borrowings into U.S. varieties of English, for instance, the word *taco*, the name for a popular Mexican food item. In Spanish, the *-o* ending is an inflectional affix indicating grammatical gender. English, which does not have grammatical gender, has borrowed the entire word as one unanalyzable unit — a content item. It has not borrowed an affix or the inflectional category of gender (which would apply to the entire lexicon).

function words, roots, or affixes, though they are among the most frequently occurring forms in any language, are clearly not borrowed on this basis (if at all). Two, it remains to be demonstrated how core vocabulary items (e.g., words for certain basic body parts, kinship relationships, everyday activities, and the like), which are particularly resistant to change (replacement or loss), correlate with frequency counts: if they are, indeed, as frequent as one might think, why are they almost never borrowed or replaced?

Three, while frequency may be a factor in the integration of particular content items into a recipient language, its overall effect may depend on other linguistic factors, for example, semantic transparency, relevance, and so on (Van Hout and Muysken 1994: 52–54). Moreover, the frequency of a particular word in a language (e.g., in corpora formally obtained from a wide range of native speakers or written texts) does not necessarily determine an individual or identifiable group of borrowers' relative exposure to that form. For example, a typical native speaker of, say, Spanish in Mexico City may not be exposed to agricultural or other terms from specific semantic fields (e.g., occupational nomenclatures) to the same degree as a bilingual speaker (of relative proficiency) of Spanish and Modern Mexicano (Náhuatl) in the relatively remote Malintzin (Malinche) region of central Mexico who may have more intense exposure to such terms as a consequence of his/her expertise in a particular occupation. In addition, many bilinguals are likely to have access to a somewhat narrower range of registers of speech in one or both of their languages as a result of socioeconomic conditions, hence, fewer semantic types (cf. Grosjean 1995: 259), especially if they are systematically restricted as a consequence of subservient or subordinate social status.

With respect to the possible effects of frequency on lexicon, one can contrast borrowing and the processes of pidginization or creolization. In the emergence of a pidgin, there is only the pull of the emerging pidgin to establish a rudimentary, core vocabulary and the complicit, uninhibited push from the lexifier (source) language. Little possibility exists of an overt blocking affect from an original (recipient) lexicon because there is no ostensible (or tangible) competition among lexical items given the separate linguistic identity and function of a pidgin against that of a native language. There is only one target, the lexicon of the donor/superstrate. However, if frequency is a main force, it remains to be seen why the most frequent items (function words and various affixes) are noticeably *absent*. In fact, their absence is even more conspicuous in the beginning stages when frequency would seem to have its strongest potential affect. Processes of equal or greater force must be present to over-ride its effects.

However, it must be acknowledged that frequency may be one of a number of factors which figure in the long term in the lexical expansion of a pidgin or creole. It is also important to note that sufficient evidence comes from studies of creole languages such as Berbice Dutch, Tok Pisin, Kikongo, Lingala, Haitian Creole, and others, to strongly suggest that there is, in fact, competition among grammatical categories from substrate languages — acting in relatively covert fashion as morphosyntactic matrices — that manifests itself in various ways, in some cases along with recognizable lexical contributions from substrate and adstrate sources.

Concerning equivalence, any formal notion must be established along some sort of sliding or gradient scale. This is especially necessary due to the multitude of ways lexical and grammatical meanings are represented in the languages of the world. The morphological character of each language will vary, but a scale for each language needs to be proposed to identify more precisely where the two languages may indeed have potential correspondences and mismatches among their diverse form–meaning sets. Insofar as nouns are consistently reported to be the first and most frequently borrowed items (followed by verbs or adjectives), perhaps one can conclude that it is easier for Y nominals to match up with X nominals both semantically and formally. After all, nominal classes appear to be more homogeneous across languages. Considering variable levels of proficiency in each language, identifying corresponding nominals seems to require a relatively low level of proficiency in either (or, perhaps both) languages. Conversely, borrowers may have the greatest difficulty finding equivalences in specific areas where a greatly decreased likelihood of formal and semantic correspondence exists. The most obvious example would be situations in which one language encodes a relatively opaque grammatical concept with an affix (or, even a zero or unmarked form) and the other with an individual function word. In such cases, correspondence may be difficult to establish on both formal and semantic grounds, though perhaps not a total impossibility. Nevertheless, exact equivalence is not a linguistic certainty merely because of a consensus among bilingual speakers that some kind of informal paraphrase or translation is possible between two formally distinct forms or expressions (cf. Gutknecht and Rölle 1996: 1–10).

More sophisticated ability in translation (seeking equivalent expressions) obviously requires a much higher degree of proficiency in both languages. It is also clear that bilingual proficiency will fluctuate among members of a given community, producing a diluting affect that might skew borrowing to areas of greater possible equivalence, reducing language borrowing to the lowest common denominator, and, perhaps, obfuscating structural borrowing (one aspect of convergence). Any number of individual forms from Y, however, will diffuse even to monolingual speakers of X through the agency of more proficient bilingual members of the community (the most likely conduits of lexical innovation). As a logical consequence, any and all members of a speech community in which borrowing is a productive process can actively participate, irrespective of bilingual ability.

1.1 Borrowing as bilingual performance

Two key figures in the study of language contact are Einar Haugen and Uriel Weinreich.[5] It is to their credit that much of their work still stands as the basis for current approaches. Although certainly not the first to do so, Haugen pointed out the obvious difficulties in the use of the term "borrowing". The recipient language is not expected to give or pay the word back; neither can the process be called "stealing", in that nothing is actually taken or removed from the donor. Despite the inherent inadequacies of such analogies, a more recent one may better illustrate the character of the processes involved. Taking a concept from the realm of computers, lexical borrowing can be seen as the *copying* of a form from one language system (the lexicon of Y) into another (X) (Johanson 1992), with or without all the associated meanings or concepts it typically expresses in its source language.[6]

In one of his most cited works, Haugen (1950: 211–220), in an attempt to clarify then current terminology, divided borrowed elements into a number of classes depending on phonological and semantic characteristics. For example, he made distinctions among (a) *loanwords* — which show the importation of form and meaning with degrees of phonological integration (all, none, or partial); (b) *loanblends* — hybrids or combinations of foreign and native forms, e.g., co-worker (Hartmann and Stork 1972: 133); and (c) *loanshifts* — in which a foreign concept (meaning) is represented by a native form. This last term includes "loan translations" (calques), e.g., English *superman* from German *Übermensch* (Crystal 1991: 205), and "semantic loans" (semantic extensions), in

---

5. See, for instance, Haugen 1950, 1953, 1989 and Weinreich 1953.

6. Obviously, concepts can be imported without their associated labels, as well, in what Haugen (195)) termed "loanshifts" — discussed in the following paragraph.

which the range of meanings expressed by a native form is extended to include a new, usually related concept, e.g., U. S. Spanish *grados* "degrees" extended to include the meaning of English "grades" (Spanish *notas*) (Silva-Corvalán 1994:170).[7] Relevant to the present work, loanwords can be further classified into (a) *additions*, those that provide labels for objects and concepts newly introduced to the culture,[8] and (b) *substitutions*, those for which forms are already available in the recipient language (also known as a kind of relexification) (Albó 1970). Much attention is paid to (b) because the question naturally follows as to why speakers of one language would select forms from another when corresponding forms already exist in theirs. Speakers of a recipient variety must derive sufficient benefit to warrant the selection and usage of competing forms from a lexical donor.

It is apparent that the phonetic shape of only one morphological unit is taken in cases of "drastic allomorphy" such as in so-called strong (radical changing) verbs (e.g., Spanish *tengo* < *tener*) or suppletion (Spencer 1991:8). This may produce the appearance of simplification in the recipient language, though interpreting borrowing as a form of simplification can only be made from the perspective of the donor language and its speakers and not from that of the borrower. This applies in cases of relexification, as well. When only the form or label is borrowed, the semantic content is assumed to be more or less the same as the native word it replaces. However, inherent in this is the possibility of further semantic splits where both native and borrowed forms exist but their meanings become more specialized (Sánchez 1982:37–40).

Regarding the actual starting point of the borrowing process, for example, whether or not spontaneous borrowings in the speech of proficient bilinguals are better viewed as "speech" or *nonce* borrowings or as instances of code-switching (cf. Myers-Scotton 1993a, 1993b, 1995; van Hout and Muysken 1994; Muysken 1995; Poplack and Meechan 1995), it seems reasonable to assume that "...every loan starts as an innovation..." (Haugen 1950:212); the borrowing process — from isolated, one-time usage of a copied form in normal bilingual speech to its complete acceptance and integration into the recipient system — has to start somewhere. Some sort of progression must exist from speech borrowing to language borrowing (in Grosjean's terminology). For the present

---

7. Silva-Corvalán 1994 (170ff) refers to these semantic extensions as "single-word calques".

8. See, for example, Karttunen and Lockhart (1976), Hill and Hill (1986) and Hill (1988) for reference to Spanish loans into Náhuatl (Mexicano), Bavin (1989) for English loans in Warlpiri, and Sánchez (1982) for English loans in Chicano Spanish (especially, 37ff).

purposes, forcing distinctions among terms like "innovation", "nonce borrowing", "lexical interference", and "single-item code-switch" does not significantly affect the course of our discussion (cf. van Hout and Muysken 1994:40).

By defining language contact in the context of *speakers*, Weinreich brought to the fore the possible roles that individual members of a bilingual community play in the various contact phenomena. As a consequence, the focus shifts to the mental processes (or "interferences") that can be inferred to operate. Accordingly, those showing greater proficiency in the two (or more) languages are assumed to have a heightened ability and opportunity to draw upon the resources of either (or all) language system(s) and perhaps keep them separate. Specifically, Weinreich made general distinctions among Types A (coordinate), B (compound), and C (subordinate) bilinguals (1953:9–11). Type A bilinguals have, in effect, acquired their languages in such a way (in separate environments) that they appear to possess two distinct linguistic systems. In Saussurean terms, each language has its own set of signifiers (forms) and signifieds (meanings); viz., the forms of each language remain separate with their own associated meanings. Type B bilinguals have learned their languages in such a way that only one set of meanings underlies two sets of forms; this may occur when both languages are acquired in the same contexts. Type C bilinguals, in contrast to both Type A and Type B, can only access meanings of weaker language forms through their stronger one, effectively succeeding in certain (limited) communicative functions only when engaging in continuous mental translation. More recent work suggests, as Weinreich was quick to note, that the form recognition abilities (word memory) of individual bilinguals cannot be accurately described in such strict terms, i.e., as exclusively A, B, or C. An individual's representational system(s) that can affect lexical access may be situated anywhere on a continuum between extremes (i.e., from types A to C), determined by such social and linguistic factors as bilingual acquisition history (sequential or simultaneous), levels of proficiency in each language, form type (content items versus inflections), and so on (de Groot 1993:46).

These distinctions and the conclusions that can be drawn with respect to the ways in which the bilingual lexicon might be organized become important when attempting to understand how such things as code-switching, borrowing, simultaneous translation, and other abilities that only proficient bilinguals appear to possess can actually occur. A number of issues broached by Weinreich remain the focus of much current psycholinguistic research into bilingualism: (a) Just how closely associated is lexical material from each language stored — is there one lexical system or two (Hoffmann 1991:75–79, Romaine 1995:205–210)?

(b) To what degree is each language activated during performance (Grosjean 1995:270–272, 1997:227–229, 2001:1–2; Romaine 1995:98ff)? (c) How do morpheme types figure into differential access in bilingual performance (Myers-Scotton 1995:235–237; Myers-Scotton and Jake 2001:97; de Groot 1993:37–41)?

1.2 Mixed languages — Language intertwining or extensive borrowing?

With respect to the kinds of language varieties that arise out of situations of deep contact, Thomason (2001) states the following: "Linguistically, a contact language is identifiable by the fact that its lexicon and grammatical structures cannot all be traced back primarily to the same source language; they are therefore mixed languages in the technical historical linguistic sense: they did not arise primarily through descent with modification from a single earlier language" (158). Any discussion of linguistic borrowing and/or contact phenomena must include that of so-called mixed languages (bilingual mixtures), if for no other reason than their rather special status in the literature. (The reverse should be equally true, that any discussion of bilingual mixtures should include that of borrowing.) A number of these contact languages — for instance, Media Lengua, Ma'a, Mednyj (Copper Island) Aleut, and so on — appear to consist mainly of the lexicon (i.e., lexical items) of one language held together and acted upon by the grammatical elements of another. Each appears to push borrowing to the extreme, undoubtedly one of the reasons why they spark so much interest and perhaps even curiosity.

Clearly, another important facet of mixed-language studies is the apparent interaction of lexicon and grammatical system; they seem to be able to operate fairly independently of each other. In these bilingual mixtures, the grammatical system into which lexical items are grafted (the recipient) essentially acts as a grammatical matrix, retaining its original grammatical categories and so on, at least in some fashion. For example, it may keep its original verbal tense–aspect system and number, gender/class, and case distinctions on nominals (perhaps exemplified most clearly in Media Lengua, with its clear Quechua grammatical system and Spanish-derived lexicon). Imported lexical items appear to be inserted into syntactic frames generated by the underlying morphosyntactic system, thus preserving both its grammatical categories and the patterning of lexical and grammatical elements. Accordingly, the basic character of the recipient language grammar stays more or less the same while the vast majority of its original lexicon is replaced by the newly appropriated elements, a process sometimes referred to as relexification.[9]

Thomason (2001:158) states matter-of-factly that "... bilingual mixed language genesis is akin to, and in effect actually is, borrowing," an assessment that is not always accepted with unanimity by specialists in the field. Apparently, borrowing is generally regarded as such an innocuous, mundane kind of process that it may be difficult to imagine that it can have such powerful and sweeping effects. It should be immediately noted that the *intensity* of contact (both participant languages spoken in the same home and in the same neighborhood, by members of a single social group) and the *relatively small size* of the speech communities undoubtedly play influential roles in the apparent speed with which such varieties are said to emerge, claimed to be within a single generation in some very acute cases. Various kinds of borrowing (not merely the borrowing of isolated lexical items) can and do have the ability to motivate significant externally-motivated change.

Regarding genetic classification, mixed language/bilingual mixtures present definitional problems even (or especially) among specialists, particularly regarding genetic classification. For instance, Thomason and Kaufman (1988) claim that bilingual mixtures cannot be related genetically to *either* component language. Normal, pure, and unadulterated transmission of an individual, ancestral language has been broken in some fashion, and there is no "normal" genetic link to speak of. Greenberg (1999) claims that there are *no mixed languages* based on his reasoning that transmission of one component language is always evident even in the most extreme cases, and that the other component(s) came along side within that original community. Radical change is, therefore, the result of the influence of this second variety on the original, ancestral language (632). Bakker (1997) states: "A mixed language is a language that shows positive genetic similarities, in significant numbers, with two different languages" (195). Nevertheless, whenever a clear matrix language is present, it may be preferable to refer to the characteristics of the variety that are in fact *inherited*, those directly handed down from ancestors to whom and from

---

9. The degree of similarity of the new, mixed system to the original may depend on a number of factors, e.g., the amount of time speakers of the languages that have mixed have been in contact and the knowledge these speakers have of the respective languages, the relative status of each language and community, the types and amount of borrowed material (structural and lexical), and the degree to which grammatical elements of the languages have been integrated (or intertwined).

whom they can be traced. This seems quite plainly the grammatical matrix system in the vast majority of cases. So, bilingual varieties may be genetically related in a sense to the grammatical progenitor, while embedded characteristics are related in some other, more environmental way, say, lexically.

1.2.1 Defining mixed language

In defining the term *mixed language*, Bakker and Mous (1994b:5) offer the following (repeated in Golovko 1994:119 and Bakker 1997:213):

a. bound morphemes (always of a grammatical nature) are in language A.
b. free lexical morphemes are in language B.
c. free grammatical morphemes can be in either language.
d. syntax is that of language A.

These four criteria, however, need to be modified somewhat to describe more accurately many of the actual results of mixing. First, it is certainly not the case that all free-standing lexical items can come from language B (the donor). Even taking into consideration the difficulty of distinguishing among lexical and grammatical elements crosslinguistically, it still remains to be demonstrated that *every* content item of a language can indeed be replaced. This would mean that every single topic, including situations, events, and all participants, is identified and expressed by a non-native (i.e., not original) form despite the fact that it is encased in native morphology. Second, given the fact that the originators of a mixed language were members of a bilingual community exhibiting various acquisition scenarios and continua of proficiencies in the relevant varieties, one a number of significant effects of contact can be expected on the matrix (recipient) system itself. Hence, one should be somewhat circumspect in accepting both (a) and (d) in their extreme forms. Only (c), which leads us to expect forms from either language, allows for the assumption of variation and implies that a mixed language may be mixed at any (or all) level(s) of grammar.

There have been other attempts to define the term *mixed language* from a structural perspective. For instance, Weinreich (1953) refers to the work of Rosetti (1945/49), who used a qualitative distinction: "the interpenetration of two morphologies as the criterion for defining a *langue mixte*, which he contrasts with a *langue mélange*, containing but isolated borrowings" (29). Bakker and Mous (1994b) speak of a quantitative measure, i.e., in terms of the percentages of borrowed lexical items, which, they claim, may be as high as

90% (5ff).[10] In the long run, Bakker tends to restrict the number of languages he classes as mixed languages, perhaps to the most noteworthy cases. In the present work, language mixing/intertwining is viewed more as a process rather than a product, a process which may occur in a broader range of contexts. The differences seem to be terminological, more or less. While a true mixed language may ultimately be "in the eye of the beholder," the unique characteristics of Michif, Media Lengua, and other documented mixed varieties are remarkable from any standpoint. The terminological issues are not a matter of acknowledging their existence; they are more in accounting for their unusual characters.

For the present purposes, the following definition is proposed, which represents a synthesis of sorts of those above: A *mixed language* is one whose morphosyntactic matrix — including the majority of its most highly grammaticalized form–meaning sets — has essentially survived from an identifiable progenitor and whose total lexicon (e.g., content items and function words) has been substantially augmented and replaced (i.e., relexified) by a lexical donor, with borrowings of a more grammatical and/or structural nature to be expected. That is, its characteristic morphosyntax is inherited more or less intact from an original language system (indigenous to the specific speech community) while significant numbers of its content items and, perhaps to a somewhat lesser extent, free-standing function items are drawn from another, heretofore foreign source. Implicit in this particular attempt is that mixed-language status is gradient; some languages are more mixed than others.

By adding quantitative criteria, this definition can be made considerably narrower, for instance, by proposing that a majority of the native content items (e.g., core vocabulary) must be replaced along with many function items and some inflectional morphology. However, such factors still can be used only on a case-by-case basis, if for no other reason than one or both languages may have no inflectional morphology at all (in the case of highly analytical languages, for instance). It accords with Rosetti's definition of *langue mixte*, which points to the likelihood that true mixing involves grammatical (whether free-standing or not) as well as lexical elements. It can also be inferred that such items as function words, which occupy midpoints along continua of forms, can be from either language. In fact, one might suspect that free-standing function words

---

10. Thomason (1997a) cites the need for societal levels of bilingualism (to which reference is made later in Chapters 5 and 6) as a precondition for mixing of any sort. At this point, however, strictly linguistic criteria are discussed despite the obvious importance of the speakers' perspective, the linguistic and social environment, and so on.

that have a high degree of semantic independence and identifiability (i.e., they are not obligatorily selected in response to a syntactic requirement) may be integrated into the mix in ways similar to content items but with important implications regarding the syntactic organization of the variety that emerges.

1.2.2 From product to process

So far, the discussion has done little to explain the systematic nature of the results. As surprising as they may be, they are still remarkably uniform. Two (perhaps more) language systems interact with each other in dynamic ways and the results are systematic. One need not look far for plausible physical and biological analogies (cf. Mufwene 2001: 1–24). The very first step in understanding such linguistic interaction is the examination of each participant language relative to the other. The operation of one system upon another may systematically allow or limit the form types which can or cannot be part of an eventual mix, and in a sense delineate the qualities of the form–meaning sets that are actually borrowed. Regarding the latter, some words and morpheme types are obviously easier to borrow than others and are, therefore, borrowed more frequently and in greater numbers (e.g., nouns relative to, say, adpositions). To account for this, the current study proposes a set of principles, the Principle of System Compatibility (or PSC) and its correlate, the Principle of System Incompatibility (PSI), which set basic limits on borrowable and unborrowable morpheme types (Section 2.3, below). It also argues that the relative numbers of items borrowed from within individual word classes and morpheme types are predictable on the basis of their formal and semantic characteristics, i.e., how their forms and meanings are identified and picked out of the speech stream by speakers of the participant languages (Sections 4.1 and 4.2.).

Proximate causes for mixing of any kind undoubtedly lie in the interaction of social, psychological, and linguistic conditions, but the actual mechanisms seem to be restricted to a relatively short list of language contact phenomena, e.g., borrowing and possibly some sort of code-switching (discussed in later sections). Many studies have certainly provided much interesting data and thought provoking discussion.[11] However, while adhering to a rather strict

---

11. For example, mixed languages such as Michif, Javindo, Pecu' (Petjo), Island Carib, and possibly Mednyj Aleut reportedly emerged from mixed marriages of indigenous people and foreign, in many cases European, settlers (Bakker and Mous 1994b: 8). For more detailed information concerning these varieties, see Bakker and Mous, 1994a.

dichotomy between lexicon and underlying grammatical (matrix) system, they have yet to provide sufficient evidence that the primary mechanism by which such varieties originate is anything other than extensive lexical and/or structural borrowing. Consequently, mixed languages may be more accurately seen as cases of extreme borrowing — a claim that is, in principle, falsifiable. They clearly offer unique windows into the limits of borrowing and the nature of a morphosyntactic matrix system due to the clarity with which the relationships between grammar and lexicon can be examined. As a consequence, it may not be necessary to posit additional mechanisms or processes. What is actually needed is a better understanding of the effects of borrowing.

1.2.3 The concept of matrix language

The term *matrix* is also used in code-switching models that view the switching process as insertional.[12] That is, one language is the main or base language into which elements from the other(s) are embedded (Myers-Scotton 1993a:3, 20, 75). Thus, the matrix plays the greater role in determining such matters as word order and the appearance of grammatical (i.e., "system") morphemes (Myers-Scotton 1995:235). Such models stand in opposition to those which assert that code-switching is alternational and symmetrical, with each language taking part equally in the shaping of the utterance (Haugen 1950:211; Muysken 1995:177ff). In this respect, some researchers consider types of code-switching and borrowing as constituting a kind of continuum of phenomena, from clear instances of inter-sentential code-switching to various kinds of intra-sentential switching and from one-time borrowings (nonce borrowings, lexical interference, and so forth) to fully adapted loanwords (e.g., Poplack, Sankoff, and Miller 1988:52f; Poplack 1982:231ff; Pfaff 1979:295–297). As a consequence, whether or not a particular phenomenon is strictly alternational or insertional is probably best viewed as situated along a similar, corresponding scale.

The concept of matrix is quite easily applied to borrowing, which is clearly insertional. However, in addition to its function as a morphosyntactic matrix, the recipient (or borrowing) system will likely operate in phonological and semantic aspects of language, as well (cf. Haugen 1950:217 and Weinreich 1953:39). Emphasizing the role of the recipient language, Haugen (1950) divides the phonological aspects of borrowing into two complementary

---

12. See Muysken 2000 for a comprehensive overview of work on code-switching.

processes: one termed "importation", and the other "substitution", both of which originally referred primarily to the phonemic shape of a borrowed form. Importation signifies the seizing of a linguistic expression (a morpheme or aggregate of morphemes) from a donor system by an individual speaker or group of speakers and its crossing over into the borrowing system (it becomes a member of the borrowing lexicon). If the only concern were one-time borrowings (which may retain their original phonological forms), then the process is basically complete and perhaps transitory. Reaching broader currency requires a form's diffusability, that is, its general adoptability (including semantic transparency) to the borrowing linguistic community.

Because precise phonemic correspondence (i.e., equivalence) is rarely (if ever) the case between two individual languages, the borrowing system must adapt the borrowed form/label to be consistent with its native phonemic inventory by substitution, at least in the vast majority of cases (barring the direct borrowing of the donor phoneme). In other words, individual phonemes constituting the borrowed morpheme(s) are interpreted according to the matrix phonology and occur in production as substitutions for (or alterations of) the original segments. Some phonemes are replaced relatively easily as a result of their more or less exact correspondence in place and manner of articulation with native phonemes. Others may require perceptually more distant substitutions (for which examples abound in the literature) that may render the borrowed string (the entire form) unrecognizable to speakers of the original donor language, e.g., Spanish *virgen* in Taos pronounced as [*m'ilxina*] (Haugen 1950: 215ff). This scenario is consistent with current views of relexification in mixed languages (cf. Muysken 1988, 1994, and 1997; van Rheeden 1994; Bakker and Mous 1994b; de Gruiter 1994; and so on).

Loanwords, by definition, are fully integrated into the matrix language system. That is to say, all fully adapted borrowings must be tagged and organized as belonging to matrix language form-classes for participation in phonological and other grammatical processes. Perhaps analogous to the ways in which borrowed elements are phonologically adapted, the morphological character of borrowed items appears to be analyzed (at least initially) in accordance with the nearest matrix language equivalents — Y nominals as X nominals; Y verbals as X verbals; and so on. One question to be addressed, therefore, is as follows: to what degree must foreign elements be identified with matrix form classes? It is not unusual to find Y items from one form class reanalyzed as belonging to a different class in X. For example, some Spanish adjectives (e.g., *loco* and *rico*) are borrowed into Chiricahua as verbs (Haugen 1950: 217).

One must first ask whether or not an equivalent form class exists in X (for the borrowed Y form). An additional (confounding) factor is semantic: perhaps in Chiricahua, such concepts are traditionally (linguistically) represented by verbs. This reflects the possibility that forms belonging to one semantic sub-type in Y (in this case, the form class Adjective in Spanish) may need to be reanalyzed as belonging more properly to a corresponding semantic sub-type in X that belongs to an entirely different form class (in this case, Verb in Chiricahua).

The current work concludes that morphological equivalence must be interpreted at the level of morpheme type and not at the level of language particular word classes, which is significantly complicated by the fact that individual languages construct words in various and contrasting ways, as any cross-linguistic survey will attest. By casting a wider net, we get a broader view of the kinds of forms that are actually borrowed (which in many instances may be whole words), and, by implication, what forms are borrowable. Again, mixed language data illustrate the kinds of limits or constraints that can be set on borrowing. For instance, Media Lengua, with a clear Quechua matrix, allows Spanish prepositions (the case-marking functions of which are accomplished through suffixation in Quechua, which has no adpositions). This also holds true modern forms of Mexicano (see Subsection 5.3.2). Neither original grammatical matrix possessed classes of words properly called adpositions of any kind prior to the incorporation of Spanish prepositions. Both marked such relational concepts as location, direction, and so on by means of suffixation or other adverbial elements (Field 1997b; Hill and Hill 1986: 186). In addition, the integration of these foreign elements was according to donor word order patterns (i.e., as prepositions), not according to the position of the affix in the recipient. Perhaps the most plausible explanation is that all three already had general classes of function words whose members consisted of free-standing grammatical morphemes. As a consequence, it appears that semantic characteristics (in a broad sense) are more relevant to any case for equivalence than word class or, perhaps, any other formal characteristics.

1.2.4 The correlation of transfer, substrate, and matrix

Whenever bilingual performance data come under careful scrutiny, the concept of an underlying (matrix, base, or substrate) linguistic system is always a "reasonable inference" (Myers-Scotton 1997a). For this reason (i.e., for its potential for explanation), the present work pursues a line of inquiry that assumes links between processes of bilingual language acquisition and bilingual performance phenomena (e.g., language transfer, interlanguage, language mixing, etc.). A good deal of recent research in second language acquisition (SLA) points to the persistent residual effects of an underlying (native or first) linguistic system which leaves an unmistakable imprint on the language (second or secondary) being learned subsequently. The most likely things to be transferred to a second, non-native language are (a) phonology, which has a physical basis (Gass 1995:31; Corder 1993:19), and (b) deeply ingrained grammatical concepts that can influence all areas of production (e.g., Selinker and Lakshmanan 1993:197–216; Schachter 1993:32–46), for example, the ways in which reference to past or present time are expressed. In addition, transfer may involve the classification of words in an alien language (the target) into syntactic and semantic classes according to classificatory principles already known (i.e., based on the learner's L1) and include grammatical processes (when the learner assumes that native processes and those of the target are the same or similar) and the transference into the target language of linguistic elements, forms, rules, and strategies (Gass and Selinker 1993:234).

In either pidgin or creole genesis, members of a community which at one time possessed its own indigenous language(s) were brought into direct contact with a foreign community and its language(s). Learners (and creators) of pidgin varieties (which, by definition, have no native speakers) are in the process of learning a second/subsequent language in some fashion even if that learning is primarily restricted to lexical items of the presumed donor (cf. Mufwene 2001:7). Consequently, the effects of an original language system (the substrate) are clear and unequivocal. Transfer is obvious and visible. Concerning creoles, a number of current works have concluded that the emergence of many of these varieties is the consequence of adult second/subsequent language acquisition based on the investigation of historical records (Singler 1993; DeGraff 1999a:4–6; Mufwene 2001:7ff; cf. Field 2001). Native language acquisition (NLA) by children of relatively small numbers — via simultaneous bilingual acquisition with the language(s) of their parents — appears to be a significant contributor to the stabilization of the creole, but not necessarily its creation (DeGraff 1999b:526; Mufwene 1999:120).

Discussion of such creole languages as Haitian Creole French (HC) (Lefebvre and Lumsden 1989; Lefebvre 1986, 1993; Lumsden 1994) and Tok Pisin (Siegel 1997; Reesink 1990; Mühlhäusler 1990, 1980) often focus on the interaction of an underlying substrate (substrata) and superstrate (donor), especially regarding phonological, syntactic, and lexical (semantic) characteristics (cf. Holm 1986:261–264; Mufwene 1986; Alleyne 1986:303ff). Apparently, evidence of a substrate is evidence of transfer.[13] The fact that creole lexicons are typically composed of donor content items (including core vocabulary) and free-standing function words despite the (near) complete lack of donor inflectional morphology appears to support the idea that complete acquisition was not attained, that is, when compared to that of monolingual native-acquirers. This is precisely what one would expect in processes of second/subsequent acquisition, particularly under the kinds of social circumstances exhibited in many creole communities (DeGraff 1999b: 480–481). Linguistically, the end product under various social circumstances will, nevertheless, depend on the amount and quality of exposure to the donor/superstrate and its native speakers (Field 2001). When a creole has completely displaced the original language(s) of the community, descendants of the founding population may then become monolingual in the creole, and they will have learned the creole natively.

The visible presence of a matrix in a mixed language suggests a number of things. First, if the mixed language emerged as the result of the sequential acquisition of two (or more) languages (on a community, hence, individual level), the one already established in/indigenous to the community is more likely to form the grammatical matrix. It also implies that this native language was acquired through normal processes of transmission — in the home, among family members, and so on. The language learned subsequently very likely may be (or was becoming) culturally dominant within the community at large, and was most likely learned under an entirely different set of circumstances. Each language in such a bilingual's repertoire is typically acquired and used in complementary ways, that is, with different people, in different social domains, for different purposes (Grosjean 1997b). It is also a possibility that the participant languages were acquired more or less simultaneously, but, even in this case, one is the language of the home and primary in some sense (see Cutler 1994).

Mixed languages may also be the consequences of processes operating during (or accelerated by) language shift, a situation in which portions of a

---

13. Overt morphosyntactic features attributable to specific substrate languages often appear to dissipate completely, leaving behind only subtle (covert) traces whose actual origins can only be inferred. As a consequence, substrate identification may be rendered quite problematic. In fact, the lack of clear and unambiguous evidence for particular substrate languages has generated much controversy in creolistics, providing considerable grist for important alternative theories of their origins, for instance, those defended by proponents of so-called universalist positions (e.g., the language bioprogram hypothesis of Bickerton 1981, 1984, 1987, and so on).

community are shifting away from an original, ethnic language to the use of a culturally dominant one, and, therefore, represent attempts at preserving an original language and the ethnic identity associated with it. However, shift obviously cuts two ways, each showing the effects of an underlying matrix or substrate system. For instance, in the language that was acquired first, one expects borrowings and the effects of attrition in terms of numbers of speakers, functions, and forms (see, for example, Dorian 1989). In the language being adopted, the culturally dominant variety that has been acquired as a second/ subsequent language, evidence of transfer is expected, perhaps to the extent that the adopted language resembles an individual interlanguage.[14] The evidence clearly suggests that transfer can have community-wide effects, especially when that community is relatively homogeneous (i.e., when all members speak the same first language).

Each of the above possibilities (transfer in processes of SLA, substrate in pidgin and creole genesis, and matrix system in various mixing phenomena) reinforces the original premise: there are significant connections among different acquisition scenarios, the nature of the bilingual lexicon (including representation and lexical access), and various bilingual/contact phenomena, which includes the emergence of entirely new varieties (whether or not they can be truly classified according to a family tree model). As an important consequence, all have the potential to shed light on the language faculty, itself. In any situation of intense contact, borrowings of various kinds and conversational (intra-sentential) code-switching may be quite common in the speech of community members who are under similar social and linguistic circumstances (see Subsection 6.3). And, just as performance errors and other apparent anomalies by native language acquirers illustrate how language is constructed anew by each child (cf. Slobin 1985:1158ff), the integration of features and elements of two entirely different language systems into one (that systematically diverges from standard usage in either participant variety) may show the ways language is constructed anew in communities characterized by such intense

---

14. See Lipski (1994) for a comprehensive discussion of contemporary Latin American varieties of Spanish — some of which he terms interlanguage varieties. Significant substrate influence, unquestionably the result of transfer from original indigenous Amerindian languages, is quite transparent. This is also likely in the case of particular varieties of English, for instance, Hiberno-English (see, for example, Harris 1985; Thomason and Kaufman 1988: 42–43, 47–48), Indian English (Hock and Joseph 1996: 375–380), Chicano English (cf. Penfield and Ornstein-Galicia 1985: 34–36) and so on.

cultural and linguistic contact. This, in turn, has the potential to shed light on the ways bilingual competence (e.g., during acquisition) can be represented.

1.3 The plan of this book

A number of studies have proposed hierarchies of borrowability (nouns are borrowed more frequently than and before verbs, for instance), including some whose applicability have been restricted to the specific cases from which they were derived (Whitney 1881; Haugen 1950; Singh 1981; Muysken 1981; van Hout and Muysken 1994:41). The many counter-examples present in a wider range of data have made the generalizability of individual hierarchies somewhat problematic, though clearly there must be something underlying their fundamental similarities. Moreover, hierarchies denoting borrowability bear striking resemblances to those proposed in work on morphological typology (the synchronic analysis of word and morpheme types), e.g. Sapir (1921), Greenberg (1974), and others, and later applied to grammaticalization (the diachronic), e.g., Hopper and Traugott (1993), Heine et al. (1991), C. Lehmann (1986), and so on. The similarities among the various indices, scales, clines, or hierarchies suggest correspondences that go beyond mere coincidence.

A major goal of this study is to account for these correspondences. To this end, the approach taken here is based on the following: the similarities among the various scales and hierarchies are likely to be the result of the general nature of language — i.e., the morphological types that actually occur and their characteristics. Individual differences are likely to be the result of language particular formal and semantic factors. A viable theory of borrowability, therefore, must be constructed to include both the general and particular, along both formal and semantic lines. As a first step, Chapter 2 discusses morphological structure and its role in comparative linguistics, the diachronic study of grammaticalization, and the establishment of scales of borrowability. While hierarchies representing quantitative and/or temporal claims to borrowability may elucidate which forms are borrowed (and, therefore, made compatible with the borrowing morphosyntactic matrix), they, nevertheless, fail to explain why other forms are not. An absolute cutoff point is proposed along a scale of morpheme types relative to the typology of both or all the languages involved beyond which forms cannot be borrowed (as embodied in the Principle of System Incompatibility); hence, they are not borrowable. Truly borrowable forms can only be seen in an absolute sense against forms that are (absolutely) unborrowable.

Hierarchies also accurately illustrate observations that members of certain borrowable form classes are borrowed more frequently than those of other form classes (e.g., nouns more than either verbs or adjectives) and that members of particular semantic sub-types within a general class are borrowed more frequently than those of other sub-types (e.g., concrete versus abstract nouns). Hopper and Traugott's (1993) cline of grammaticalization represents a path along which a content item travels in its evolution to grammatical element (function word, then affix). One directional aspect of this cline involves the diminution of form and the other loss or change of semantic content (so-called "semantic bleaching"). This, in turn, provides the motivation for discussion (in Chapter 3) of both form classes and semantic types and their possible roles in borrowing. Potential points of conflict are, therefore, indicated, suggesting that form and content conspire in processes of borrowing.

Chapter 4 continues this line of reasoning and proposes that explanation lies in the gradient notions of perceptual salience and semantic transparency (as herein defined). Referring to studies of native and secondary language acquisition (e.g., Slobin 1985), it is postulated that any language learner's task is to map forms in the speech stream onto associated concepts or meanings. Clearly, an individual grammar provides a particular form (through the interface of syntax and phonology) with relative prominence based on its significance in an utterance (Caplan 1992:338). Perceptual salience, therefore, refers to the characteristics of a form and the degree to which it can be recognized and isolated, corresponding to the implications contained in clines of grammaticalization which suppose that morpheme types generally consist of significant degrees of phonological form. Semantic transparency, defined broadly as the successful linkage of form to meaning, includes degrees of perceptual salience, but it also introduces types (hence, degrees) of meaning or semantic content — therefore, the association of the concept of semantic bleaching with semantic types. Because individual languages link form and meaning in a multitude of ways — viz., they distribute meanings along indices of synthesis and fusion, and among the various form classes and semantic types in accordance with the morphological structuring of their lexicons, the transparency of meaning of a particular form from Y (to speakers of Y as well as to speakers of X, given the assumption of bilinguality) is seen as crucial in its relative borrowability into X.

Chapter 5 applies the insights and principles gained from Chapters 2–4 to an analysis of data from Malinche Mexicano, a variety of Modern Mexicano (Nahuatl), an indigenous American (First Nations or Amerindian) language of Mexico heavily interlarded with borrowings from Spanish — in various registers said to be in the range of 60% of its lexical material. Mexicano is one of the most thoroughly documented of the indigenous languages of North America as a result of careful record keeping from the very beginning of the Spanish Conquest. This documentation provides the present work with two positive rewards. First, temporal claims of borrowability can be examined in light of historical evidence with the potential to disprove particular claims (e.g., that certain grammatical affixes are not borrowable). Second, the effects of length and intensity of contact can be investigated with regard to the amount and types of borrowing one expects to occur. After nearly five centuries of close contact, a great deal of convergence, borrowing, and so on is to be expected.

The concluding chapter (Chapter 6) contains discussion of the proposed lexical-typological model against a backdrop of language contact phenomena. It centers around the programmatic nature of the model and its extension to other contact situations, including code-switching and the emergence of various contact languages. Hypothetical contact situations of various possible recipient (X) and donor (Y) languages are discussed along with specific examples from known contact situations. Finally, a proposal is made for future research on the role that different kinds of meanings are likely to play in contact phenomena.

CHAPTER 2

Morphological structuring and system compatibility

This chapter begins with a brief discussion of the analysis of morphological structure and the ways it has been applied in various branches of linguistics, from comparative and descriptive studies to those concerned with language typologies and the establishment of language universals. The kinds of distinctions that have been formulated over the years have provided researchers involved in a variety of disciplines with the terminological wherewithal to observe and discuss patterns that emerge in the various processes and phenomena they investigate. Obviously, accurate descriptions of processes and the elements affected by them are a necessary prerequisite towards explanation. Relevant to the present work, the terms derived from descriptive and typological studies have made significant contributions to the many recent advances in the diachronic study of grammaticalization and to work in bilingual/contact phenomena, including lexical borrowing, code-switching, and the emergence of entirely new language varieties.

The analysis of words into types of morphemes (free-standing versus bound, as well as word, root, stem, and affix) has remained fairly constant in recent years, although there still may be some controversy concerning the general criteria for distinguishing among certain types of bound morphemes, e.g. between derivational and inflectional affixes, and so on. There is also some discussion regarding which types of elements figure most significantly in language contact phenomena: should we look at open- versus closed-class or lexical versus function elements? While there is an obvious high correlation between the kinds of entities to which these terms are meant to refer (e.g., lexical items usually belong to the open classes and functional elements are normally members of closed classes), some researchers prefer a third set of terms, for instance, content versus system morphemes (Myers-Scotton 1993a and 1993b), which takes note of the fact that some so-called grammatical words act like lexical items. This usage is at least partly due to observations that some independent function words are selected for semantic reasons and participate in thematic role assignment, a function usually reserved for lexical items. Moreover, in languages such as English, pronouns may exhibit NP-like behavior by filling slots as grammatical subjects, objects, and so on, and modal auxiliaries can take the place of entire VPs.

From a Sapirian perspective, it may be difficult to imagine a complete and intelligible sentence composed of only so-called function words ("I do!") and no content (concrete or radical elements) items, though he did recognize the possibility (Sapir 1921:93). Nevertheless, with these caveats in mind and to avoid creating additional terminological confusion that might possibly obscure subsequent discussion, the present work will stick to the use of terms more typical of studies in borrowing and grammaticalization, even though their definitions may appear a little squishy to those accustomed to clear, unequivocal categorical distinctions; but, given the gradient nature of the phenomena being treated, such terms may be hard to come by and difficult to sustain. Attempting to preserve more traditional terminology, we will use the terms lexical and content (item) more or less synonymously, as well as the terms grammatical and function (word or element). Of course, examples will be given in the case of ambiguous reference.

One of the express aims of this work is to account for hierarchies of borrowability — why some things are borrowed more frequently than others. An additional goal is to demonstrate that, while many of the hierarchies discussed here may, indeed, be cognitively based (owing their characteristics to such recognition and production factors as perceptual salience, semantic transparency, and so on), they cannot reconcile two apparently contradictory observations: anything is or should be, in principle, borrowable, but not everything is borrowed, especially to the same extent. Haugen (1950:224) states, "All linguistic features can be borrowed, but they are distributed along a scale of adoptability... [emphasis his]". It is true that all sorts of elements have been borrowed at one time or another (see, for example, Thomason and Kaufman 1988:83ff). It seems that whatever is learnable should be borrowable (see, also, Hudson 1980:60 and Bynon 1977:255). At least a portion of the total number of bilingual speakers of the two (or more) languages participating in contact situations will be proficient enough in both (or all) to be able to draw freely upon the resources of either (all), viz., to use their elements, structures, and processes alternatively or simultaneously (e.g., in inter-sentential or intra-sentential code-switching, or for short- or long-term borrowing), for whatever sociological and/or psychological reasons that might be present.

2.1 Scales, indices, hierarchies, and clines: Continua of forms and meanings

Formal distinctions such as those established in comparative and typological studies allow us to observe the ways language systems are organized and to identify what aspects of language are involved when it is said to change. Regarding the nature of linguistic systems, Sapir (1921) helped turn attention away from languages as "wholes" (to be typed variously according to clusters of morphological properties) and onto the significance of the word in generalizations of the structure of language as a mental faculty; he noted that language "struggles towards two poles of linguistic expression — material content and relation — and that these poles tend to be connected by a long series of transitional concepts" (109). Sapir's work became the seed for many conceptualizations of language that have followed. Many of his basic distinctions have endured into studies of grammaticalization, language acquisition, and language processing.

The conception of a continuum or index of forms assumed a fundamental correspondence of independent words (or radical elements) and basic (concrete) concepts. It is at the other pole, with regard to secondary or relational concepts, that we find that they are "sparsely developed" in some languages and "elaborated with a bewildering exuberance" in others (Sapir 1921:95). It is precisely in the matching of meanings and forms that we find that languages possess their own unique logic, or "genius". This is true when looking at them synchronically as coherent systems and diachronically, as always in the grip of change, for both form and meaning are "ceaselessly changing" (98); what is evidenced now is the result of previous processes. The different scales, indices, hierarchies, and clines are fitting conclusions to these insightful observations, concerning both synchronic states and diachronic processes.

2.1.1 The indices of synthesis and fusion

In the synchronic analysis of language, we see that meanings are distributed among the forms available in a language in ways which are particular to that language. Some elements may consist of direct (one to one) mappings of specific concrete meanings (concepts) onto discrete phonological forms, while others appear to have no actual, primary meaning (or definition) at all, except to indicate purely grammatical concepts such as tense, number, case, and so on. The description of how languages distribute kinds of meaning among forms constitutes one basis by which they have traditionally been classified. For example, the fundamental character of some varieties can be distinguished along an index of synthesis, i.e., of isolating-analytical versus polysynthetic character. An isolating language (e.g., Vietnamese, Mandarin, etc.) is one that exhibits the maximal correlation of morpheme and word. That is, each word consists of one, discrete morpheme representing a single semantic concept or distinction with no affixal morphology whatsoever. At the other end of this index, a continuum of language types, are polysynthetic languages (including a subset that are incorporating) characterized by relatively long words composed of a number of morphemes, from one to many (e.g., Inuit varieties such as West Greenlandic and such Algonquian languages as Cree).

A second index, that of fusion, types varieties according to agglutinating versus fusional character, that is, according to how much lexical or grammatical information can be represented in one morpheme. On the one hand, words in an agglutinating language (e.g., Turkish) typically contain a sequence of discrete morphemes. However, distinct boundaries exist between individual morphemes, and each one expresses only one lexical or grammatical concept. On the other hand, in a fusional language (e.g., Spanish), such clear boundaries may not exist. A particular morpheme may represent a number of categories that have fused into one, unsegmentable (morphophonological) unit. To characterize the diversity of the world's languages, most (if not all) are best typed according to each of these indices, especially in view of the fact that an individual language will occupy a position relative to other languages between the extremes of both indices (Sapir 1921:120ff; Comrie 1989:47).

Within an individual language, lexical and grammatical distinctions can be represented in diverse ways. For example, in English, which is more isolating and less fusional than, say, Spanish, some grammatical forms are expressed by individual words while others are expressed through inflectional affixes (e.g., comparatives expressed by the affix *-er* versus those by the independent word *more*). Crosslinguistically, the lack of precise correlations of form and meaning creates potential mismatches in such areas as the translatability of individual lexical or grammatical items from one language to another (see, e.g. Croft 1990:11–18). To illustrate the often subtle effects of possible mismatches, some researchers consider the ways words are structured in the lexicon of a first or native language (morphological structuring) to be significant factors in bilingual comprehension and production and the relative ease with which a second (or subsequent) language is acquired. It is apparent that the more a second language resembles the first in the ways that words are structured, the easier it is to learn (Ard and Homberg 1993:62–3; Green 1993:250; cf. Schreuder and Weltens 1993 and Frauenfelder and Schreuder 1992).

In general, morphological structuring may have a number of consequences on the lexicon of a specific language. For example, a more isolating language may have a relatively large number of discrete content items — i.e., content-bearing roots and words (e.g., the Romance languages), while a (poly)synthetic language may have a relatively small number of these (e.g., Inuit varieties). In languages of the former type, referential capacity may be realized through sheer numbers of content words and morphemes, while in the latter types, it may be accomplished morphologically through the systematic application of larger numbers of derivational and inflectional affixes to a more limited number of roots or stems. What constitutes synonymous or antonymous expressions in one language may be accomplished through a diversity of radical elements — in Sapir's terminology, and in another by means of morphological complexity. This will obviously be reflected in the paradigmatic relationships among items within particular semantic domains in their respective lexicons. In an isolating language, such a paradigm will most likely consist of a variety of distinct roots. In a highly synthetic language, corresponding paradigms may consist of a single root attached to a variety of affixes; borrowing a separate root from an outside source may produce competition among forms and eventually act to break up a paradigm (one of many possible structural effects of borrowing). It seems clear, then, that patterns of borrowability will depend on the ways specific languages structure their lexicons (lexical structuring).

2.1.2 The cline of grammaticality

A number of other scales or continua of forms and/or meanings have been proposed in diachronic studies, as well. Hence, one finds in much work on grammaticalization a continuum of meanings, from purely lexical (with clear sense and reference to unique objects) to purely grammatical (which represent language-particular grammatical categories — from one to a fusion of several). This continuum of meanings, in turn, is represented by a corresponding continuum of forms and structures that extends from free-standing forms (morphemes) to bound forms (including zero forms) and structures or positions within structures. Midpoints between purely lexical (concrete or primary) and purely grammatical (relational or secondary) include elements expressing a range of less concrete semantic distinctions, e.g., certain types of modifiers (e.g., quantifiers) and expressions of mood or modality whose meanings are secondary (or relational) to the forms they usually accompany — in the case of the former, nominals, and in the case of the latter, verbals.

Among researchers specializing in grammaticalization theory, Heine et al. (1991a) apply this reasoning as a basis for their descriptions of the gradual "thinning out" of meaning (referred to as "semantic bleaching" in earlier studies) in historical processes of grammaticalization (9–10). In a similar vein, Hopper and Traugott (1993) focus on the inherently gradient character of these continua and the dichotomy between meaning and form implied in Sapir's statement in their notion of the cline (or scale) of grammaticality (7):

(1) content item > grammatical word > clitic > inflectional affix

This cline represents the process of grammaticalization, the gradual historical development of a grammatical form from content word to inflectional affix, as exemplified in (2), below:

(2) Vulgar Latin *amare habeo > Spanish amaré

Moving from left to right, there is a gradual diminution of form, from free-standing, autonomous word to grammatical affix. There is also a concomitant lessening of semantic content ("semantic bleaching"), or, rather, change from narrow lexical meaning to broad grammatical meaning. As a consequence, the meanings associated with linguistic expressions are distinguished in ways similar to the forms of language, as oppositions of lexical (or content) versus grammatical (or functional) meanings. The cline of grammaticality serves to illustrate that the various form and meaning types evinced in a particular language constitute a continuum whose individual members may be quite indistinguishable except on the basis of an abstract set of formal and semantic characteristics.

Terms like "continuum" or "cline" refer to some kind of abstraction, a theoretical line containing certain focal points at which clusters of formal properties may occur (Hopper and Traugott 1993:7). Cross-linguistically, boundaries between such focal points may seem quite arbitrary — one language makes a distinction in one place while another makes it elsewhere. However, in an individual language, relevant characteristics marking the relative positions of various form classes on a scale or index are, nonetheless, somewhat less subject to dispute (for example, the distinction between adposition and inflectional affix). A cline of grammaticality also captures the general insight that there is an opposition of specific, concrete lexical meaning often expressed by words or other "radical elements" and an increasingly generalized and abstract set of meanings expressible by grammatical elements. Even though, in a particular language, there is a high coincidence of discrete (content, open-class) word and transparent lexical meaning on one end of the scale and inflectional affix and grammatical information on the other, there is a significant lack of exact correspondence across languages at potentially matching points along the length of each continuum.

This conceptualization of a cline brings to the discussion the natural separation of form and meaning.[1] What may appear to be an idiosyncratic, perhaps random allocation of (a) a range of meanings and meaning types on to (b) a variety of forms and form types turns out to be quite systematic, nevertheless. In addition, the mapping of form onto meaning (and vice versa) surely indicates that they are, indeed, distinct and separable. Consequently, meaning and form are more properly investigated individually, bearing in mind that they are inherently and inextricably linked in a particular language. In fact, current psycholinguistic research is uncovering the many ways that forms and concepts can be accessed independently by the individual language user (Kroll and de Groot 1997:171). When investigating a previously unknown language variety, especially during its initial stages, a precise linkage would be unpredictable and would have to be apprehended through principled suppositions and on the basis of actual evidence.

When attempting to establish cross-linguistic bases for equivalence of any kind, it may be helpful to consider that the exercise of translation, which often involves renditions ranging anywhere from word-for-word interpretations to broad paraphrases, rarely involves exact formal equivalence; it is typically based on a number of ad hoc factors employed for the sake of expediency (cf. Gutknecht and Rölle 1996:2). Potential mismatches and incongruence of types of form and types of meaning are especially conspicuous in the comparison of two separate language systems that differ widely with respect to such lexical structuring (e.g., that are typologically situated at differing points along the indices of synthesis or fusion). If, within an individual language (X), there are formal criteria that provide distinctions among elements, and these criteria prevent us from equating function words and inflectional morphology, then we have even less of a basis to equate, say, adpositions in one language (Y) with affixes in another (X), except by positing some very general and perhaps abstract semantic correspondence (e.g., observations that various forms share particular functions); such attempts may be very difficult to defend on any formal basis. Moreover, the formal operations applying to affixes as opposed to independent words are

---

1. Much recent work towards the establishment of monolingual and bilingual models of lexical representation stress the need for each of these to be treated in separate, yet connected ways (see, for example, Smith 1997 and Kroll and de Groot 1997).

obviously distinct in individual languages; this fact alone may be even more telling when attempting to compare or contrast forms from distinct systems.

2.1.3 The cline of lexicality

The cline of grammaticality, stated in (1) above, portrays formal aspects of the process of grammaticalization in the gradual progression of a form from content item (word or root) to inflectional affix and captures the observation that a continuum of forms exists synchronically (at any one point in time) within a single language. In the same way, Hopper and Traugott (1993:7) illustrate the gradient quality of semantic content and the gradual evolution of a concept from one that is strictly lexical (its occurrence restricted by discourse factors such as choice of topic) to one that is increasingly grammatical (its generalized, abstract meaning enabling it to occur in a greater number of contexts) with their cline of lexicality in (3), below:

(3) a basket full (of eggs...) > a cupful (of water) > hopeful

A number of researchers working in grammaticalization studies mention an increase in abstractness (though this does not necessarily lead to grammaticalization), but also describe the semantic processes as a gradual emptying or loss of semantic complexity, pragmatic meaning, syntactic freedom, and phonological substance (Heine and Reh 1984:15; Traugott and Heine 1991:3–5; Traugott and König 1991, 189ff; Greenberg 1991:301ff; Hopper and Traugott 1993:68, 87–93; Heine et al. 1991a:39–45). It is not simply the case that the concept represented by a particular word or morpheme is merely fading to nothing; once again changes are gradual and quite likely invisible to strictly synchronic analyses.

Regarding the most likely elements to undergo grammaticalization, recent cross-linguistic studies of change have uncovered considerable evidence that only certain sub-classes of lexical items within fairly restricted semantic domains are potential candidates. Often cited examples are adpositions from body parts or verbs of motion, tense and aspect markers from spatial expressions, modals from possession terms, and so on (Traugott and Heine 1991:8). It is also evident that the progression from one type of form to another is step-by-step rather than in leaps and bounds across larger formal or semantic domains (Heine et al. 1991a:112–113; Heine et al. 1991b:161ff). Two additional examples, cited below in (4) and (5), characterize the path of grammaticalization of noun-to-affix and verb-to-affix, and serve to illustrate gradual changes in meaning and a concomitant diminution of form. The noun-to-affix cline (C. Lehmann 1986:3), however, shows that there is not only the loss of specific, concrete meaning, there may also be an increase in the amount of abstract, grammatical information contained in a single form. That is, an individual form may become the repository of a number of concepts (that may have previously been represented individually) that have coalesced (or fused together) onto that form (perhaps a phonological remnant of fusional processes).

(4)   relational noun > secondary adposition > primary adposition > agglutinative case affix > fusional case affix

This gradual decrease in lexical content is also illustrated in the verb-to-affix cline (Hopper and Traugott, 1993, p. 108):

(5)   full verb > (vector verb >) auxiliary > clitic > affix

An often cited example of the latter is the development of an inflected future tense (in various Romance languages) from a verb + have construction (Hopper and Traugott 1993:42–5; Bynon 1977:249) as represented in (2) above, repeated as (6):

(6)   Vulgar Latin *amare habeo > Spanish amaré

A scale, or cline, based solely on lexical meaning generalizable from (4) and (5) above can now be expressed as (7):

(7)   primary lexical meaning > secondary semantic distinction > single grammatical category > fusion of categories

The point at which the processes of grammaticalization eventually stop may be determined by the morphological character of the individual language (see, also, Bybee 1995:227–229). For example, in the case of postposition to case affix, pictured in (4), above, such developments have yet to be documented in a language of the isolating-analytic type, prompting claims that language internal processes of grammaticalization are not likely to motivate the development of inflectional morphology (of any kind) (Traugott and Heine 1991:9). Presumably, there is an intermediate stage in which clitic elements gradually evolve (perhaps as a result of phonological processes). However, this would entail the (more or less) simultaneous emergence of obligatorily expressed inflectional categories, as well.

2.1.4   A scale (or continuum) of morpheme types

To sum up the discussion of clines of grammaticality and lexicality to this point, it is evident that the units (morphemes or words) that link form and meaning, that are involved at all points in the construction of language, nevertheless, consist of a fairly restricted set of general forms and form types which combine to form utterances in highly idiosyncratic, language-particular ways, for instance. Moreover, it is possible to generalize further from the clines in (1)–(7) above and propose an additional hierarchical ordering of forms (i.e., at any point in time) to represent the relevant morpheme types available to any language. Therefore, the Scale (or Continuum) of Morpheme Types (stated in (8), below) is proposed. This hierarchy, consistent with both the grammaticalization clines of C. Lehmann (1986), Heine et al. (1991a), and Hopper and Traugott (1993) and with observed language particular patterns of borrowing (discussed in Section 2.2 below), is set forth as follows:

(8) independent word, bound root > agglutinating affix > fusional affix

Though the scale of morpheme types presented in this way is similar to the cline represented in (1), above, the emphasis has shifted to reflect a somewhat wider view of language types and the types of morphemes they consist of. Specifically, on the far left, the category "independent word, bound root" is inclusive of all so-called content items (independent words and contentive roots[2]) and function words (likewise, words and roots) that can be realized as independent words in their respective languages. These are the particular morpheme types permitted in isolating-analytical languages and consequently realized as discrete words. Agglutinating languages have these (independent words and roots) and types one position to the right, and fusional languages have the full complement of morpheme types.

2.2 Hierarchies of borrowability

Turning now to issues of borrowability, the striking parallels between (diachronic) clines of grammaticality and lexicality, on the one hand, and (synchronic)

---

2. In the Sapirian sense, these are "radical elements" or content-bearing morphemes of a language that can be distinguished by its speakers, whose linguistic knowledge includes the identification of "...words, significant parts of words, and word groupings" (Sapir 1921: 25ff). Whether particular radical elements are actually realized as independent words or not (the vast majority may not be in synthetic languages), they are, nonetheless understood and acquired as identifiable, non-derived stems (see Fortescue and Lennert Olsen 1992, especially 136–7 for a discussion of the acquisition of polysynthetic morphology in West Greenlandic).

hierarchies of borrowability, on the other, should become immediately evident. Taken together, there is a rather obvious inference that degrees of grammaticalization and degrees of borrowability are somehow intimately linked. This, in turn, suggests that the parallels are much more than coincidental and points to underlying causes. There appears to be substance to observations that the more structural (or grammaticalized) an element is, the less likely it will be borrowed from one language to another.

It has long been noted that some linguistic elements are borrowed more freely than others. The linguist most often cited as the first to make this observation was the Sanskritist William Dwight Whitney, who in 1881 noted that nouns are the most frequently borrowed elements of language, followed by other independent words ("other parts of speech"), then suffixes, inflections, and individual sounds (in that order). A hierarchy based on these orderings would appear as (9) below (van Hout and Muysken 1994:41):

(9) nouns > other parts of speech > suffixes > inflections > sounds

Haugen (1950) suggested a similar ordering in his scale of adoptability, based on a synthesis of data from American Norwegian and American Swedish (224):

(10) nouns > verbs > adjectives > adverbs, prepositions, interjections

In this scaling, nouns are borrowed more frequently than verbs, and verbs more frequently than adjectives, the latter an order not reflected in a report on English borrowings in Hindi (Singh 1981, cited in van Hout and Muysken 1994:41), illustrated in (11):

(11) nouns > adjectives > verbs > prepositions

In general, such hierarchies illustrate borrowing patterns that are specific to certain contact situations, and they are consistent with the statement that speakers of subordinate varieties borrow from a dominant variety content items more frequently than grammatical items and grammatical words more frequently than inflectional affixes (Comrie 1989:209–210). In (9) above, there is a much broader generalization that includes among form types nouns at one extreme end of the scale and inflections at the other. In (9), (10), and (11), nouns occupy the same positions (as the most often borrowed), but the discrepancy that appears in (10) and (11) among content items concerns which form class should follow nouns with respect to frequency (and so on) of borrowing (discussed below).

2.2.1 Borrowing hierarchies: Lexical items

It is also possible to make finer distinctions among each of the three categories (lexical items, grammatical words, and inflectional affixes). For instance, all hierarchies appear to agree that the most likely content items to be borrowed are nouns, followed by either adjectives or verbs. Similar observations can be made concerning the relative borrowability of diverse types of function words, as well.[3] It is very likely that explanations for many potential discrepancies (e.g., whether verbs are intrinsically more borrowable than adjectives) will be found by closely comparing lexical structuring and the allowable form classes in each of the participant languages. Hence, while nouns (labels for people, places, things, and so on) are reportedly the most frequently borrowed in all cases, what comes next in a proposed subhierarchy of content items may vary. Consequently, the following subhierarchy is proposed:

(12) nouns > adjectives, verbs

Some have suggested that verbs follow nouns in frequency of occurrence as a result of their relative semantic and syntactic complexity. Whether verbs precede or follow adjectives in a particular hierarchy "may just reflect the distribution of grammatical categories in native-language materials rather than the propensity of specific items to be borrowed" (Romaine 1995:65). For example, some languages (e.g., Cree and other Algonkian languages) have no adjectives; attributes of nouns are expressed through verbs, relative clauses, and so on. This may make borrowing adjectives from a donor language that may be rich in adjectives (or, "adjective rich") problematic, though not necessarily impossible.[4] In addition, it may be possible that the complexity of the processes that lead to the highly synthetic (and incorporating) verbal morphology of some languages inhibit the incorporation of borrowed verbal roots (Bakker 1994:21). Irrespective

---

3. Van Hout and Muysken 1994 investigates borrowing preferences based on probabilities of Spanish content and function words into Bolivian Quechua and make a number of distinctions among both classes of words. See, also, Muysken 2001 (73–75 and 166–167) for discussion of that particular study.

4. There are two possible ways these foreign adjectives may be handled. First, if they are reinterpreted according to matrix form-classes, of course, they can not be adjectives. They would have to be treated as belonging to an already existing form class (perhaps as verbs in this case). The second is the creation of a new form class (identifiable as having a foreign source). In either case, the borrowed morpheme will be analyzed according to the morphological possibilities of the borrowing language (content item, function word, and so on).

of the status of adjective versus verb, however, nouns (or nominal roots/stems) are the more frequently borrowed of any other class of content item.

2.2.2 Borrowing hierarchies: Grammatical items

The hierarchy in (9) also points to the fact that languages may also borrow grammatical elements; more specifically, languages are known to borrow independent function words and different types of inflectional affixes though not as frequently or extensively as content items. Characteristically, borrowing hierarchies (to date) identify a general category of inflectional affix as occupying one end point. However, they stop short of differentiating between agglutinating-type affixes, with one-to-one correspondences of form and meaning, and fusional-type affixes, which represent a coalescence of a number of grammatical categories onto a single, often phonetically minimal, form. With respect to kinds of inflectional affixes and degrees of borrowability, morphological typology is obviously key: it is"...more likely that clearly segmentable [i.e., agglutinating] affixes will be borrowed than fusional morphology..." (Comrie 1989:210). Therefore, the following subhierachy is proposed:

(13) function word > agglutinating affix > fusional affix

The hierarchical relationship of grammatical forms thus stated is consistent with a number of observations of borrowability and various grammaticalization hierarchies.[5] It also serves to illustrate implicationally that the more grammaticalized a form is, the less likely it is to be borrowed. Being located to the far right of the hierarchy, fusional affixes are clearly the least likely of all forms to be borrowed.

2.2.3 Summary of hierarchies

As anticipated, borrowing hierarchies reduce in much the same ways as grammaticalization clines and appear to be identical with the Hierarchy of

---

5. See, for example, Croft 1990:191 and his tentative hierarchy of grammatical concepts; the noun-to-affix cline of C. Lehmann, 1986:3–4 (already cited in this text); and Hopper and Traugott 1993:108ff (also cited above). The link between grammaticalization and borrowability is made more obvious when considering both reduction of form (salience) and concomitant semantic bleaching (loss of specific, concrete meaning), which can be linked also to degrees of semantic transparency.

Morpheme Types in (8) above. Thus, it is now possible to propose a preliminary scale of borrowability, stated as (14) below:

(14)   independent word, bound root > agglutinating affix > fusional affix

Items furthest to the left are the (a) content items and (b) independent function words, i.e., those free-standing and/or bound morphemes (acting as roots or stems) that are involved in the formation of classes of Noun, Verb, Adjective, and Adverb, and independent function words (free grammatical morphemes and/or bound roots capable of receiving markers of inflectional categories), including sub-classes of Determiner, Pronoun, Auxiliary, Adposition, and Connective (inclusive of Coordinators, Subordinators, Complementizers). Based on degrees of grammaticalization, we can divide the morpheme type "independent word, root" into the following:

(15)   content item > function word

Once again linking grammaticalization and borrowability, we can characterize the borrowability of function words versus affixes as (16) below (repeated from (13), above):

(16)   function word > agglutinating affix > fusional affix

Combining (15) and (16) into a single hierarchy, we have the more specific Hierarchy of Borrowability, as represented in (17):

(17)   content item > function word > agglutinating affix > fusional affix

The implicational nature of the hierarchy in (17) is two-fold. First, there is a quantitative claim which states that X will borrow (from Y) a greater number of content items than grammatical words, more grammatical words than agglutinating affixes, and so on. Secondly, there is a temporal claim which states that if language X has borrowed fusional affixes from Y, then it has already borrowed agglutinating ones; if it has borrowed agglutinating affixes, it has already borrowed grammatical words; and, if it has borrowed grammatical words, it has also (previously) borrowed content items.

The investigation of borrowing in a specific language will always depend on the particular languages involved, the word and morpheme types that exist in each language, and the ways meaning is distributed across the forms available in each. On the one hand, there are simple, one-to-one correspondences of salient phonetic forms that possess readily identifiable (transparent) meanings. These specific form–meaning sets require little or no language particular knowledge and are among the form types most frequently borrowed from one language into another. On the other hand, there are general markers of grammatical concepts that are typically less salient and less semantically transparent, as well. These markers may take a variety of forms, from free-standing function words to bound inflectional affixes, and represent more generalized, abstract meanings. Consequently, function words are less likely to be borrowed than content items. Inflectional affixes are the least likely forms to be borrowed. Stated implicationally, if a language has borrowed inflectional affixes, it will have also borrowed some grammatical words; and if it has borrowed grammatical words, it will have borrowed lexical items (Comrie 1989:210). Such a scaling is consistent with Thomason and Kaufman's "borrowing scale" (1988:74ff) and statements concerning form types from typologically distinct languages and possible mismatches of form that can affect patterns of borrowing (hence, borrowability).

The strongest argument for a strictly cognitively based explanation seems to be with respect to fusional-type affixes. In the donor system to which they belong, fusional affixes typically occupy positions within tight paradigms, and they are not generally interpretable outside of their paradigms; their identification, therefore, requires a more intimate knowledge of the donor language, including knowledge of entire paradigms and the oppositions of form and meaning they serve to indicate. They have no one-to-one mapping of form and meaning, which undoubtedly affects the efficiency and speed with which their (relational) meanings are retrieved. In addition, a single borrowed fusional affix must either become part of an existing recipient paradigm (replacing a native form) or augment the paradigm by creating a new position and a new distinction (i.e., barring a complete reanalysis of the borrowed form). In either case, the make up of original paradigms of the recipient language will be altered and the processes which distribute individual paradigm members will be necessarily affected. This involves a much greater degree of change than the simple addition of a borrowed lexical item, especially factoring in the frequency in which inflectional forms are likely to occur. We can also assume that such change takes a longer period of time to diffuse within a community-the larger the community, the longer it would take.

It has been implicit in studies of mixed languages that matrix inflectional affixes of any type are not included in processes of relexification, that is, according to a dichotomous view of language forms as either lexical or grammatical, and that the reason for this is cognitively based (in some yet to be defined way). The search for a universal cut-off point to borrowing based on such a vague notion of cognition, however, may be a red herring — after all, everything should be borrowable that is, in fact, learnable. And, assuming that in a bilingual/contact situation, at least a subset of fluent bilinguals have the ability to know and use both languages (in principle, not restricted with respect to type), such a claim may be somewhat difficult to defend. The solution proposed here is that the limits to borrowing and borrowability are established by the language systems themselves, and are, as a consequence, linguistic in nature.

2.3 The Principle of System Incompatibility

It is possible to take into account both the implicational nature of proposed borrowing hierarchies and the individual characteristics of the participating languages and formulate a principle that will be able to identify precisely the forms that are borrowable in the broadest sense. Due to its bilateral nature, its negative formulation will also expose morpheme types that are not borrowable. The identification of compatible form classes is done by superimposing the morphological typology of language X (a borrowing variety) over that of Y (a lexical donor) (see Figure 2.1). Consequently, if X is isolating-analytical (i.e., contains only independent words), all independent words in any Y are, in principle, borrowable. If X is agglutinating (contains independent words and roots and agglutinating affixes), all independent words or roots and agglutinating affixes are borrowable from any Y. Finally, if X is fusional (contains independent words and roots and both agglutinating and fusional affixes), all morphemes are borrowable from Y (see Figure 2.2).

Based on the morphological structuring of the languages involved, we can state the Principle of System Compatibility (PSC) as follows:

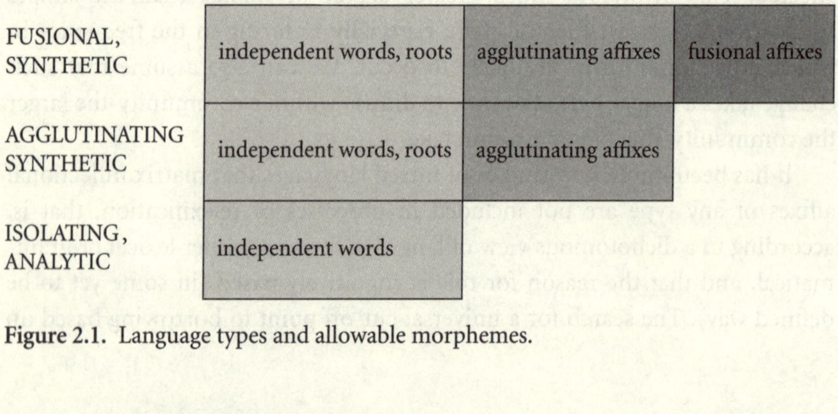

FUSIONAL, SYNTHETIC	independent words, roots	agglutinating affixes	fusional affixes
AGGLUTINATING SYNTHETIC	independent words, roots	agglutinating affixes	
ISOLATING, ANALYTIC	independent words		

Figure 2.1. Language types and allowable morphemes.

TYPOLOGY OF X	Y FORMS COMPATIBLE WITH X	Y FORMS INCOMPATIBLE WITH X
FUSIONAL, SYNTHETIC	independent words, roots agglutinating affixes fusional affixes	zero (all Y forms are borrowable)
AGGLUTINATING, SYNTHETIC	independent words, roots agglutinating affixes	fusional Y affixes, only
ISOLATING, ANALYTIC	independent words, roots (analyzed as discrete words in an isolating X)	any Y affix (including agglutinating and fusional forms)

Figure 2.2. Compatibility and incompatibility.

(18) The Principle of System Compatibility (PSC):
Any form or form–meaning set is borrowable from a donor language if it conforms to the morphological possibilities of the recipient language with regard to morphological structure.

All content items are borrowable from one language to another as are grammatical morphemes (free or bound) that can fill slots typically occupied by elements of the borrowing (recipient) language (irrespective of their meanings). As a consequence, compatibility may include any item from content word to inflectional affix. While hierarchies of borrowability assign grammatical affixes to positions that reflect the degree of difficulty with which they are borrowed, there is no principled basis for their exclusion other than to say that, in a specific language X, forms from Y are systematically blocked that cannot be recognized and processed according to the formal characteristics of forms in X. In other words, as possible forms in X, they do not exist (at least in the ways they exist in Y).

Following from the PSC as formulated in (18) above, the Principle of System Incompatibility (PSI) can be stated as follows:

(19) The Principle of System Incompatibility (PSI):
No form or form–meaning set is borrowable from a donor language if it does not conform to the morphological possibilities of the recipient language with regard to morpheme types.

Using the typology of X (the recipient language) as the basis for comparison, forms in Y that lie to the right on the hierarchy of morpheme types are rendered unborrowable. This formulation captures the fact that some agglutinating inflectional affixes are, indeed, borrowed by other agglutinating varieties (Heath 1981) (or from fusional ones, for that matter) despite claims that inflectional affixes are not borrowed (e.g., in mixed languages). In essence, the PSI states that borrowability, in a broad sense, is constrained by the morphological structuring of the languages in contact. To be more specific, strictly analytical languages (with no affixal morphology) are blocked from borrowing affixes of any kind (without perhaps reanalyzing affixes as independent words), and agglutinating languages are blocked from borrowing fusional affixes (without reanalyzing the fusional affixes as possessing one-to-one correspondences of form and meaning). Actual cut-off points will undoubtedly vary in language-specific ways relative to the typology (of morphological structuring) of the participating varieties and the ability of the recipient language (viz., its speakers) to identify donor forms and meanings.

2.3.1 Predictions within general classes

According to the PSI, language X (a recipient or borrower) can borrow from Y (a donor) any form that is consistent with its own morphology (that of X), providing that Y exhibits such forms. In other words, though change may be inevitable (especially as a result of contact), a borrowing language will act within its own typological parameters to preserve its morphological integrity: it will not borrow items that are morphologically incompatible (to the right on the indices of synthesis and fusion). The PSI simply points to formal typological constraints that define an individual item's borrowability — violations would result in typological anomalies in the borrowing language that would need to be reconciled.

To illustrate, if X is predominantly isolating, it can, in theory, borrow independent words and roots freely from Y.[6] If Y is primarily synthetic (some of its forms lie to the right in the hierarchy of morpheme types), all inflectional (and derivational) affixes will be constrained from the mix. In addition, the

---

6. Borrowed words or roots are typically treated as stems in the recipient language and take the usual affixes for the appropriate form class (Thomason and Kaufman 1988:37). These stems may contain derivational affixes or other elements (e.g., clitic articles in the case of borrowings from French) that are analyzed as part of the root, for example in Michif *zafer* "business" from French *les affaires* (Bakker 1997:103).

hierarchy expressed in (13), above, (which expresses relationships among classes implicationally) predicts that X will not borrow function words from Y unless it has borrowed content items first.[7] The reverse, however, is excluded. Even if X has borrowed content items from Y, it may not borrow grammatical words. The frequency of borrowed items will always be gradiently skewed to the left of the hierarchy — viz., X will borrow content items more frequently than function words.[8]

Synthetic languages, depending on their position along the index of fusion, may borrow content items, function words, and some types of inflectional affixes. If X is primarily agglutinating, permitting content items, function words, and agglutinating affixes, all independent words, roots, and agglutinating affixes occurring in Y are borrowable; the only items formally constrained from borrowing are fusional affixes (if they are permitted in Y). It is also implied that, if X borrows agglutinating, inflectional affixes from Y, it has already borrowed function words and content items. If X is fusional, all forms in any Y are theoretically borrowable. In each case, items gradiently positioned to the left along the hierarchy of morpheme types will be borrowed more frequently.

In theory, all content items and function words in any Y are potentially borrowable by speakers of any X irrespective of morphological typology because all languages have content items and function words.[9] In practice, X will not borrow all the forms of Y (whether they are borrowable or not). Perceptual salience and semantic transparency, in themselves relative notions, will conspire together to promote individual forms from among individual form classes. Other factors, for example frequency and intensity of exposure and relevance, will further restrict the list of possible candidates. Obviously, the actual list of

---

7. The implicational nature of the hierarchy does admit the theoretical possibility that a particular function word may be borrowed at the same time as a particular content item. The likelihood of elements from different general classes (e.g., content items and function words) being borrowed simultaneously is much reduced compared to elements from neighboring subclasses of borrowable types (e.g., nouns and adjectives).

8. There may also be a cumulative effect of the frequent borrowing morphemes of the analytical types; for instance, Modern Mexicano and Michif (with a Cree matrix), highly synthetic languages, have become more analytical as a consequence of borrowed content items from Spanish and French, respectively.

9. Recall that the discussion concerns languages in contact in which degrees of proficiency in Y by speakers of X are presumed. Content items (nouns, verbs, adjectives) are acquired first in both NL and SL acquisition. Thus, the correlation of learnability and borrowability may hold with respect to compatible items.

borrowed forms may, in fact, vary from speaker to speaker depending on such factors as degree of education (and, therefore, familiarity with and exposure to Y), occupation (restricting exposure to certain semantic domains), and so on.

2.3.2 The occurrence of anomalies: Reanalysis

In the naturally occurring speech of bilingual (X, Y) speakers, one might expect to find the occurrence of a number of apparent anomalies, for example in the case of so-called nonce borrowings or during code-switching when the switch is constituted by a single lexical item (with or without inflection) from Y embedded into an utterance in X.[10] The PSI's basic predictions refer specifically to processes that necessarily occur subsequent to such isolated occurrences that may lead to the integration of heretofore foreign elements into the recipient language. Just as phonological anomalies are resolved phonologically (perhaps by some process of imitation), morphological anomalies must be resolved morphologically. We, therefore, propose that the PSI be taken with the following caveat, as stated in (20), below, the Principle of Reanalysis:

(20) The Principle of Reanalysis (PR):
For a foreign element to be borrowed that is incompatible with the recipient system by virtue of its position outside or to the right on a scale of allowable morpheme types, it must be assigned to a position to the left that is within the typological parameters set by the recipient system.

The process so construed is analogous in a sense to the process of substitution in the phonological reproduction of foreign items, providing the mechanism by which a morpheme can be reanalyzed (so that it can "imitate" the functions of the morphemes permitted in the recipient). It amounts to the reinterpretation of an element's morpheme status to be in conformity with the recipient system regarding morphological structure. The borrowing language must (a) locate the nearest possible point along the Hierarchy of Morpheme Types that is within its own morphological parameters and (b) assign the heretofore incompatible item to that position. Assuming that morphological character varies along the axes

---

10. The term *nonce* borrowing refers to the spontaneous, one-time borrowing of a form from Y that has yet to be fully integrated into X. It may be morphologically and syntactically adapted, but show minimal phonological integration. For opposing views of the usefulness of this term, see Myers-Scotton 1993a (e.g., 20–23) and Poplack, Sankoff, and Miller 1988 (e.g., 47–50) or Sankoff, Poplack, and Vanniarajan 1990.

of synthesis and fusion, reanalysis requires the assignment of the incompatible element to a position far enough to the left along one (and only one) of these axes to be within the morphological parameters set by the recipient, hence, matrix system.

Accordingly, strictly isolating languages cannot borrow affixes, per se, because the occurrence of even one affix (i.e., via processes identifiable as affixation) would constitute a systematic anomaly. In order for this incompatible element to be fully integrated into an isolating-analytical morphosyntactic system, it must become compatible: it must be reanalyzed to the left of the index of synthesis, as an independent word, thus preserving the morphological integrity of the recipient language. Similarly, synthetic languages that are primarily agglutinating cannot borrow fusional affixes, per se. In the event that a fusional-type affix occurs in an otherwise agglutinating language (e.g., as part of a nonce borrowing or single-item code-switch), it cannot be fully integrated into the recipient language unless or until it is reanalyzed as agglutinating-it must be assigned to a position to the left on the index of fusion. Semantically and morphologically, this amounts to its reinterpretation as having a one-to-one correspondence of meaning and form, which is likely to appear as a case of simplification. One can imagine that reanalysis of this sort is quite rare; however, it has been said to occur, for instance, in Mednyj Aleut, which "reduces Russian sets of endings, unifies their range of meanings, etc..." (Golovko 1994:116).

2.3.3 Predictions within subclasses

It is yet again possible to be more specific within smaller subclasses; however, predictions cannot be made solely according to general morphological structure; it is much more likely that individual semantic characteristics will play the greater role. For example, within subclasses of noun, concrete nouns are borrowed more often than abstract nouns (see Chapter 4). While the frequency of occurrence of an individual item in the language may be a factor with respect to content items/roots (i.e., as measured in various corpora), frequency of exposure and relevance undoubtedly play greater roles in whether or not a form is learned by an individual speaker.[11] That is, for a particular content item to

---

11. Salience may be associated with and reinforced by frequency; the more times a person hears a particular form, the easier it will be to recognize and recall. Likewise, the desire to attach a meaning onto a form will most likely depend on its relevance (how important

be learned, a speaker needs to be exposed to it, and it will need to be relevant (there is a need to learn it). Consequently, those who work in an environment in which nautical terms are in frequent usage learn nautical terms; those who are involved in agriculture (e.g., on farms, co-operatives, plantations, and so on) learn agricultural terms. As a semantic domain, the nomenclature associated with a particular occupation, social institution (e.g., religious terminology), and so forth will be familiar and relevant to those involved in such areas. The same can be said of other content words (verbs, adjectives) as a whole, though nouns will be more frequently borrowed than verbs or adjectives.

With respect to function words, individual inflectional affixes, and grammatical categories in general, their diversity and language specificity present numerous problems in borrowing and acquisition. Nevertheless, some forms may be easier to pick out of the speech stream and associated onto meanings because they are more salient than others (as a result of certain content-word-like behaviors) and/or because they are more semantically transparent. For example, pronouns in English can behave in NP-like ways. They have reference, occupy grammatical subject position and are assigned semantic role, can receive phrasal and clausal stress, participate directly in syntactic processes, and so on. In comparison, the articles of English carry out numerous and sometimes conflicting discourse and semantic functions, e.g., indicating such distinctions as old versus new information, definite versus indefinite, specific versus nonspecific, count versus non-count noun, etc. As a subclass of pronominals, personal pronouns in languages such as English appear quite early in second language acquisition, while mastery of the articles (i.e., a/n and the) is notoriously problematic leading to later acquisition.[12]

2.3.4 The relative timing of borrowed elements

The hierarchies and subhierarchies of borrowability predict that when contact is initiated, the first elements to be borrowed will be content items. The current work also points out that they are borrowed first as a general class because they are the most salient and transparent of all potentially borrowable elements. Forms (labels) with visible, tangible referents are the easiest to learn; so, nouns

---

knowing its meaning is to perform a particular job and so forth).

12. See Chapter 4 for a comprehensive discussion of the formal and semantic characteristics that pertain to degrees of identifiability and, hence, borrow ability of items within various subclasses.

(as a subclass within the class of content items) will be among the first content items to be borrowed. Nouns will then be followed by other content items, for instance adjectives or verbs, depending on the morphological structuring of the languages in contact. It is very unlikely that any X will borrow verbs (and only verbs) from Y without having already borrowed nouns; consequently, languages whose contact is fairly limited may borrow only nouns.

There is a certain amount of logical necessity involved in this ordering, as well, especially with respect to the order of acquisition in a particular language. In order to attribute qualities to a thing, it is well to know what that thing is and what it is called, although it is not a logical necessity — the label for a general attribute may in many cases be acquired before the name of all particular persons, things, and so on that may possesses that attribute. Because actions involve complex relationships among participants (human, animate, and inanimate agents, themes, and instruments) and things acted upon (patients, goals, and so on), the prior knowledge and possession of names for these participants will be required, even though it should be obvious that when two languages are involved (i.e., in bilingual/contact settings), the actual labels may originate from either X or Y.

The hierarchy formulated in (2) essentially rules out the possibility that any X will borrow adjectives (or verbs) more frequently than nouns from any Y. However, it may be possible (though not likely) for X to borrow, say, a particular adjective or verb from Y before a particular noun (assuming that any element is, in principle, borrowable), but it will have to do so without violating the general tendency to borrow nouns more frequently. Another possibility naturally follows that is consistent with the implicational nature of such hierarchies: particular adjective-noun or verb-noun pairs may be borrowed simultaneously. That is, a particular adjective may be borrowed at the same time as a particular noun, or a particular verb may be borrowed at the same time as a particular noun. This may be especially likely when their co-occurrence is the norm, as in cases where frequent collocations occur within relatively restricted semantic domains, for instance, involving occupational nomenclature (agricultural, nautical, religious, and so on).

Borrowing, especially that which may lead to relexification, is necessarily a gradual process. Consistent with observations of doubling phenomena in language change, in general (Hawkins 1990: 98), it is quite likely that X will pass through stages in which single referents have two labels existing side by side. Each label can become more specialized and acquire more exact, differentiated meanings; the labels may split the semantic load, each inheriting only one of the possible meanings. In other cases, "older" forms may be remembered only by older (or more conservative) speakers, while the "new" forms may increase in currency for a variety of reasons. Original (X) forms may be completely forgotten (especially in cases of language shift) and lost. Differences between garden variety borrowing and relexification are seen here as essentially quantitative. Intense contact along with the acute nature of shift in some former colonial communities has had the obvious capacity to accelerate change of all sorts, especially within particular domains, and borrowing is no exception. What is remarkable about relexification is that vocabulary replacement is so complete that — where both continue to exist — relexified X may no longer be understandable to speakers of conservative varieties of X (that are not relexified to the same extent), even to those speakers who may be familiar with Y.

CHAPTER 3

Form classes and semantic types

To briefly sum up what has been covered to this point, we can say that lexical borrowing appears to involve the importation of form–meaning sets from one language into another. How these form–meaning sets are assembled into words to be used in everyday speech will, of course, depend on the morphological structure of the recipient language. Some sorts of reanalysis may be necessary as borrowed forms are integrated into a new linguistic system, which may be accomplished in a number of ways and at different levels of grammar (phonologically, semantically, morphologically, and syntactically), perhaps in parallel fashion. It is also clear that some donor forms are borrowed more easily than others (e.g., content versus function items) and that not all words or morphemes from a donor will be borrowed in practice (there appears to be a saturation point, most likely determined by social factors), despite the fact that any word or morpheme (content or grammatical) that is learnable may be borrowable.

Observations such as these have led to the postulation of the Principle of System Incompatibility (PSI), based on morpheme type, which identifies a single cutoff point in any borrowing situation past which forms cannot be borrowed. Adherence to the PSI preserves the morphological integrity of the recipient language for the sake of continuity and stability, though the cumulative effects of borrowing may eventually lead to morphological and syntactic change. As stated in previous sections, boundaries between morpheme types and, hence, among word classes (e.g., on clines of grammaticality) are not always distinct. This situation becomes more complex when looking at different systems in contact because exact form class correspondences at the morpheme or word level may be relatively difficult to establish. An important question to be posed at this juncture, and which should be answerable by any framework purporting to offer a model for borrowing, may be the following: what exactly is borrowed when a form, morpheme or word, goes (is copied) from one system to another? The answer to this must include instances in which an item appears to undergo a change in class membership, as in the case of a Spanish adjective being reinterpreted as a Chiricahua verb (see Section 1.2.1, above).

The overriding theme of this chapter is the centrality of meaning in processes of borrowing. It is argued that borrowing involves form–meaning sets irrespective of word-class membership. Obviously, borrowed elements originate as either words or parts of words (morphemes) in the donor language. Individual speakers of relative proficiencies in either or both donor and/or recipient must identify form–meaning sets from among an extensive inventory of linguistic elements for incorporation into the recipient, a list of potential candidates that is essentially the donor lexicon minus incompatible forms. This necessarily involves word and morpheme recognition and a degree of morphological analysis of candidate forms in the donor. Nevertheless, this is quite distinct from issues of morphological reanalysis that are addressed by the PSC and its correlate, the PSI.

3.0.1 The relationship of word class and semantic type

Despite the readily apparent diversity in particular languages and potential for cross-linguistic discrepancies, any bi- or multi-lingual contact situation that involves the interaction of distinct linguistic systems brings with it the tacit understanding that there are equivalences or correspondences of some kind in such areas as the translatability of individual words and phrases from one language into another, even if this can only be done through broad paraphrase.[1] For translation to be possible at all, bilingual speakers must assume that they can find corresponding utterances in each of their languages-irrespective of typological distance. It would be naive to think that any two languages could exist having exact morph-for-morph equivalents (beyond perhaps particular subclasses of noun or verb). This is true between languages that are close genetic relatives or dialects of the same language, as well. Subtle differences will occur despite any close typological fit. A rough translation based on functional equivalence (for expedience in communication) is not formal linguistic equivalence. Conversely, it would be unreasonable to speak of formal equivalence as a rough translation, at least in the vast majority of cases, partly because lack of direct correspondence of individual forms cannot block effective translation (see Croft 1990: 13). The two issues are clearly separate despite the

---

1. Recall that two (or more) languages are said to be in contact when they are spoken by members of a single community (Chapter 1); the internal interaction of linguistic systems — in the heads of individuals — manifests itself as performance phenomena (transfer, borrowing, code-switching, and so on).

fact that they may occasionally coincide. Based on these observations, we may assume that bilinguals find at least some intuitive grounds for their determinations of correspondence.

The present work proposes that the primary basis is, in fact, semantic by positing that what is actually borrowed is a core meaning or concept and the label (a phonetic string) for that concept, that is, a form–meaning set. Previous word class membership (being assigned by the donor morphosyntax) is rendered moot by the very act of borrowing. Such a view is compatible with a number of current models of morphological processing that consider morphemes (and perhaps words) as epiphenomenal and lacking independent status (Bybee 1995:233).[2] It seems much more likely that assignment to particular word-classes comes later, as a result of borrowing. Granted, in most cases this means assignment will be to a similar class (e.g., nouns in a donor language usually function as nouns in a recipient). If donor items were to be imported strictly on the basis of syntactic affiliation, a language could only borrow those items for which it already possessed equivalent (sub)classes. For example, a language without a class of adjectives (identified by its unique distributional and morphological characteristics in the donor) would not be able to borrow an adjective without, perhaps, bringing the class designation along with it. This hardly seems plausible for a single item. Even in cases where a word class is apparently borrowed (as in Michif), there may be a number of factors in play, including obvious structural borrowing.

However, if the borrowed form is first associated with a particular semantic type or subtype, its assignment into an appropriate word class for appropriate distribution and/or morphological marking will be automatic and analogous to other members of that semantic (sub)type in the recipient system. This can occur whether the recipient word class is identifiable as equivalent to that from which it originated or not. Lexical borrowing, then, may begin when an individual speaker (or group of speakers) of the recipient language associates a desired form–meaning set with an equivalent semantic type or subtype on the basis of semantic congruence.[3] For instance, a "name for a concrete object" is

---

2. For additional discussion of these proposed models, see, for example, Anderson 1992 (56ff), Matthews 1991 (21f), and Spencer 1991 (52, 434).

3. Semantic congruence is probably best viewed as gradient. The degree of congruence may be significant when, for instance, the meanings of two forms overlap in certain situations, as in cases of hyponymy and near synonymy. Minimal semantic congruence may be construed as (merely) belonging to the same semantic subtype.

interpreted as belonging to the same semantic subtype as other "names of concrete objects" and emerges as a morpheme of the appropriate type in the recipient. Because it is identified with other morphemes of a particular subtype, it can be assumed to have certain basic morphological properties (free or bound, root or affix) in accordance with its type in the recipient language system. On-line determination of exact cross-linguistic word-class equivalence becomes irrelevant. In addition, morphological (re)analysis is relatively unencumbered and natural-according to the recipient system.

3.0.2 Form–meaning sets and semantic types

While the number of form–meaning sets ("concepts" in the Sapirian sense) represented by individual words and the morphemes they are composed of is in principle limitless due to their sheer numbers and potential for specificity, the number of semantic types constitutes a range of possibilities that is significantly reduced as a consequence of its more general character. For instance, names of people and objects can be classed as concrete nouns, concepts of time as abstract nouns, and so forth. We can represent these relationships according to a somewhat simplified version of set theory, avoiding, for the present, matters of cross-classification, overlaps, multiple sets, and so on. This is portrayed in (1), below:

(1) form–meaning sets → semantic type (morphemes or words)

Semantic types and subtypes cluster (as subsets of a sort) into word classes (so-called parts of speech) which compose a list of classifications even more restricted in number resulting from its considerably greater general character. For example, names of people, objects, and places are commonly represented by only one general form-class, Noun. In fact, every major form class can be divided into collections of semantic types (cf. Dixon 1991:6ff). We see these relationships illustrated in (2), below:

(2) semantic types (morphemes, words) → word class (N, V, Adj...)

The path that a borrowed form–meaning set takes as it enters a recipient lexicon and is consequently integrated (morphologically and syntactically) into the recipient system can be represented according to these same basic organizing principles, as pictured in (3), below:

(3) form–meaning set → semantic type → word class

Across languages, groupings may be quite similar, though we have learned to anticipate that there will be differences as a consequence of language-particular grammatical characteristics. What may be a proper subset of one word class in X may be a subset of another in Y (Sapir 1921:117; Dixon 1991:9,77). The ways concepts (form–meaning sets) are assigned to syntactic (word) classes may be subject to some variation. The starkest examples of this are grammatical concepts (e.g., function words), but that does not necessarily preclude the possibility, or even likelihood, that lexical concepts (content items, whether independent words or bound roots) will be subject to similar classification problems, as well.

3.0.3 Organization of this chapter

The discussion begins with an overview of notions of word and word class and on descriptions of and comparisons among morpheme types and their roles in the construction of words. Consequently, formal contrasts are presented between items occupying extreme ends of the Scale of Morpheme Types, i.e., content items versus inflectional affixes, moving on to the comparison of the remaining types, content items versus grammatical words, and grammatical words versus inflectional affixes (and clitics). From there, we proceed to more specific discussion of various form classes (noun, verb, adjective, etc). Subsequently, general semantic contrasts are made, first between content items and grammatical affixes-focusing on the Sapirian distinction between primary ("material content") and secondary ("relational") meaning. Function words, at midpoints between content items (words and bound roots) and inflectional affixes are discussed at length, especially in light of the fact they constitute obvious points of conflict (or mismatch of forms) between two languages in contact. Finally, discussion shifts to semantic types, representing the kinds of meanings that are allocated into various, language-specific form classes. This semantic approach allows us to characterize linguistic borrowing as the copying of semantic entities with accompanying labels from one lexicon into another, which affords the recipient language maximum freedom of reanalysis in the preservation of its morphological integrity.

3.1 Notions of word and word class

The most significant units of language (written and spoken) are words, and these are composed of different types of morphemes. Discussion of one necessarily involves the other. Sapir (1921) portrayed the meaningful elements of language according to fundamental "notions" of subject or content matter (so-called radical elements) and additional concepts of a more abstract nature (grammatical elements), "of person, number, time, condition, function, or of several of these combined" (Sapir 1921:25). In general, words can be independent entities (consisting of individual, free-standing morphemes), combinations of bound roots representing primary, concrete meanings joined with language-particular subsidiary or relational concepts (represented by types of affixes), or other language-specific aggregates of morpheme types (e.g., inflected function words composed of a bound root plus various grammatical markers, etc.). The possibilities intrinsic to a particular language are determined by its morphological typology (Chapter 2). In any case, words form the essential building blocks of speech, representing the topics (content), attitudes (intent), and concepts that must be expressed if language is to fulfill its referential and expressive functions.

Sapir (1921) discusses the integrity of the word in terms of a native speaker's own intuition. For instance, whether it consists of one or several morphemes, a word is not divisible without rendering the parts "meaningless" in some sense: "[A word] cannot be cut into without a disturbance of meaning, one or the other or both of the severed parts remaining as a helpless waif on our hands" (Sapir 1921:34). He also refers to phonological properties, specifically "accent" (stress), as marking the internal cohesiveness of the word, even though the boundaries between words may become rather blurred in actual speech (as a result of language-particular prosodic patterns).[4]

Bloomfield (1933) describes form-classes as determined by function. For example, substantive expressions (nouns) share many functions, e.g., the positions of actor or goal with a verb, point of reference with respect to adpositions, underlying the identification of pronouns and possessives, and so on (265). Thus, he distinguishes form classes, for example, according to the English actor-action construction in which the form class of nominative expressions (in languages such as English) precedes the form class of finite verb expressions. Bloomfield equates position with function in that the positions that forms may occur in indicate their functions, and, collectively, their function. Forms that

---

4. In this respect, a number of current approaches offer definitions of phonological word that appear to be at odds with those that are primarily syntactic or morphological (e.g., Di Sciullo and Williams 1987; Levelt 1992; Bierwisch and Schreuder 1992). Phonological factors affecting word boundaries may have additional consequences in the on-line recognition of forms.

can fill given positions, therefore, constitute form classes: any English word or phrase that can fill the actor position in the actor-action construction is, therefore, a member of a "great form-class" called nominative expressions; any word or phrase occupying the action position is a member of another great form-class, finite verb expressions (Bloomfield 1933: 185). Thus, word class can be defined along the lines of function or role within a sentence and position with respect to other expressions (words and phrases). In other words, a word is primarily classified by its characteristic relationships with other words and their distributional properties. That is, nouns or verbs appear in certain contexts (e.g., as heads of NPs and VPs, respectively).

There may be a degree of circularity in this reasoning (nouns appear where nouns appear), though it is clearly true that context restricts the occurrence of nearly every linguistic unit or class (except sentence) that may characterize its distribution. However, in many cases there is a certain degree of ambiguity involved, as when members of different form classes can occupy identical slots (e.g., following a copula in languages such as English or Spanish).[5] Distributional criteria also reflect the fact that members of a particular class may be distributionally equivalent, where each member occurs in similar contexts, or in complementary distribution, where particular elements have no common contexts, which can apply to certain phonemes, affixes, and words of particular semantic subtypes (Lyons 1968: 70–72). Nevertheless, functional and distributional characteristics apply to any morpheme type in a given language; this applies to affixes, as well. For example, one distributional restriction on inflectional affixes is that they can only appear on members of particular word classes: nominal affixes denoting such categories as number, case, and gender/class usually appear only on noun stems (or are spread by processes of concord), and verbal affixes denoting tense or aspect appear only on verb stems.

Patterns of occurrence lead to the paradigmatic relationship of one form with all other forms that may appear in the same context and syntagmatic relationships with various forms that constitute its context. Certain subsets of nouns, for instance, form paradigms (e.g., units of measurement, ounce, pound, and ton, that may occur in such expressions as an ounce of coffee and a pound of coffee...). Syntagmatic relations lead to the precise patterning of these terms within the expression "a/n ___ of coffee". As a direct consequence of such

---

5. This is typical of the difficulty in distinguishing between members of noun and adjective classes in languages such as Spanish. See Chapter 6 for discussion.

grammatical patterning, these forms or words (ounce, pound, and ton) are said to belong to the same grammatical class (in this case, a sub-set of noun).

Obviously, notions of word and word class can be looked at from a number of perspectives, which may be in large part due to the fact that there are usually clear connections between distribution (i.e., position and word order) and grammatical function. Moreover, function is typically linked to meaning (semantic agents are often grammatical subjects). Theoretically, the two (semantic role and grammatical function) remain distinct (Lyons 1968: 73), a fact that is clearly demonstrated by the diverse strategies with which languages encode grammatical and semantic relations, e.g., through word order, morphological markers, and so on.[6]

Because the surface appearance of forms does not change from class to class in more isolating/analytical languages like Vietnamese, it might be difficult to distinguish to which word class a particular form belongs, especially in the absence of a grammatical and/or semantic context. Unless form-class membership is specifically and uniquely marked (i.e., morphologically), there is always the potential for a certain amount of ambiguity. The form–meaning set qua word *love* in English seems to belong to both great classes of noun and finite verb expressions, as in the following: (a) *Love is kind* and (b) *John and Mary love each other*. In (a), according to positional, functional, and distributional criteria, "love" belongs to the form-class of noun, while in (b), it is a finite verb. It is apparent that the former inflects for the form class Noun, while the latter, the form class Verb. What is the same about them is a core meaning and its associated phonetic string [lʊv].

Whether each individual occurrence of a form in different syntactic contexts must be treated as a manifestation of a separate lexical entry or not may be somewhat controversial. It most likely depends more on one's viewpoint of the nature of the mental lexicon and so forth than anything else. Whatever the final outcome of this debate might be, the vast majority of the morpheme types in any language are, nonetheless, classifiable as either freestanding words (or bound roots, stems, or bases) or various types of affixes according to fairly unambiguous morphological criteria.

---

6. We would be remiss if we failed to mention ergative languages as an example of this potential for diversity.

3.2 Contrasting points on a continuum

Establishing and comparing types of morphemes (as we have seen in Chapter 2) is, in fact, an attempt to contrast points on a continuum. Distinctions between adjacent members may seem somewhat arbitrary at times. It is considerably easier (and clearer) to look first at points at opposite extremes of a spectrum, in essence, contrasting black and white, rather than shades of gray. Points toward the middle can be said to more greatly resemble one extreme or the other. The criteria will be formal, based, for example, on distributional and morphological characteristics, and semantic, perhaps, a more specific and explicit measure regarding major word classes.

3.2.1 Formal characteristics: Grammatical affixes versus content items

The number of inflectional affixes that a language possesses depends in some measure on the number of inflectional categories it obligatorily expresses (cf. Bybee 1995:228), mediated by the number of categories expressible in a single morpheme in that language. As with function words, they constitute closed classes, whose membership is generally fixed. In fusional languages, grammatical affixes may represent a coalescence of categories whose multiple (simultaneous) meanings can only be determined in opposition to other members in their specific paradigm; this stands in stark contrast to content items which can be associated with individual visible, tangible referents (and so on).[7]

With respect to their internal characteristics, affixes are bound, by definition, and are, therefore, subordinate in form while content items can be either separate words or constitute bases or stems to which affixes attach. They lie within word boundaries and are systematically removed from stems and replaced by equivalent morpheme types (affixes) or other members of their paradigms.[8] Inflectional affixes typically do not draw word stress except as a result of normal, language-specific patterns on words; the capacity to receive primary word stress is generally reserved for the radical (or content) elements

---

7. This is discussed at length in Chapter 4.

8. In this respect, the Semitic languages behave similarly to Indo-European ones even though, generally speaking, inflectional morphology is primarily expressed by changing vowel (and some consonant) patterns of a word and not directly by application of discrete affixal morphemes (Bybee 1995:233).

to which they are affixed (Hopper and Traugott 1993:145ff). As a consequence, they quite often lack perceptual salience.[9]

Contributing to a relative lack of on-line phonological prominence, their realizations are often characterized as brief sequences of sounds typically ranging from a single syllable to a single phoneme, in contrast with content items, which can be of varied length and phonological complexity. There are a number of possible explanations for this: one is that the relatively simple phonological form of an individual affix results from the fact that it belongs to a limited set of single, bound morphemes whose occurrence is relatively frequent in speech, and, as a consequence, that identification requires less phonetic information (i.e., subsequent to the acquisition of the entire paradigm). Another lies in their possible historical origins (as descended from independent words) and the processes of grammaticalization (Hawkins and Cutler 1988:310; Hall 1988:335–44; Heine et al. 1991a:19–20; Hopper and Traugott 1993:145–6).

Positionally, they appear before, after, or within appropriate radical elements (bases); viz. they are prefixes, suffixes, or infixes. Their placement within a phrase, clause, or other larger unit of discourse is derived exclusively from the positional character of the word class members to which they customarily attach. In general, they apply "outside" all derivational processes; i.e., they are affixed to stems or bases subsequent to the application of derivational morphemes (in the formation of a stem) and may even be applied to larger syntactic units (such as phrases) acting as formal, semantic units, even though they may adhere to only one of the collection of elements. For example, the genitive marker *'s* in English phrases like "*the Mayor of Lancaster's limousine*, where, although the *mayor* is the possessor of the *limousine*, the *-'s* inflection is attached to *Lancaster*" (Katamba 1993:209). Finally, regarding position, they may be configurational: "These are so called because the choice of a particular inflection is determined by the place occupied by a word in a syntactic configuration, i.e. its position and function as a constituent of a phrase, or some other syntactic structure" (Katamba 1993:209).

With respect to their functional roles, inflectional affixes may serve a variety of language-specific grammatical and semantic functions (while content items carry the basic semantic content of an utterance):

---

9. The inflectional affixes of English are a case in point. There are, however, a numerous exceptions: nearly all verbal markers of tense/aspect in Spanish receive primary word stress with the exception of the basic present tense (but not most present forms of *estar*, to be).

a. they mark grammatical or semantic role, enabling content forms to fit into particular syntactic slots;
b. they provide markers of language-specific tense, person, or number distinctions without changing the referential or cognitive meaning or word class of the stems they attach to;
c. they indicate inherent properties such as the gender, animacy, or other class of a noun, that must be accessed by agreement rules;
d. and, their application is obligatory when required by syntax, e.g., when marking agreement of grammatical categories across or within phrasal boundaries.

Distributionally, selection may be made according to the inherent properties of the particular content items to which they attach, e.g., according to specific conjugation classes in such languages as Spanish (whose so-called theme vowels serve to designate such classes). They may apply to members of broad paradigms. For instance, some affixes apply only on certain kinds of nouns while others apply only on particular verbs or verbal auxiliaries. The content items (or radical element) to which particular inflections are joined are allowed, as a consequence, to become members of a relatively broad, grammatical paradigm: *sea* and *seas* are opposed within a paradigm constituting the opposition of singular and plural, which (only) applies to countable nouns (Matthews 1991:38). While the word class that is affected by this distinction is large (in fact, as an open class, its membership is theoretically unlimited), the number of inflections necessary to mark this very general distinction is two (one typically being a zero form). Generally, then, the smaller the number of grammatical affixes belonging to a specific paradigm, the larger the potential number of items (or class of items) that can be morphologically marked. The alternate use of a singular or plural form (especially in subject position) will trigger agreement patterns that are strictly grammatical and language specific (e.g., in the case of English, upon certain demonstratives within the noun phrase — *this/that* with singular count or mass nouns and *these/those* on plural — and on the tensed verb within finite verb phrases).

3.2.2 Semantic characteristics: Grammatical affixes versus content items

On the one hand, content items are generally understood to carry the primary semantic content of an utterance, identifying the topic(s) under discussion (the persons, objects, activities, etc.), and so on. On the other, inflectional affixes function to specify additional information of a strictly grammatical nature. For example, some grammatical affixes may mark certain temporal characteristics such as aspect or tense that are highly relevant to the central action represented by a verb (Bybee 1985: 15). Other grammatical affixes may mark such categories as number or gender that are directly relevant to classes of noun (i.e., to identify how many of a particular semantic type are involved in an action). In either case, neither the action nor the actors change identity or reference.

Constituting the vast majority of words in any language, content items are customarily defined as having stateable lexical meaning. Forms that designate people, places, things, and so on, traditionally called nouns, make reference to concepts that exist (at least in the imaginations of speakers) in some objective or subjective way (i.e., having a physical, visible, and tangible referent or referring to psychological states such as sentiments, emotions, etc.). Items that typically indicate activities or actions, states of being, and are the main elements of VPs (Lyons 1968: 423ff) are traditionally called verbs. A third class, Adjective, includes items that specify certain attributes of nouns. It is assumed that all languages have classes of Noun (nominals) and Verb (verbals), less frequently classes of Adjective (the attributes of nouns being expressed by alternative, e.g., verbal, means).[10]

Content items are often characterized metaphorically as vocabulary items or entries in a dictionary (to indicate clear links to people, objects, visible qualities, etc.). Such characterizations lead to the awareness that they do, indeed, have identity outside of any syntactic context though actual usage may limit the possible meanings an item can have in a specific utterance. This property is particularly significant when investigating word or morpheme meaning in synthetic-fusional language types such as Spanish or Italian in which nouns and verbs typically receive various inflections. In each, nouns obligatorily express gender and number and finite verbs tense–aspect and agreement of person and number with grammatical subject via inflectional morphemes which attach to word roots. The associative meaning of a particular

---

10. Many traditional grammarians identify a fourth major class, Adverb, which in a language like English is said to modify the meanings of verbs, adjectives, and other adverbs; others prefer to lump adverbs and adjectives together into a single classification. To enter into this particular controversy is, needless to say, beyond the scope of this work, even at the risk of creating a deafening silence. Linguists, however, often refer to certain classes of words indicating temporal distinctions in various languages as adverb(i)al elements (e.g., derivational affixes, particles, words, phrases, etc.) whether or not they wish to distinguish a special (open) word class in a specific language.

content item must be acknowledged apart from its inflection, as "existing outside of any particular syntactic context" (Aronoff 1994:11).[11] Content items are also organizable into semantically based groupings (or fields) such as color terms, verbs of saying, relational terms (e.g., kinship terms), taxonomies (hierarchies such as *animal, mammal, dog, spaniel* including such part-whole hierarchies as *finger–arm–hand–body*), complementaries (e.g., *right–wrong*), antonyms (gradable pairs such as *tall–short*), directional oppositions (e.g., *bring–take*), synonyms, polysemies, and so on (Hopper and Traugott 1993:97).

Semantic content is formally associated with open-classes. Human experience informs us that the range of possible referents is open-ended (perhaps inexhaustible), and our linguistic devices need to reflect that reality. In some approaches, adpositions (members of a more grammaticalized closed-class) are included as lexical (or content) items (Katamba 1993:41). However, the concepts they express are always relational and secondary (in the Sapirian sense), even in instances when they are semantically selected — marking location in space or time, for example — and not obligatorily expressed as a result of a syntactic rule or selectional restriction.[12] As likely products of grammaticalization processes, they may show a range of semantic independence; the increased abstractness and generality characteristic of their meanings may straddle some sort of lexical-grammatical frontier (between function word and grammatical affix), perhaps being represented in one morpheme type or another depending on the degree of grammaticalization.[13]

Grammatical affixes, as noted above, are associated with inflectional categories, although it may be difficult at times to distinguish among inflectional and derivational processes. Fusional affixes, the most grammaticalized of the morpheme types, are always (by definition) members of tight-knit grammatical paradigms, and, as such, cannot be understood except in context (i.e., when

---

11. The fact that content items have identity that is separable from language particular morphology and syntax undoubtedly contributes to the increased likelihood of borrowability.

12. The term "lexical" is sometimes used with a slightly different sense, also in opposition to "grammatical", but referring more to independent word status. For example, a lexical (or analytical) strategy refers to the practice of employing a word (unit of vocabulary) to convey a specific meaning which may also be (in some equivalent sense) represented by a grammatical affix. An example of this would be *a picture of my mother* versus *my mother's picture*. The use of the genitive marker -'s does, however, create an ambiguity that is not present in the lexical version. (See Crystal 1991:200f)

13. See Chapter 4 for a more comprehensive discussion of grammaticalized meanings.

attached to an appropriate root) and in relation to other members of their paradigm. Obviously, the kinds of meanings that are expressed by inflectional affixes are quite different from the meanings associated with the words they help to form (cf. Beard 1981). While content items maintain the relationship of signifier and signified (in the Saussurean sense) to the fullest possible extent, inflectional affixes, especially those that are fusional, have no tangible referent possible-they mark language-particular inflectional categories. Even agglutinating affixes, which may appear to be semantically simple in a sense by virtue of their one-to-one linkage of meaning and form, deal with the "bound realization of syntactic categories" (Aronoff 1994: 15) and remain outside possible derivations of their lexical hosts.

3.2.3 Function words: Formal and semantic characteristics

Standing at midpoints between content items and inflectional affixes are function words. The behaviors they exhibit (i.e., their functional and distributional characteristics) and the meanings they express run the full gamut of those shown by nearly every other type of element, from content (lexical) to inflectional. Upon careful examination, they clearly occupy points stretching nearly the entire breadth of a continuum of morpheme types. However, in all cases, they are members of closed classes. Positionally, functionally, and distributionally, they represent perhaps the most diverse group in that they constitute numerous language-specific subclasses with a wide variety of functions and distributional characteristics. Perhaps their only unifying characteristic is their status as independent words, even though some of them may receive markers (or assume suppletive forms to complete paradigms) for tense, person, and so on (e.g., the various forms of the English auxiliary "to be").

In any comparative study of languages, function words pose special problems, especially in view of the fact that what may be expressed by an affix in one language (e.g., an agglutinating one) may be similarly expressed by an independent word in another, especially in varieties that are relatively high on the index of synthesis. Even within an individual language, certain redundancies may appear: Spanish *yo* as nominative, first person, singular pronoun and verbal first person, singular, present tense suffix -*o*. Languages such as English which mark number on count nouns show a similar redundancy in such expressions as "Four-score and seven years ago…".

Function words are distributed into either nominal or verbal structures or occupy positions along phrasal or clausal boundaries. For example, determiners such as articles, demonstratives, quantifiers, numerals, and possessives are relegated to positions within noun phrases while pronouns can be functional, positional, and distributional equivalents to entire noun phrases. Auxiliary verbs are considered to be subsidiary to lexical (or main) verbs, and are often included in descriptions of VP (or as occupying separate or adjacent syntactic nodes). Adpositions and connectives (various types of conjunctions) serve to link elements and to indicate logical relations.

With respect to general semantic characteristics which can affect translatability and borrowability, the articles, in languages such as English, are the "main subset of determiners" (Crystal 1991:100) and mark a number of discourse functions such as old versus new information, definite versus indefinite expression, general versus specific reference, and so on (Hawkins 1991:405ff). Others, e.g. demonstratives, quantifiers, possessives, and numerals, serve a variety of deictic and expressive functions, i.e., indicating a broad range of semantic contrasts such as quantity, number, and so on. Pronouns (some of whose membership overlaps with determiners, above) are traditionally included in the set of nominal expressions. Some approaches distinguish among personal, possessive, demonstrative, interrogative, reflexive, indefinite, and relative pronouns (Crystal 1991:281). As a group, their semantic or discourse function may be to substitute for an individual noun or entire noun phrase, but syntactically, their behaviors are typically diverse. In addition, they constitute paradigms of limited membership and may include expression of such grammatical categories as case, gender/class, person, and number corresponding to those of the noun or phrase they replace. Terminological conflicts often surface regarding demonstrative, possessive, and relative pronouns, for instance, because they characteristically have multiple functions.

Auxiliary verbs are considered a special subset of Verb, and, therefore, may be marked for such grammatical distinctions as tense and agreement (e.g., of person-number and gender). In some approaches, they are included in descriptions of VP. In languages such as English and Spanish, auxiliaries may express semantic distinctions such as mood or modality, aspect, and voice.[14] However,

---

14. In traditional descriptions of auxiliaries in English, including *be, have, do,* and the modals, it is commonly noted that they (a) have special negative forms (e.g., *isn't, haven't, don't, couldn't,* and so on); (b) participate in subject–aux inversion to form questions (and occupy V2 position after words such as hardly or seldom); (c) replace or refer back to full verbs; have cliticized forms (e.g., *I'm* and *he's*), and so on. Modals also are distinguished by the fact that they do not receive the third-person, present-tense *-s*.

the semantic distinctions made by auxiliaries in one language are often found expressed in some form of verbal morphology in another (or in the same language), especially in varieties that are high on the index of synthesis (e.g., polysynthetic languages). Auxiliary verbs do not function to designate the primary action of a phrase or clause, but may substitute for full VPs in languages that allow for tag questions or ellipsis, e.g., abbreviated responses to yes-no type questions, e.g., Spanish *¡Sí, puedo!* ("Yes, I can!") in response to, *¿Puede Vd. hablar español?* or in such English sentences as "I love reggae, and my wife does, too."

Adpositions (pre- and postpositions) are often considered to be heads of their associated phrases, which renders their identification somewhat simpler on formal (viz., functional, positional, and distributional) grounds, especially vis-à-vis the other elements with which they normally co-occur. Distributionally, they mark boundaries of phrases that can function adverbially or adjectivally, especially those performing temporal and spatial locative functions. However, as members of a closed class, they perform grammatical as well as semantic functions: they may be assigners of inherent case (as the adpositions of German), express logical relations, and indicate abstract grammatical (syntactic) relationships when subcategorized for by specific nouns, verbs, or adjectives. Some adpositions (e.g., *after, before,* and *until* in English) appear to take entire clauses as their objects, which causes some to class them as subordinating conjunctions-perhaps another instance of functional overlap. Consequently, forms recognizable as adpositions may be classed as adverbs (when they have no overt objects) or particles, adpositions (when they do), or types of conjunctions.

Various kinds of connectives constitute a diverse class and perform a range of grammatical functions. They include coordinating conjunctions (or coordinators) that conjoin syntactically equivalent words, phrases, and sentences (e.g. English *and, or, but*) and subordinating conjunctions (e.g., *because*), relative pronouns (e.g., *who, what,* and *which*) and (so-called) relative adverbs (e.g., *where* and *when*), and other complementizers (e.g., *whether* and *that*), all of which may be markers of embedded sentences (clauses). As a general rule, such connectives are also positioned at the edges of the respective elements they function to connect, that is, at phrasal (e.g., NPs, VPs, PPs, etc.) or clausal boundaries, and, as a consequence, occupy salient positions. There have been proposals to classify some subordinating conjunctions in English as prepositions with sentential complements (Crystal 1991:334–335; Radford 1988:133ff). This suggests that distinctions between certain subordinators and adpositions may be somewhat blurry in a particular language, and perhaps even more so cross-linguistically.

While it is beyond the scope of the present work to treat each type of function word individually and comprehensively, a few remarks can be made based on observations of borrowability. When the role of the function word is strictly grammatical, for instance reflexive pronouns of Spanish that are subcategorized for by specific lexical verbs (e.g. *-se* of *caerse*, "to fall", often translated into English as "to fall down"), it is much less likely to be borrowed. However, there are a number of instances of borrowed personal pronouns that can behave like nouns or full NPs-even in English (W. Lehmann 1992:136): they often express case distinctions and so on usually reserved for nominal expressions; can appear in isolation as responses to questions (as in "Who, me?"); and can refer to the principal people, objects, and qualities mentioned in discourse in ways similar to common and proper nouns. NP-like behavior ensures perceptual salience as elements capable of receiving stress, and so on (this may apply to some determiners, as well). Modal auxiliaries capable of VP-like behavior (as noted above) and adpositions that are heads of phrases expressing isolable semantic distinctions (e.g. locative *under, after, between*, etc.) are likewise capable of representing reasonably transparent and independent meaning and, therefore, can constitute potentially salient stretches of speech.

3.2.4 Function words versus content words

With respect to syntactic behaviors, the line between function and content words may seem blurred, which is especially true across languages regarding pronouns and adpositions (cf. Myers-Scotton 1993a:99). As the preceding discussion of function words points out, content (lexical) and grammatical words are in principle distinguished on a number of formal bases, most often on that of open versus closed class. Both are internally cohesive; that is, as independent words, they are identifiable according to similar internal criteria, e.g., as potential stress-bearing units and other phonological cues such as pauses or juncture points. In general, however, function words associated with nominal classes (e.g., determiners) cannot assign markers of such grammatical categories as case or number or receive agreement markers of person-number or gender independently of the specific content item with which they co-occur (or replace), signifying their structural dependence. Those associated with verbal classes (e.g., auxiliaries) are subject to similar restrictions, with the notable exception of adpositions (which, in some languages, can assign grammatical case). While main verbs automatically assign semantic roles (and associated case markers) according to their semantic type, auxiliaries (as a result of their subsidiary nature) cannot (except in cases of ellipsis and so on, noted above).

3.2.5 Function words versus inflectional affixes and elements in between

As outlined above, inflectional affixes are distinguishable from content items on numerous formal grounds, and grammatical words are distinct from content items. In any discussion of the grammatical elements/forms of a language (excluding for the time being gradations of meaning and the like), distinguishing among grammatical words, inflectional affixes, and clitics may frequently be one of shifting boundaries. The contrast in morpheme status (i.e., free versus bound) supports the conceptualization that function words are formally situated between content items and inflectional affixes (in languages that allow inflectional affixes). As independent words/roots, syntactic procedures that result in word order changes may apply to certain kinds of function words (e.g., personal pronouns and auxiliary verbs in English). However, regarding affixes in general, language-particular word formation rules will apply (e.g., inflectional affixes are applied "outside" derivational affixes). In addition, the functions of both function words and inflectional affixes are in some sense subsidiary. Function words are generally subordinate to the heads of their respective phrases (with the exception of adpositions, for example, which are heads of phrases themselves, and various pronominals which stand in the place of entire NPs). The functions of inflections are clearly secondary to the stems to which they adhere.

The remaining class in the cline of grammaticality, that of clitics, is traditionally positioned between grammatical words and inflectional affixes, and are often viewed as occupying midpoints of form between free and bound. Their characteristic degree of bonding relative to either derivational or inflectional affixes is, however, slight because they are neither inflectional nor affixes (Bybee 1985: 12).[15] With respect to their functions, they consist of phonologically reduced forms of grammatical words which coalesce with immediately adjacent forms. In some cases they attach to content items (e.g., clitic pronouns of Spanish and articles of French); in other cases they involve two closed-class function words (e.g., contracted forms of pronoun plus "be" in English; the clitic is realized as a reduced form and attaches to the preceding pronoun (as in *I'm* and *we're*).

Cliticized elements (both proclitics and enclitics) are outside the word, including its possible inflected forms, while derivational and inflectional affixes occur within word boundaries. Their peculiar mix of behaviors is more a result

---

15. Bybee includes clitics with particles and auxiliaries as free morphemes because none are obligatorily bound to any lexical item. In her approach, clitics merely resemble inflections as a result of positional restrictions and because they are obligatory in certain contexts.

of their ambiguous morphological status. For instance, they may be considered separate (but contracted) words by native speakers (or separable in their full, phonological forms). They constitute sets whose membership is very restricted, and whose distribution is correspondingly small (e.g., articles in French, certain pronouns occurring at the end of a verb in Spanish, or negative elements following auxiliary verbs in English). Therefore, they have a very limited range of functional, positional, and distributional characteristics, limited by the short list of grammatical forms they reduce from.

Apparently, their dual behavior is an indication of change towards a more general meaning (Heine et al. 1991a: 213). That is, they appear in an increasing number of contexts, and, as a result, can become phonologically reduced (recognition is assured through frequency). However, semantic change is not necessarily in the direction of a more grammaticalized meaning; that is, a new inflectional category is not being represented that might require a new set (or paradigm) of obligatory markers (cf. Bybee 1985:42–3; Hopper and Traugott 1993:150f). As a consequence (when viewed synchronically) of their position along a scale (or cline) of grammaticalization, clitics, as a general rule, are not borrowed, i.e., as clitics (cf. Muysken 1988:414 and 1981:61; Bakker 1997:226).

In situations of intense language contact, grammatical elements which have cliticized to content items are often reanalyzed as an integral part of the (content) word, i.e., inside word boundaries, for example Michif *lamur* ("love") from French *l'amour* (Bakker 1997:103).[16] This is more likely the result of language-specific, donor phonological and morphological processes that occur coincidentally with various other semantic factors. For example, clitics usually come from special classes of pronouns, copular or auxiliary verbs, discourse particles, or, in specific languages, other classes of function word (e.g., certain adpositions) from which cross-linguistic generalizations are difficult to make (Hopper and Traugott 1993:5). Any reduction of phonological form will make these form–meaning sets less salient as well (see Chapter 4 for discussion of the role of salience in borrowing).

3.2.6 Derivational affixes: Between content and inflection

There is little unanimity among linguists regarding the exact differences among types of derivational and inflectional affixes (Katamba 1993:47; Bybee 1985:81).

---

16. Phonological reanalysis of French articles plus nouns is common in French based creoles, as well. Much of this reanalysis undoubtedly is a result of French liaison and elision rules.

Nevertheless, most agree that, in the more straightforward cases, the application of derivational morphemes leads to the creation of new, discrete, words or stems to which inflectional affixes (markers of inflectional categories) may be subsequently added. (Inflectional affixes, in contrast, create so-called different versions of the same word and never change the class to which a particular word belongs.) Derivational affixes may be of two basic sorts, so-called category preserving, those that only change the meanings of the roots to which they attach in some specified way (e.g., *un-*, *re-* and *dis-* in English) and category changing, those that change the grammatical class of the root (e.g., *-ly, -tion, -ize*) (Katamba 1993:47, 51; Bybee 1985:82–83). Thus, we can easily derive adverbs from adjectives, nouns from verbs, and verbs from nouns. We can also derive both nouns and verbs from certain subtypes of adjectives, and so on (e.g. *strong → strength, strengthen*). Both sorts of derivational process result in the creation of a new word, usually of a similar semantic type (Bybee 1985:81).

In many cases, derivational morphemes have clearly stateable meanings (e.g., *bi-, supra-*) similar to content items; hence, they may be referred to as bound lexical items. For example, the English derivational prefix *un-* may signify negative with adjectives (as in *unable* and *unhappy*) or some sort of reversal of meaning in verbs (for example, in oppositions of *tie* and *untie*), but it never changes the syntactic class of a root word. Derivational affixes often make semantic distinctions that can be expressed lexically (i.e., with a separate lexical item), for example *inoperable* versus *not operable*, or *redo that, please* versus *please do that again*. While derived forms may have complex meanings (consisting of radical plus derivational concept, in Sapirian terms), derivational morphemes themselves have either one associated meaning or one function (e.g., nominalizing or verbalizing). In any case, they have one-to-one correspondences of form and meaning and resemble agglutinating affixes in that respect-one might say they are agglutinating without being clearly inflectional.

Semantically, derivational morphemes lie at points between content items (words or bound roots) and inflectional affixes, between lexical and inflectional expression (Bybee 1985:12), and may share characteristics of both. On the one hand, derivational form–meaning sets can be quite idiosyncratic (e.g., *retro-, mini-, -dom, -ship, -ful,* and so on), and, on the other, they are bound (i.e., they require bonding to a contentive root) and can never appear in isolation (as independent words). Among the usual criteria employed to distinguish between derivational and inflectional affixes is obligatoriness (Bybee 1985:27; cf. Carstairs-McCarthy 1993:174ff), which in essence reflects the grammatical status of the respective types. That is, the expression of inflectional categories of person, number, and (occasionally) class agreement and verbal categories of tense, mood, aspect, voice, and so on is required in languages that have those inflectional categories (according to some approaches, as a result of a syntactic rule or procedure). The application of derivational affixes is applied according to semantic criteria linked to their ability to provide specific semantic modification or a change in word class, and, as such, are options for which there may be a number of alternatives.

However, in the cross-linguistic comparison of derivational and inflectional processes, lines may not be easily drawn. For instance, in one language, a particular affix may be considered derivational, while in another, a semantically similar affix may be considered inflectional, thus indicating a greater degree of grammaticalization. For example, a number of languages (e.g., Diegueño and Kwakiutl) express the normally inflectional category of number derivationally (Bybee 1985:103). Even within a particular language, a particular suffix may appear to be inflectional in one instance and derivational in another (e.g., English *-ing* in *He is reading*, which marks progressive aspect, or in the derivation of a noun from a verb form, as in *Reading is fun*). As a consequence, distinctions among derivational and inflectional affixes may be somewhat less clear and subject to controversy than between affixes, in general, and stems or roots.

To illustrate the gradient nature of many such distinctions, Greenberg (1966) proposed a number of implicational universals with respect to morphological types. For example, he states, in essence, if a verb (in a specific language) is marked for person-number (agreeing with the grammatical subject), then it has categories of tense and modality (Universal 30). If the verb agrees with grammatical subject with respect to gender, then it also agrees in number (Universal 32); if a language has the category gender, it has the category of number (Universal 36). Thus, we can arrange a hierarchy of inflectional concepts according to (4), below (items to the left representing more basic, i.e., frequently encountered, categories in his sample of languages):

(4) tense–aspect–modality > number > gender

Greenberg also states implicationally (Universal 29) that any language which has inflectional morphology (i.e., inflectional affixes) has derivational morphology (i.e., derivational morphemes). As a result, the following hierarchy (adapted from Croft 1990:191) illustrates the gradient and hierarchical relationships that exist among derivational and inflectional concepts:

(5) derivational concepts > tense–aspect–modality > number > gender

Despite the fuzziness of discussions of derivational morphemes, it is still sufficiently clear that the form–meaning sets used in the application of word-formation processes that are unequivocally derivational show (a) unifunctionality (i.e., one stateable meaning or a single function) and (b) clear segmentability (distinct morpheme boundaries) whether the particular affixes involved might be considered expressions of inflectional categories or not. These are two significant factors that will figure prominently in the subsequent discussion of transparency and salience (Chapter 4).

3.3 Semantic types: Groupings of morphemes according to meanings

Linking borrowability and grammaticality assumes a twofold interaction of form and meaning. In the previous section (3.2), discussion centered on various sorts of forms (morphemes and words), morpheme types, and word classes, and their various characteristics, assuming that the principal task in a borrowing situation is to (a) identify form–meaning sets that are compatible with the recipient system and (b) integrate those form–meanings sets into the recipient language. To accomplish (a), individual proficient bilingual speakers of the recipient and donor (a subset of the total number of members of a bilingual community) must be able to recognize and isolate forms in the donor (see Section 3.1, above). We can conclude that they do, indeed, possess the requisite morphological knowledge in each of their languages, despite that fact that in most cases of borrowing, the recipient is their dominant (first or native) language. They know, however unconsciously, the roles that different morpheme types play in the formation of words and word classes and in the formation of larger discourse units (e.g., phrases), being sufficiently able to distinguish among such forms as content-bearing items (free or bound), function words, and types of inflectional affixes.[17]

However, a more semantic focus is most likely required to accomplish (b), above, that is, to successfully integrate borrowed form–meaning sets into semantic types in a recipient lexicon. It is proposed here that, in the case of loanwords, concepts and their accompanying labels are borrowed, not form-class members (see 3.0.1, above). Partly due to the questionable nature of such

---

17. As mentioned elsewhere, it is taken for granted that the individual bilingual's knowledge of each language in his/her linguistic repertoire will be situated along a continuum of proficiency.

terms as "semantic bleaching" and so on, a great deal of attention has been paid in recent grammaticalization studies to various kinds of meanings, especially as they may lend themselves to placement along scales. Meaning types, representing clusters of semantic characteristics that can be situated along a cline (hence, continuum), are especially relevant to the present work because they have the greatest potential to shed light on the semantic aspects of borrowability.

One way that has been advanced to categorize meanings is to posit a scale representing the evolution of a concept as it is abstracted away from its original concrete meaning (i.e., direct reference to person or object) towards an increasingly general, relational, and, hence, abstract concept (cf. Lyons 1968:406). To this end, for example, Heine et al. (1991a) construct a scale of meaning types (in (6), below) based on ontological categories that depict general domains of conceptualization according to which we are able to view and organize experience. Individual categories represent prototypical entities that encompass a wide range of perceptually based and, therefore, linguistically expressible concepts (49). The particular ordering is based on degrees of metaphorical abstraction; that is, one category may be used to conceptualize another immediately to its right (so-called categorial metaphors), for example object-to-space or space-to-time. It is also consistent with the ways languages typically represent entities according to kinds or degrees of animacy (cf. Croft 1990:113; Comrie 1989:42f and 185ff).[18]

(6) PERSON > OBJECT > ACTIVITY > SPACE > TIME > QUALITY

An example of this in English would be the word "back", which, as a source concept originally signifying a body part, may refer to position in space or time, and then (in compound form) to an attribute or quality, "backwards" (Heine et al. 1991b:151). These authors also posit a correlation between metaphorical (ontological) categories and both word class and constituent type (construction) (Heine et al. 1991a:53), portrayed in (7), below:

---

18. For further discussions of the role of metaphor in grammaticalization processes, see also Traugott and Hopper: 1993:86–87, Heine et al. 1991a:48ff and 1991b:157ff; Traugott and König 1991:190, 207–212; and Keesing 1991:325, 334–6 (cf. Bybee and Pagliuca 1985 and Sweetser 1988).

(7)	Category	Word type	Constituent type
	PERSON	Human noun	Noun phrase
	OBJECT	Concrete noun	Noun phrase
	ACTIVITY	Dynamic verb	Verb phrase
	SPACE	Adverb, adposition	Adverbial phrase
	TIME	Adverb, adposition	Adverbial phrase
	QUALITY	Adjective, state verb, adverb	Modifier

Numerous linguistic phenomena are used to support this generalization (and those of its type); one example is the range forms and meaning types elicited in response to the so-called Wh-words (interrogative pronouns) who, what, where, when, and how-a class of forms held to be fairly constant across the world's languages. While other categorial lists of this type have been proposed (e.g., Jackendoff 1983; Clark 1993: 43ff; cf. Landau 1993: 191ff), the categories proposed by Heine et al. (1991a) should be sufficient for the present purposes. One may wish to add a category or two for specificity (e.g., amount), but this list is specific enough to allow the organization of semantic types into ordered groups (that, incidentally, would qualify as responses to basic who, what, where, when, and how question types).

Any process of abstraction will involve the extraction of a basic or core meaning and its extension (broadening) in some fashion along a scale of this type. However, it is also necessary to view form–meaning sets (words) according to the amount of detailed information they entail. For example, people usually know more about the persons and objects that are near to them; children show this tendency by learning words for the people, things, and activities in their immediate environment first (e.g., Clark 1993: 30; cf. Markman 1989: 5ff). These items represent their most specific and concrete referents, and descriptions of them will be based on direct (specific) and tangible (concrete) experience. Close objects have clear edges and are more clearly structured; distant ones have blurred edges and are much less structured (Heine et al. 1991a: 44). Metaphorical processes allow us to apply our direct experience with tangible objects and the concepts they help organize (e.g., into taxonomies of similar objects) to more distant, therefore abstract, concepts. This tendency to go from close to far, concrete to abstract, and specific to general provides one basis for claims of unidirectionality in processes of grammaticalization (cf. Traugott and Heine 1991: 4ff; Traugott and König 1991: 192ff; Heine et al. 1991a: 50; Hopper and Traugott 1993: 94ff), though it is quite clear that not every term that becomes abstract and general will become grammaticalized.[19]

In the remaining portions of this chapter, the kinds of meanings that fall under headings provided in the above scale of metaphorical/ontological categories are combined with a comprehensive list of semantic types to portray the layered ways meanings and their corresponding forms may be organized in a language, vertically according to ontological category and horizontally according to semantic type-morpheme type correspondence. The purpose is to construct a set of criteria by which distinctions can be made among the types of words and morphemes that are starting and end points of borrowing processes, distinctions that can be used to identify more specific characteristics of borrowed forms. In so doing, it may be possible to predict more precisely which forms are the most or least likely candidates for borrowing.

3.3.1 Semantic types and subtypes of N, V, and Adj

There have been numerous suggestions concerning the ways languages (and their users) actually organize words into semantically based sets and types, for example in studies of child language acquisition (see, e.g., Clark 1993 and Markman 1989, 1994). One rather extensive study of English (upon which the ensuing discussion is primarily based) was done by Dixon (1991), who set out to identify possible groupings with an eye towards the ways languages, in general, encode concepts. One assumption (shared here) was that syntactic (word) classes may vary considerably across languages (influenced by morphological structuring), but the basic kinds of concepts to which languages must make reference and, perhaps, need to express may be quite similar based on human experience. Drawing from the 2000 most frequently used words in English (from West 1953), Dixon proposes a listing of semantic types and subtypes of content items which are linked to classes of Noun, Verb, and Adjective. About 900 of these were verbs that were organized into types based on their syntactic and semantic characteristics (i.e., similarities of meanings, number and type of semantic roles, and other characteristic syntactic behavior).

In all, there were five major Noun types, ten Adjective types, and six Verb types. Among types of Nouns, there were CONCRETE, ABSTRACT, STATES (or PROPERTIES), ACTIVITIES, and SPEECH ACTS, each divided into numerous subtypes. Among Adjective types, there were those expressing DIMENSION,

---

19. See Section 4.2.1 for a more thorough discussion of abstraction.

PHYSICAL PROPERTY, SPEED, AGE, COLOR, VALUE, DIFFICULTY, QUALIFICATION (e.g., definite, possible, etc.) and HUMAN PROPENSITY (some organized into subtypes). Major Verb types include PRIMARY-A and B, and SECONDARY-A through SECONDARY-D (all divided into various subtypes). In general, PRIMARY verbs make direct reference to an activity or state, while SECONDARY types provide some sort of semantic modification to another (main) verb (e.g., modals, semi-modals, or other auxiliary verbs). PRIMARY-A verbs are distinguished from PRIMARY-B on the basis of complement types; the former take only NPs as grammatical subjects and objects, while the latter may take either NPs or complement clauses in those grammatical functions.

Assuming that Dixon's groupings are reasonably comprehensive (at least for English), we divide again the semantic types and subtypes according to the six metaphorical categories delineated above in the following subsections (3.3.2–3.2.7). Nouns are separated according to kinds of referents, for example, whether direct reference is made to a person, object, activity, and so on. Most verbs represent activities, but can be sub-divided according to semantic roles, for example whether the semantic role that obligatorily maps onto the usual grammatical subject (external NP) must be filled by a human (a person), an animal (animate object), or other. Adjectives normally represent qualities of some sort but (as with verbs) may be restricted with respect to the types of referents to which they may be applied (e.g., person or animate object). In each section, we also include more grammaticalized forms traditionally associated with a particular meaning type. For example, included in the category of PERSON are pronouns and various inflectional affixes that are markers of person; in the category of SPACE are adpositions and an assortment of inflectional affixes. These additional forms are included because they provide a category-by-category listing of forms linked to specific meanings indicating degrees of grammaticalization and reflecting the semantic tendencies we seek to characterize.

At this point, a note about animacy seems in order. In languages such as English, there appears to be a fairly clear delineation among general semantic categories or domains: there are human, animate, and inanimate referents. It should be clear that among the world's languages, not only will these distinctions not necessarily correspond to those made in English, a particular language may possess a relatively long list of semantic categories or word classes based on such distinctions (among others) as animacy.[20]

---

20. In Manam (New Guinea), for example, has a category of animacy that includes higher

3.3.2 Person

Forms which refer to the category of PERSON may belong to classes of Noun and Pronoun, and various inflectional person and agreement markers. Nominals referring to PERSON are all included in the semantic class of CONCRETE nouns, for example kinship terms (*father, mother, sister,* and so on), social group (e.g., *nation, tribe, army, crowd*...), and rank (*chief, captain,* etc.). Most words referring to social groups cover a range of terms that are, in essence, more general than those referring to individuals and may, in many cases, require more language (and culturally specific) knowledge than basic kin terms. Terms denoting rank also require knowledge of specific patterns of social organization.

These and other similar terms can be viewed from near to far, as well, for instance from the standpoint of an individual language learner (e.g., a child): body parts, family, rank, and social group. In addition, individual subgroups like body parts (human or non-human animate) can be applied metaphorically to inanimate objects (the *mouth* of a river). Source concepts such as *foot* may occur (with metaphorical meaning) in any of the subtypes. Body parts also offer a convenient pool for terms that can be utilized in spatial orientation (e.g. points of reference), and as such, constitute possible source concepts for grammaticalized (relational) forms. As a result, this semantic subtype (within the type of person) has great potential for grammaticalization (Heine et al. 1991a: 34).

Pronouns can refer to both persons and objects; certain kinds (i.e., personal pronouns) may also occupy positions of grammatical subject, object, and so on. They can receive any semantic role that can be associated with nouns, noun phrases, or nominal complements and are also subject to the same syntactic processes or patterns of occurrence as nouns, for example in Subject–Aux inversion in English direct questions. In contrast, inflectional affixes indicating PERSON distinctions are applied according to language-specific word formation rules. In many languages, verbal markers co-exist alongside full pronouns, which may render pronouns superfluous in many (non-emphatic) contexts, for example, in so-called Pro-drop languages, though there may be other pragmatic considerations that contribute to this tendency.

In specific languages, full pronouns and affixes marking person may be contrasted in other ways, as well. For example, Spanish fusional affixes marking tense and person-number agreement do not mark gender while the full

---

order animals (pigs, dogs, birds, and so on) along with humans. Generally, animals are considered higher order when domesticated, optionally so when wild (Croft 1990: 113).

pronouns (*él, ella*) do, agreeing with their referents in person, number, and gender. Hence, in addition to being more grammaticalized than pronouns, these affixes have more generalized meanings that are capable of referring to either gender: while they often consist of only a single vowel (stressed or unstressed), they also indicate conjugation class as well as tense–aspect, resulting in a 1-to-many mapping of form to meaning(s). A different sort of verbal inflection exists in Modern Israeli Hebrew; while it preserves gender in the third person, singular, present tense (as a separate suffix marking the feminine), tense and aspect are usually indicated by certain vowel patterns that occur between root consonants (cf. Bybee 1995:233 in reference to Arabic). With different aspects of meaning distributed at different points in the word, the contrast between full pronoun and affix in Hebrew is certainly complex, clearly showing long term results of grammaticalization.

3.3.3 Object

Content items that have visible and tangible referents are normally classed as CONCRETE nouns. Most CONCRETE nouns are underived roots, but some may be derived from verbs, for example *pig, flower, moon, valley*, or *window*, but *building* from the verb "to build". Depending on their position on an animacy scale in the particular language, CONCRETE referents can be ANIMATE (from domestic to wild animals) or inanimate, which can cover a wide range, including flora (flowers, fruits and other edible plants or parts of plants, trees, and the like), celestial and weather (*sun, moon, star, wind, storm, rain, snow*...), environment (*air, water, stone, metals, forest*), and artifacts (including names for types of lodging, articles of clothing, tools and utensils, transportation vehicles, and perhaps foods).

ABSTRACT nouns, which have referents that are less visible and tangible, may refer to results, products (of processes) or abstract notions relating to various types of activities. For example, LANGUAGE terms refer to (linguistic) sounds, words, phrases, or sentences and GENERAL ABSTRACT TERMS refer to such concepts as ideas, problems, methods, results, truth, and so on. Such referents, though not visible in the sense of *stone* or *coyote*, are, nonetheless, tangible, at least in the imagination of the speaker.

In similar fashion, the category termed STATES and PROPERTIES also makes reference to entities that exist in a more psychological sense and typically refer to aspects of human existence. For example, this subtype of noun typically refers to MENTAL (e.g., emotions) or CORPOREAL (*hunger, pain, strength*) categories; many are bound roots, but others are derived from adjectives (e.g., *jealousy* from *jealous*). The direction of derivation may also be the reverse, for instance *envious* (the adjective) from *envy* (the noun). If, in a language there is some categorial variation, then, cross-linguistically, one would suspect that the syntactic category employed to represent a particular semantic type may be subject to considerable variation.

3.3.4 Activity

Words referring to an ACTIVITY generally belong to two separate syntactic classes, Noun and Verb. Words referring to (i.e., naming) activities, acts, or states as entities are nouns, and, as such, they can occur as grammatical subjects, objects, and so on and be morphologically marked as other members of the Noun class. While most nouns (independent word or roots) are derived from the word class Verb (e.g., *division*, *thought*, and *seat*) some are basic, non-derived forms (e.g., *war* and *game*). For nearly every ACTIVITY noun, there is a corresponding verb, whether that verb is a cognate (i.e., represented by the same, basic phonetic label) or not (e.g., *game* the noun and *play* the verb).

Included here are nominal expressions referring to SPEECH ACTS and STATES (and PROPERTIES) because many of the concepts they represent can be referred to as (a) entities and function as nouns or as (b) acts, activities, events, or processes (terms used traditionally in descriptions of classes of Verb) and function as verbs. With respect to SPEECH ACTS, in every instance, there is a corresponding, often cognate, verb, e.g., *response-respond* and *command-command*, but *question/request-ask* and *story/the truth/a lie-tell*. Regarding basic sorts of STATES (and PROPERTIES), there are two main types: MENTAL (e.g., *pleasure, joy, honor*...) and CORPOREAL (e.g., *hunger, thirst*, etc) with subtypes of ACHE and STRENGTH. Some terms for STATES (and PROPERTIES) are derived from adjectives (e.g., *jealousy* → *jealous*) while others may be derived from verbs (e.g., *delight*).

In most instances, however, ACTIVITY and its closely related types belong to the general class Verb, and occur as the central elements of verb phrases (or predicates). Verbs are clearly the most diverse of the major word classes in terms of syntactic behavior (most likely resulting from the ways semantic roles map onto grammatical relations). Semantically (and, consequently, syntactically), PRIMARY VERB types usually require other elements-the bare minimum perhaps being some sort of grammatical subject (which, if understood by context and so on, may be left unexpressed). They may also require grammatical objects, complements, and so on, which function according to specific semantic roles (e.g., agent, instrument, etc.). SECONDARY VERB types (e.g., modals or other auxiliaries) most often co-occur with PRIMARY types and may be morphologically marked for (verbal) inflectional categories such as tense or aspect, thus resembling primary verbs. However, their meanings will be subsidiary in some fashion to the main (or PRIMARY) verb.

Among the PRIMARY-A verbs, MOTION verbs may be the most relevant for the present purposes, being identified as a semantic type with potential for grammaticalization (Hopper 1991:20; cf. Hopper and Traugott 1993:109). Many of the members of this particular subclass are everyday activities (i.e., core vocabulary) and often have accompanying semantic roles that must be filled by CONCRETE, ANIMATE subtypes (e.g., as grammatical subjects), and are, presumably, among the most frequently used forms (Hopper and Traugott 1993:114).

3.3.5 Space

Forms representing spatial concepts can belong to a number of grammatical classes and morpheme types. Cross-linguistically, they can cover a variety of meaning types from concrete and abstract reference (e.g., place names and directions, respectively) to relative position (adverbials such as *here*, *there*, and *somewhere*) to more grammaticalized locative meanings linked to adpositions and certain case markers. It is safe to say that words and morphemes relating to spatial concepts may cover a full range of form–meaning sets contained on a cline of grammaticalization or hierarchy of borrowable types.

Concrete place names can serve as points of reference; they include reference to environmental objects such as *forest*, *river*, and *hill* or artifacts such as *house*, *market*, *city* (particularly when marked for definiteness, as in *the river* or *the market*, respectively). ABSTRACT nouns represent such concepts as position or direction (e.g., *front*, *edge*, *north*) or units of measurement (e.g., *meter, mile, foot*). Function words such as adpositions can indicate location (*on, beneath,* and *at*) or direction (*to* and *from*), but only relationally, i.e., one object in relation to another.

3.3.6 Time

Similar to spatial concepts, forms representing temporal concepts belong to a number of grammatical classes from noun to affix. They span a range of meanings from ABSTRACT reference to units of time (e.g., *month, day, night, season*) and more general terms indicating time (as an abstract notion) and position in time (e.g., *time, present, past, future, yesterday*) to abstract notions of tense and aspect. At midpoints between these two extremes are adverbials (e.g., *now* and *then*); forms that can be adverbs, subordinating conjunctions, or adpositions in languages like English, depending on grammatical function (e.g., *before* and *after*); and such function words as conjunctions (e.g., *while*) and adpositions (e.g., *during*) and those adpositions that occur with temporal complements whose meanings have been metaphorically applied from spatial expressions (e.g., *in, on,* and *at* used with such NPs as "the morning", "the third day", "five o'clock", respectively).

3.3.7 Quality

Form–meaning sets that refer to QUALITY may refer to a broad range of loosely related concepts (cf. Heine et al. 1991a:49). At one end of the spectrum are ABSTRACT entities (organized into classes of Noun) such as variety (e.g., *type, kind, character, shape,* and types of shapes such as *circle, line,* and so on) and concepts referring to a wide variety of qualities conceptualized as ABSTRACT entities. In languages like English, some QUALITY nouns are derived from adjective classes (for example, *redness, happiness,* and *narrowness* from semantic subtypes COLOR, HUMAN PROPENSITY, and DIMENSION, respectively). One particular type, QUALIFICATION, is composed of several subtypes that are obvious semantic relatives to MODALS (SECONDARY-A verbs). These are the subtypes of DEFINITE (e.g., *probable, true*), POSSIBLE (e.g., *impossible*), USUAL (e.g., *normal, common*), LIKELY (e.g., *likely, certain*), SURE (one member), and CORRECT (e.g., *right, wrong, appropriate,* and *sensible*).

Various qualities (or types of QUALITY) may be associated in semantically restricted ways to only particular sorts of entities. For example, the HUMAN PROPENSITY type can only be used to add particular semantic information to (modify) CONCRETE (HUMAN and ANIMATE) referents, to refer to states of mind, emotions, and so on. This type consists of a number of subtypes, for example FOND (*fond of...*), ANGRY (e.g., *angry, jealous of, sad*), HAPPY (e.g., *anxious, keen, happy, thankful, careful, sorry, proud, ashamed, afraid of*), UNSURE (e.g., *certain, sure, unsure, curious about*), EAGER (e.g., *eager, ready, prepared, willing*), clever (e.g., *stupid, luck, kind, cruel, generous*).

Generally speaking, the following types also refer to qualities attributable to CONCRETE (ANIMATE or INANIMATE) entities: DIMENSION (e.g., *big, small, narrow, short, tall*), PHYSICAL PROPERTY (e.g., *hard, strong, sweet*), SPEED (e.g., *quick, slow*), COLOR (e.g., *red, yellow, blue*). A subtype of PHYSICAL PROPERTY, CORPOREAL, most often refers to ANIMATE types (e.g., *well, ill, absent*). However, a number of types may modify a wider range of CONCRETE or ABSTRACT referents, for example AGE (e.g., *new, old, young, modern*), DIFFICULTY (e.g., *tough, simple, complex*), and SIMILARITY (e.g., *unlike, different from*), VALUE (e.g., *good, bad, odd, necessary, lucky*).

As a general semantic type, meanings associated with classes of Adjective appear to be more general as a whole than those of Noun; viz., an adjective may appear in a greater number of contexts. The concepts (attributes) they represent can be applied to more than one noun or grouping (subtype) of nouns (e.g., COLOR terms with almost any CONCRETE noun). Even though one would never wish to say that adjectives are grammaticalized from nouns (in the sense referred to in the current work), there is, nevertheless a certain asymmetry that underlies their relationship as modifier and modified that surfaces in cross-linguistic patterns of gender/class, number, and other sorts of agreement (Hawkins 1988:7–9), in languages that have such agreement, adjectives will agree with the nouns they modify and not vice versa. As mentioned above, one can find frequent nominalized forms of the concepts contained in subtypes of Adjective in English; a number of verbs are derived from adjectives, as well (e.g. *redden, strengthen,* and *widen* from COLOR, PHYSICAL PROPERTY, and DIMENSION subtypes, respectively). If a set of meanings can freely move from word class to word class (derivationally) with relative ease and frequency in English, then we can look for similar processes to operate cross-linguistically, as well.

As categories of concepts attributable to a wide variety of referents, those types that refer to QUANTITY may, indeed, need to be considered a separate category.[21] However, because of their importance in the description of PERSONS and OBJECTS (of various types), QUANTITY is included here as a subcategory of QUALITY. Form–meaning sets also range from making reference to concepts of QUALITY as abstract entities (e.g., *number, amount, age, width, depth*) to the expression of various semantic contrasts associated with the classes of Determiners (function words), to grammatical categories of number (e.g., singular, dual, plural, paucal, uncountable) that map onto inflectional nominal, and (by agreement) verbal affixes. In languages that have a grammatical

---

21. As does Jackendoff (1983), whose ontological categories include THING, ACTION, EVENT, PLACE, DIRECTION, MANNER, and AMOUNT. Without arguing for or against this listing as opposed to any other (or a synthesis of any sort), we include QUANTITY as a type within QUALITY, for the stated reasons.

category of number, QUANTITY terms may be distributed (in complementary fashion) among objects that are countable or uncountable (for instance, in languages like English).

3.4 Summary and comments

In this chapter, it has been proposed that lexical borrowing involves the association of borrowed form–meaning sets into recipient semantic types and their subsequent assignment into syntactic word classes. In steps, this includes (a) the recognition of system compatible forms, (b) the linkage of appropriate meanings onto those forms, (c) the assignment of form–meaning sets into semantic types, (d) subsequent allocation into word (form) classes, (e) and the full integration of the borrowed form into recipient morphosyntax. It is likely that every borrowed form–meaning set undergoes degrees of reanalysis (phonological, morphological, etc.) when being integrated into the new (host) system. With respect to word class, they will probably occur in recipient classes that are similar or equivalent to those from which they originated, but this may be only coincidental. The degree of similarity of donor and recipient word class may merely be a function of the type of meaning expressed by the borrowed form.

The synchronic investigation of relationships between word classes and semantic types has given indirect but significant support for this proposal by pointing out that certain concepts can be represented by members of a number of syntactic classes whose forms may function in various ways, even in languages like English. Types of ACTIVITY, for example, can be members of the two great form classes, Noun or Verb, depending on their grammatical function in a sentence; some QUALITIES may be members of any major word class (e.g., *strength, strengthen, strong, strongly*). Certain types of meanings (e.g., terms for body parts and so on) appear to weave their ways through a wide range of form types from content items with concrete reference to inflectional affixes with highly grammaticalized meanings. Other concept types may become more abstract and general, but never actually become fully grammaticalized (as in processes of derivation). It can be inferred, then, that the ways concepts organize into syntactic classes may depend in large part upon language-specific morphological structuring—and there is no reason to assume that similar investigations of other languages would yield significantly different results.

Patterns have emerged in many studies such as the one done by Dixon suggesting that the creativity of human language has certain specific characteristics and limitations. For instance, form–meaning sets that undergo grammaticalization pass through a gradual evolution of form and meaning: forms become more frequent and phonetically less complex (in general); their associated meanings become more general (allowing them to occur in a greater number of contexts), more abstract (moving away from reference to visible, tangible referents), and eventually associated with obligatorily expressed grammatical (inflectional) categories. Borrowability mirrors grammaticalization: the more grammaticalized an element is in the donor language, the less likely it is to be borrowed into a recipient. Hence, the links between processes of grammaticalization and those of borrowing are most likely the result of the systematicity of language and the language faculty-correspondences are too close to be random.

We now examine the characteristics and properties that are linked to grammaticalization, especially those that may help account for the striking parallelism. With respect to form, phonetic substance has the ability to influence the recognizability of specific forms and form classes; diminution of form, therefore, is a factor. Regarding meaning, generality and abstractness of meaning and linkage to inflectional categories are semantic concomitants. Consequently, the next chapter goes into greater detail regarding these properties and their roles in borrowing.

CHAPTER 4

The identification of form–meaning sets

Apart from the social forces inherent to all bilingual/contact situations, any comprehensive model of linguistic borrowing and borrowability needs to offer some sort of plausible explanation for observations that the more grammatical(ized) an item is, the less likely it is to be borrowed (all borrowed forms being necessarily compatible with the recipient morphosyntax). Even after defining which donor forms are potentially compatible with the recipient/matrix system and those that are not, questions remain regarding why, among all borrowable (i.e., system compatible) forms, certain types of form–meaning sets are preferred over others. Moreover, the evidence suggests that individual speakers do not borrow members of abstract, language particular classes. Initially, they borrow form–meaning sets (i.e., new concepts with associated labels) and then, perhaps, forms only (new labels for concepts already known and for which forms already exist in the recipient); they may also borrow new and unfamiliar concepts that can be represented with native forms (loan translations and semantic extensions). In any case, for borrowing processes to take place at all, forms must be picked out of the linguistic environment and linked to appropriate concepts. In other words, form–meaning sets must be learned; then they can be put to use.

It certainly does not seem to be coincidental that intense bilingual/contact situations also show a variety of contact phenomena involving different kinds of language mixing (Grosjean 1982, 1995, 1997a, 1997b). The more intense the bilingualism, the more one expects bilingual phenomena. With respect to how bilingualism is attained, there are only two basic routes: (a) the sequential acquisition of a first (native L1) and then subsequent language (second or L2) and (b) the simultaneous acquisition of both languages.[1] Hence, in any contact situation (on individual and societal levels), the first stage in bilingual acquisition necessarily includes the identification of forms in each language and the

---

1. Distinctions between the two acquisition scenarios obviously depend on the age of onset of L2 learning, which can vary. Consequently, phenomena associated with one or the other may differ in individual cases.

successful matching of meanings onto those forms. This, of course, applies to all kinds of learning/acquisition situations, primary, secondary, or other. In simultaneous acquisition, certain form–meaning sets in both languages are learned more or less simultaneously, while in sequential acquisition, forms (i.e., from the L2) will be learned for concepts that already possess labels (in the L1). In the latter case, significant effects of transfer are to be expected; in the former, various kinds of mixing behaviors are likely to occur. In addition, the more proficient speakers become in their languages, the more their individual resources (forms and structures) become available (cf. Kroll and de Groot 1997:170).

One can say intuitively that content items are easier to identify and incorporate into a borrowing system than, say, inflectional affixes. Among other things, they are generally more semantically transparent and salient and, therefore, easier to pick out of the speech stream. Because this undertaking appears to be essentially the same irrespective of the source language, it can be inferred that candidates for borrowing (donor forms) and original, native forms may be learned in many of the same ways.[2] Consequently, the current chapter follows a basic learner's strategy (cf. Slobin 1985) regarding spoken language and attempts to identify particular properties that may coincide in varying types and degrees to render one form–meaning set more readily identifiable than another. Isolating the phonological properties of items that facilitate identification appears to be a logical place to start. Analyzing the types of meanings constituting the semantic arsenal of a particular language naturally follows — especially in view of the fact that, in practice, the two are inextricably linked.

4.0.1 The spread and integration of borrowed form–meaning sets

There are a number of issues of a practical nature to consider with respect to the integration of borrowed items into a recipient/matrix language. For instance, content items become members of open classes where overlaps of meaning (degrees of synonymy), hyponymy, and so on are quite usual. In fact, the hierarchical organization of many semantic fields allows the addition of new terms on a number of levels, for example, in names for individual, characteristic

---

2. Degrees of attainment will ultimately depend on a number of factors such as acquisition history (i.e., according to sequential or simultaneous acquisition), function (i.e., with whom and for which purposes the languages are acquired), modality (e.g., through spoken and written media), and so on, but most likely on an interplay of all the above (see Grosjean 1995; Kroll and de Groot 1997; Smith 1997; Green 1993; de Groot 1993).

parts, or groups of entities (including persons, animals, objects, places, and so on). In contrast, borrowable function words and inflectional affixes constitute significantly shorter lists as members of closed classes. In addition, they may face stiff competition from native forms, which are also relatively few in number, already solidly entrenched, and very frequent in normal speech patterns as a result of their roles in the structural organization of the language. The emergence of new grammatical distinctions (i.e., obligatory inflectional categories) on the basis of borrowed forms seems, on its face, to be a much more difficult and complex process, one that would take a relatively long period of time, if it were to occur at all (cf. Section 2.1.3, above).[3]

Another factor affecting the spread of donor forms and form–meaning sets throughout an entire community is the borrowing population's gradient levels of proficiency in the donor language. So-called "balanced bilinguals" (a classification generally accepted as ideal rather than actual) should be able to borrow freely from either language, lifting the upper limit on borrowability to those forms that are learnable to them. However, not every member of the bilingual community, a large portion of whom are assumed to be primary speakers of the subordinate variety, will have the proficiency required to command and borrow any and all forms of the donor language. In fact, it is rare that an individual (let alone a community) is equally proficient in both (or all) languages, especially with respect to a broad range of genres and registers (Romaine 1995:19; Hoffmann 1991:21; Grosjean 1982:232). Even supposing that relatively proficient bilinguals are the initial conduits of borrowing (a relatively small sub-set of the total set of bilinguals), individual borrowed forms must diffuse throughout the community among speakers of a wide range of proficiencies.

While it may not be completely accurate to say that borrowing is, therefore, reduced to the lowest common denominator (e.g., to the borrowing of concrete nouns by monolingual speakers of the recipient), a lack of proficiency in the donor may inhibit some members of the bilingual community from having complete access to the more grammaticalized form–meaning sets. That is to say, the list of potential candidates for borrowing appears to be constrained by the collective abilities of another perhaps greater sub-set of the community of

---

3. Clearly, inflectional affixes have been borrowed. Thomason and Kaufman (1988) point out the borrowing of an aspectual marker from Balochi into Brahui (93), and Heath (1981) mentions numerous instances of borrowed case markers among the Australian languages of Arnhemland (336).

bilingual speakers to (a) successfully identify donor forms and (b) associate appropriate meanings onto those forms. Exposure to these forms may come from three sources: monolingual speakers of the donor; bilingual speakers of donor and recipient (speaking either language or in code-switches); and monolingual speakers of the recipient who have already borrowed the forms. If this reflects a sequence of any kind (as forms from Y gradually pass into the speech of monolingual X speakers), one would expect a kind of filtering or sifting effect: only the strongest forms will survive.

There may be a number of reasons why a donor form wins out over a more traditional, native one in such situations. Frequency in the donor language, the relative prestige and social dominance associated with donor forms, and the waning influence of a recessive, perhaps dying, language (among other things) all undoubtedly play important roles.[4] However, distinguishing between donor and native forms is not necessarily simple. At times, forms considered to be native by the most proficient speakers (i.e., according to folk etymologies) were themselves borrowed at more remote points in the history of the language, their origins obfuscated through the cumulative effects of phonological and morphological integration (i.e., reanalysis).[5]

4.0.2 Identifying clusters of properties

To begin, a general definition of semantic transparency is proposed as the successful matching of an acoustic signal (a phonetic form or amalgam of forms) with a semantic interpretation, "with the least possible machinery and with the least possible requirements regarding language learning" (Seuren and Wekker 1986:64). The optimal or ideal case is associated with a one-to-one correspondence of meaning and surface representation. A number of researchers refer to a direct one-to-one linkage as primary in acquisition and in processing. For example, Roger Andersen's One-to-One Principle (1989: 385–393 and elsewhere) asserts that children assume that there is only one clear and invariant

---

4. It may well be that the donor, because of its cultural and economic dominance, is used more often and in a greater number of contexts by bilinguals of varying competencies than the original (ethnic) language of the community. In such situations (characteristic of advanced shift), old native forms, victims of neglect, may be forgotten by younger speakers (Field 1994a), providing a practical incentive to borrow seemingly ubiquitous donor labels.

5. Which is certainly the case with Spanish borrowings in Modern Mexicano that have been around for centuries (e.g., Hill and Hill 1986: 124–141: 157).

form or construction for every intended meaning.[6] Consequently, the meaning of a novel form must contrast in some fashion with one already known. If a new form does, in fact, refer to a familiar object or other referent (perhaps to a specific attribute or characteristic of that object), ascertaining its precise meaning may involve taking on a different conceptual perspective, an ability that apparently is present in very young learners (Clark 1997). At any rate, the one-to-one mapping of form and visible, tangible referent is maintained even when that visibility is primarily conceptual (mental).

Levelt (1989) states unequivocally that a one-to-one mapping guarantees speed and accuracy in connecting a word-meaning with an appropriate form (200). Semantic transparency, therefore, must include the ability to map a form onto a meaning and the reverse, the ability to find a form for a particular concept (see, also, Heine et al. 1991a: 119). This sort of conceptualization of a one-to-one mapping, however, may need to be modified or elaborated in some sense to account for the possibilities inherent in different kinds of form–meaning sets. Implicit in the various scales and continua discussed so far is that mappings of any sort will be somehow dependent on the nature of the form (e.g., how easy it is to separate out of the speech stream). They will also depend to a degree on the nature of the referent (e.g., from concrete to abstract and so on).

It is assumed that the content of human communication is relatively constant across cultures (i.e., the types of meanings that are encoded into language) even though the formal characteristics of individual languages may vary considerably. Content items in all languages make reference to entities that exist in some fashion from concrete to abstract or from specific to general. On the one hand, they express meanings that are concrete (in the Sapirian sense); they link to visible and tangible referents that represent the primary concepts of all human discourse that can be classed into semantic types and subtypes (e.g., topics, participants in activities, etc.). On the other hand, inflectional (i.e., fusional) affixes have highly abstract and generalized meanings that link to language-specific inflectional (grammatical) categories. Being language-specific, these categories are by definition not found in all languages and are not common to all human discourse. By identifying the relevant characteristics of

---

6. Because there may be more than one toy, brother, friend, and so on, children apparently assume that words can refer to types of objects and not necessarily individual ones (Clark 1993: 50). There is no reason to think that adult learners of a second language would assume anything to the contrary, though it is likely that they will be influenced by the ways their primary language organizes items into semantic types.

forms and meanings at both extremes, the stage is set for the analysis of the formal and semantic properties that may cluster in varying strengths or combinations at different points along the scales.

4.1 Form identification characteristics: The role of salience

The term salience is often used to refer to the phonological prominence afforded to certain words or bound roots in the speech stream relative to various kinds of function words and/or affixes. That is, some forms receive greater phonological stress or certain other prosodic features (e.g., intonational contour) that make them more conspicuous than others as a result of their intended significance or functional role within a word, phrase, clause, or sentence (cf. Lyons 1968:273, 435–8). Discussions of the syntax-phonology interface (e.g., Pullum and Zwicky 1988:255; Carr 1993:228) point to the ability of phonology to respond to syntax to indicate word groupings and relationships among words (Hawkins 1994:3–4, 116), distinguishing such forms as content items (e.g., identifying specific topics, objects, and actions) from function words (expressing more general semantic distinctions) and so on. Moreover, grammars afford salient positions to members of particular syntactic (word) classes relative to their modifiers, for example, to those that function as heads of phrases (i.e., heads extreme left or right).

Words may receive stress according to normal word-level prosodic patterns and additional phrasal and/or clausal stress. For example, the status of a noun as a stress-bearing content item coincides with its salient position within the English NP.[7] Words in so-called focus positions may also receive extra phonological emphasis to increase their prominence in relation to other elements in a clause. Word, phrase, and clausal stress can work together or in conflicting fashion to contrast members of particular word classes and/or morpheme types in an utterance for a number of reasons. The converse is also true: salience can be accomplished in diverse ways. For instance, in some languages, the relative importance of a specific form can be indicated by other grammatical or

---

7. While this may seem a bit circular, it is not. The fact that syntactic position and phonological stress may, indeed, coincide is a built-in, systematic redundancy that undoubtedly increases intelligibility. Moreover, in languages such as Japanese, where phonological stress is played down to an extent, one would expect word order and other morphosyntactic devices to pick up the slack.

morphological means, through the use of particles or the reduplication of forms or syllables to mark emphasis, intensity, and so forth. Nevertheless, it is clear that these strategies also add to the perceptual prominence of the marked form.

As a result of language particular lexical and metrical prosodic patterns (Cutler 1989:352), certain words are easier to pick out. However, whether a particular form is salient or not, the ability to correctly identify it, that is, to associate it with an appropriate meaning, involves more than general prominence. It does not necessarily follow that a form will be any easier to comprehend just because it is made louder or more conspicuous by a combination of phonological foregrounding strategies. It still needs to possess properties that make it unique and recognizable. Ultimately, form identification is dependent on the makeup of the individual form. All other factors being equal, however, salient forms stand a greater chance of being noticed, thus providing a kind of incentive to hearers. Salience, therefore, appears to be the result of a number of aspects of grammar that conspire together to provide clues to the hearer concerning the relative significance of selected forms in the speech stream (that s/he desires to understand).

Salience typically favors content items. Some function words can also become salient, for example, personal pronouns in various argument positions; less frequently will affixes of any kind be perceptually salient in systematic ways (e.g., Spanish tense markers with the exception of those indicating present). In the event that an affix is allocated primary word stress, that stress may be the result of normal word stress patterns or triggered by inherent characteristics of the affix itself (and other members of its paradigm). In either case, the affix is an integral part of the full content item to which it attaches and occupies a position within phonological and syntactic word boundaries (Levelt 1992:10ff). It provides one basis for the identification of word class membership and, perhaps, among other things, the grammatical and semantic function of the content item. The fact that various affixes substitute for one another also provides an important perceptual clue by which a speaker/hearer can distinguish between the bound root and the particular form-type that marks any and all inflectional categories and their respective category values that are obligatorily expressed on words of that class.

4.1.1 Transparency versus opacity

Forms at either end of the scales of borrowability and grammaticalization can be contrasted in a number of respects regarding identifiability. True transparency encompasses the ability to distinguish one form from all others together with the assumption that an individual form has one (and only one) intended meaning (one form → one meaning; one meaning → one form). Consequently, the bidirectional nature of semantic transparency entails not only ascertaining a unique meaning for an individual form (in perception), but also the ability to recover an appropriate form to indicate a specific meaning (in production). Speakers, therefore, are able to retrieve appropriate meanings or concepts when presented with particular forms; they can also select from their lexicons the individual forms representing the entities to which they wish to refer and the ideas they intend to express. Opacity, at the other end of a spectrum of relative transparency, denotes the inability to adequately connect an individual form to a particular concept or meaning and/or the reverse, to link an individual meaning with a single, appropriate form.

One of the reasons given for the relatively detailed phonetic shape of content items is that specific phonological information (a collection of distinguishing characteristics) is required to make accurate identification. In order to retrieve the correct meaning of a particular content form, a hearer will likely attend to specific portions of the phonetic string or label. For example, in languages such as English, words are often recognized at or before the point at which they are different from all other words in that language beginning with the same sequence of phonemes — their so-called uniqueness points.[8] The fact that forms are often correctly recognized before this point is a remarkable feat undoubtedly facilitated by semantic context (Marlsen-Wilson and Tyler 1980; Marlsen-Wilson 1989: 4–6; Hawkins 1994: 4). Considering the speed with which an item is encountered in the incoming speech stream and the sheer number of possible meanings that could link to a specific content item, there must be an equally rapid and efficient mapping procedure that is capable of identifying forms based on initial sound sequences (from left-to-right), at least in many cases. Other relevant portions (middles and endings) may be important for full and accurate identification (Hawkins and Cutler 1988: 295ff; cf. Cutler 1989: 343–344).

The amount of phonological information necessary for identification is undoubtedly dependent on the number of possible meanings to be retrieved.

---

8. Even assuming that lexical access is ultimately a complex process involving "narrowing-in and monitoring stages, correcting strategies, post-access decision stages, and even look-ahead and look-back operations..." (Grosjean 1995: 264–265; Grosjean and Gee 1987), form recognition seems hardly possible without at least some sort of one-to-one mapping.

The larger the number of possibilities (in a sense, limitless with respect to content items), the greater the amount of detailed information required by individual identifying labels. In other words, the label needs to contain enough phonetic information to achieve the uniqueness that is required to pull up the correct (equally unique), corresponding meaning. This is similar to the requirements of telephone numbers or social security numbers for individuals or license plates for cars. The mathematical possibilities represented by the symbols themselves stand in direct proportion to the number of items to be identified. This also suggests that an efficient system employs labels that possess optimal amounts of phonetic information for the purpose of economy. On the one hand, a system composed of forms with too little phonetic substance would yield a high degree of homonymy, making the retrieval of appropriate meanings problematic, at best. On the other hand, too much information can make retrieval inefficient, as well. Returning to the analogy of telephone numbers, it certainly seems that too many unwarranted digits would make the recognition and association of numbers to appropriate persons unnecessarily tedious. Sequences of phonemes, as phonological addresses (see, for example, Butterworth 1992:264), possess similar characteristics, for instance in the form of sequential constraints, which can be viewed as optimizing form–meaning associations and maintaining the efficiency of retrieval processes.[9]

Concerning the amount of detailed phonetic information that may be available for the construction of morphemes, English, for example, has between 6,500 to 7,000 syllables (Levelt 1992:17).[10] Taking the lower figure and excluding form–meaning sets that are not syllabic (for the purpose of discussion), as many as 6,500 unique meanings can be linked to individual, unique forms, with no resultant synonymy, homonymy, or polysemy. The number of possible two-syllable form–meaning sets soars well into the millions, which can be added

---

9. Phonological processes that streamline labels by reducing superfluous or redundant segments or features certainly may also be seen as improving the efficiency of the system by reducing the amount of information that must be processed. This is particularly consistent with views of individual languages diachronically as "expression-compacting machines" (Langacker 1977:106; cf. Hopper and Traugott 1993:64–65).

10. According to Levelt (1992), English and Dutch (which resembles English in the number of possible syllables) can be contrasted with (Mandarin) Chinese, which "has no more than about 400 syllables" (17). Obviously, not all possibilities and combinations of phonemes in languages like English or Dutch play equal roles. Certain combinations occur with much greater frequency; hence, Levelt proposes language-specific frequency effects in various on-line tasks.

to the original number of one-syllable possibilities. Needless to say, a language that possesses such potential in the formation of morphemes or words has the capacity to refer to an enormous number of concepts. With affixation (derivational and/or inflectional), compounding, and other word-formation strategies (all restricted by language-particular word-formation processes or rules), the potential is clearly inexhaustible in principle — the exact requirement that needs to be met.

Uniqueness of form also implies that the form itself has definition; it possesses limits. That is, it must contain beginning and end points which can serve as morpheme boundaries of some sort, irrespective of language-specific metrical patterns that can shift syllable and even word boundaries (see Levelt 1992: 10–16). Consequently, some sort of segmentability (by speaker/hearers, not just linguists) must be part of any conceptualization of identifiability. Accordingly, one property that is clearly applicable to transparent forms is sufficiently detailed and segmentable phonetic information that can function as a unique phonetic fingerprint that is, consequently, traceable to an appropriate, individual meaning.

The discussion of uniqueness of form also directly leads to its necessary co-factor in transparency, uniqueness of meaning (e.g., there is one, unambiguous referent). Uniqueness of form serves no logical purpose unless that uniqueness also indicates a clearly identifiable meaning. Therefore, the second property that is specified has to do with the mapping possibilities provided by the intrinsic properties of the form: one unique form maps onto one unique meaning. Perhaps the recognition of other form types (e.g., inflectional affixes) that normally consist of minimal phonetic information (a consequence of the so-called diminution of form in processes of grammaticalization) is based on something other than detailed phonetic shape, which may not be as critical when the form is obligatory and drawn from a very limited pool of candidates (e.g., members of such tight-knit paradigms as specific conjugation classes in Spanish).[11]

We now come to the postulation of a third property pertaining to selectional possibilities: as a consequence of a clear one-to-one mapping of form and meaning, transparent items can be selected on the sole basis of the particular meanings they convey (identifying topics, participants, and so on). Such forms

---

11. Given the systematic complexity of language in all its aspects, it is difficult to accept that this clear contrast is not a result of something and serves no logical purpose. This analysis also provides implicit support for processing models of language that suggest content items are processed differently from inflectional affixes.

stand in opposition to those whose selection is obligatory, that are assigned to positions within an utterance to satisfy some grammatical requirement, which applies to inflectional affixes and certain function words that fulfill the subcategorization requirements of certain nouns, verbs, and so on. Instances of homonymy and polysemy, in which there are multiple but not simultaneous meanings for a single form, and synonymy, in which there may be more than one form for a single meaning, may make form recognition and the interpretation of particular utterances somewhat tricky at times. However, any resultant ambiguity is generally temporary and quickly resolved by the eventual effects of context (see, for example, Frazier and Clifton 1996: 4).

Nevertheless, just as there are unequivocal cases of semantic transparency (e.g., regarding concrete nouns with clearly visible and tangible referents), there are cases of complete opacity where there is no possible bidirectional linkage of form and meaning. As shown in the following subsection (4.1.3), there are forms that do not make direct reference to unique entities of any kind (they refer to abstract inflectional categories), and their multiple, simultaneous meanings cannot be linked back to a single form (i.e., many categories are fused onto one form).

Table 4.1 portrays the three properties that may cluster in various numbers and degrees to render specific forms relatively transparent or opaque.

Table 4.1. Form–meaning interpretation characteristics (FMICs): Forms

Transparency	Opacity
(a) shape: unique (detailed, segmentable)	(a′) minimal, no (or zero) form[12]
(b) mapping: 1-to-1 link to meaning and back to a single form	(b′) 1-to-many simultaneous links to multiple meanings; no return link to a single form
(c) selection: optionally selected on the sole basis of particular, individual meaning	(c′) obligatory; occur in response to the requirements of language-specific grammar; give appropriate syntactic form

---

12. The phonological requirement also refers to the fact that zero (or unexpressed) form and no form are not the same. For example, while the regular plural is marked (with -s) in English, an unmarked form can indicate two separate grammatical conditions, either singular (when it is countable) or uncountable noun. In the former, the absence of a particular marker is, nonetheless, an indication of singular number; in the latter, there is no form for either plural or singular. There are also instances of unmarked plurals, as in *sheep, fish, reindeer*.

Form–meaning sets sharing all characteristics represented in the left-hand column, (a)–(c), are content items (for example, members of the major classes Noun, Verb, and Adjective). Those sharing all the characteristics in (a′)–(c′) are fusional affixes. However, function words and affixes that are derivational and/or agglutinating may have characteristics of either column. For example, agglutinating-type inflectional affixes maintain 1-to-1 linkage of form to concept even though they typically have minimal phonetic shape and their application may be obligatory. In a similar vein, various kinds of function words (as a diverse group) generally have 1-to-1 form–meaning correspondences resembling those of content items, but are occasionally required by the grammar (e.g., particular prepositions in languages such as English, German, Dutch, etc.).

Fusional affixes have a 1-to-many mapping of form to meaning, but this should not be confused with synonymy. For example, the Spanish verbal affix *-o* represents a coalescence of present tense and person-gender agreement (with the intended grammatical subject).[13] These three meaning types are mapped onto the single form simultaneously. The ambiguity resulting from the kinds of synonymy and polysemy that occur with content items are normally disambiguated by semantic and/or grammatical context, and meanings can be found one after the other that are appropriate only in a given context. They are not simultaneously expressed on a single form in the same sense that the discrete inflectional categories are on a Spanish affix (see Figure 4.3). They are integrally fused together and cannot be teased apart or segmented (clearly the result of grammaticalization processes). The phonological segmentability characteristic of bound roots also acts to isolate affixes (of any type), even though affixes, as phonologically and semantically subordinate (bound) forms, bond in different ways to their roots. In some cases, there is a high degree of phonological bonding (sometimes referred to as fusion) resulting in a shift of word stress and so on. However, with respect to the internal characteristics of fusional affixes as discrete forms, there has been both complete phonological and semantic fusion so that neither phonological nor semantic segmentability is possible.

4.1.2 The opacity of fusional affixes

As a consequence of the intricate web of mapping possibilities created by their fusional character, fusional-type affixes are completely opaque and represent

---

13. There is a homophonous form, *-o*, which marks masculine gender on nouns. However, their separate grammatical contexts prevent any ambiguity that could conceivably arise.

the extreme opposite form type from concrete nouns. There are no phonetic fingerprints that can be used to identify any one of their individual meanings; all meanings associated with a particular form have to be retrieved simultaneously (not one after another depending on any kind of semantic or grammatical context). Therefore, hearers cannot segment an affix of this type to locate a single meaning; no portions of the Spanish -*o* referred to above can mean first person, or singular, or present tense sequentially (the way agglutinating affixes can) because all of them are expressed at the same time. Neither can speakers select an individual meaning and locate a single form (first person maps onto eight separate forms that also express singular or plural in four separate tenses, in the first conjugation class alone). Multiple mapping possibilities exist in each direction that cannot be disambiguated by a formal (i.e., strictly grammatical) context, at least in the same sense that "love" the noun can be distinguished from "love" the verb in English by position or function within a sentence. Fusional affixes can substitute freely for members of their respective paradigms.

There are other cases of one-to-many and many-to-one mappings on grammatical affixes that are, nonetheless, relatively transparent. English has three grammatical affixes that are homophonous in identical phonological environments (realized as [s], [z], or [ɪz] depending on the preceding phoneme): -*s*, marking plural, noun; -*s*, a possessive marker; and -*s*, marking third person, singular, present tense on verbs. All three appear in distinctly different grammatical contexts, and, therefore, can be disambiguated relatively easily. In German, plurality on nouns can be expressed by a number of complementary forms, e.g., by the pluralizing affixes -*e*, -(*e*)*n*, or -*s*, or by means of a vowel change in the root (i.e., umlaut), combination of umlaut plus suffix (e.g., umlaut +*er*), and so on: Pferd → Pferde; Frau → Frauen; Auto → Autos; Haus → Häuser representing horse(s), woman/women, car(s), and house(s), respectively. However, in each instance, one, and only one, concept is expressed: plurality. Both English -*s* and the German plural can be contrasted with the Turkish plural -*lar*, portrayed in Figure 4.1.

The Turkish plural marker -*lar* shows a clear 1-to-1 mapping; there is no ambiguity possible. English -*s* has a 1-to-3 form–meaning linkage that can be disambiguated by context (e.g., in comprehension tasks).[14] German plural has (at least) 4-to-1 form–meaning mapping, but in each instance, the meaning of

---

14. Note that, in English, there are so-called strong forms (e.g., *foot-feet, tooth-teeth*) and zero forms (*sheep-sheep, deer-deer*), but they are not numerous enough to say that they are in direct competition with one another as are the various plural forms of German.

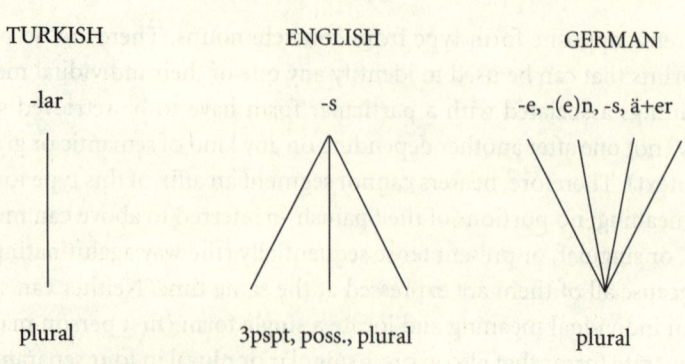

TURKISH	ENGLISH	GERMAN
-lar	-s	-e, -(e)n, -s, ä+er
|	/|\	\\\|//
plural	3pspt, poss., plural	plural

Figure 4.1. Mapping patterns of grammatical affixes.

the form is clear and unambiguous (also) in context. The correct forms marking plural must be individually learned (which may make second language learners wince in production), but they still make up a relatively small number of possibilities.[15] The Spanish fusional affix -*o*, however, maps 1-to-3 (form to meaning), but those 3 meanings simultaneously map back to a minimum of 25 possible forms (i.e., excluding suffixes representing subjunctive mood and/or conditional). Suffice it to say that this is not a simple case of semantic transparency. The complex mapping scheme of the Spanish fusional affix -*o* is summed up in Figure 4.2.

Among all fusional affixes indicating four tenses, a total of 8 forms express first person; 12 mark singular number; and 5 indicate present tense (only).[16] Summing the number of possible mappings for the members of a single tense paradigm expressing three persons, singular and plural (plus second person, singular, informal), there are 138 mapping possibilities involving five forms, as depicted in Figure 4.3.

---

15. German may not be the best example here. Clearly, there is a homophonous form -*en* which occurs on verbs; however, the two forms are easily disambiguated by syntactic context. And, genitive -*s* is also homophonous with the plural marker, but, again, is disambiguated in context. In addition, some nouns do not change form when expressing plurality (e.g., *der Wagen* "the car" and *die Wagen* "the cars") — plurality being indicated by plural forms of definite and indefinite articles, through the expression of agreement in other phrasal constituents, and so on. Nevertheless, each of these individual markers has a direct link to the category of number and marks plural on nouns.

16. For the purpose of this calculation, the present-tense suffix -*amos* is taken as homophonous with that marking preterite because it is a member of a separate paradigm and can be counted separately as a consequence. However, the affix -*a* marking the singular version of both second-person, formal and third-person belongs to this one paradigm only, and is, therefore, not divided into two homophonous forms, one marking second-person and the other third.

The identification of form–meaning sets 97

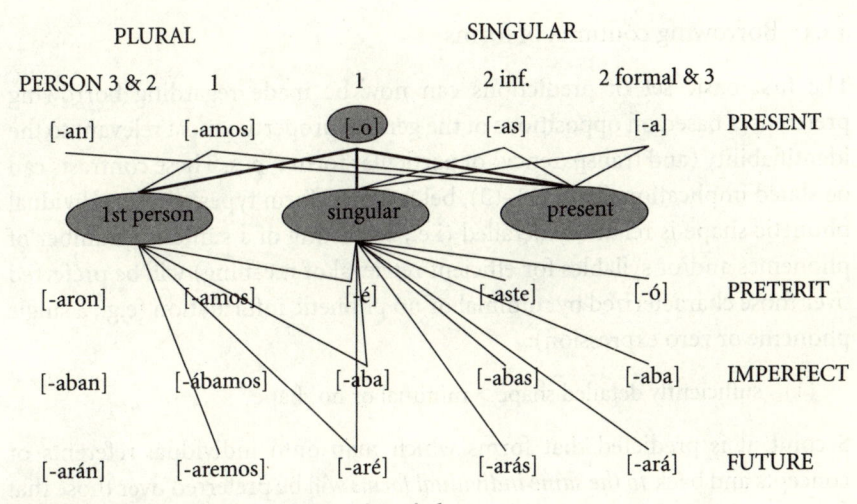

```
         PLURAL                          SINGULAR
PERSON 3 & 2      1           1        2 inf.        2 formal & 3
  [-an]         [-amos]     [-o]        [-as]         [-a]        PRESENT

                1st person        singular           present

  [-aron]       [-amos]     [-é]        [-aste]       [-ó]        PRETERIT

  [-aban]       [-ábamos]   [-aba]      [-abas]       [-aba]      IMPERFECT

  [-arán]       [-aremos]   [-aré]      [-arás]       [-ará]      FUTURE
```

Figure 4.2. The mappings of Spanish verbal -*o*.

singular			plural		
form	meaning	no. of forms for given meaning	form	meaning	no. of forms for given meaning
-o	first person	8	-amos	first person	8
	singular	12		plural	8
	present tense	5		present tense	5
		3+25			3+21
-as	second person, informal	4			
	singular	12			
	present tense	5			
		3+21			
-a	second person, formal	8	-an	second person, formal	8
	third person	8		third person	8
	singular	12		plural	8
	present tense	5		present tense	5
		5+33			5+29
totals		80			58

Figure 4.3. Calculating mapping possibilities (present tense, first conjugation class)[*]

[*] The leftmost column lists the forms; the middle column represents the types of meanings expressed by that form; and the rightmost represents the number of forms that express that particular meaning (mapping backwards from meaning to form).

4.1.3 Borrowing continua of forms

The first basic set of predictions can now be made regarding borrowing preferences based on oppositions of the general properties most relevant to the identifiability (and transparency) of particular form types. These contrasts can be stated implicationally in (1)–(3), below. First, form types whose individual phonetic shape is relatively detailed (i.e., consisting of a sufficient number of phonemes and/or syllables for efficient retrieval of meaning) will be preferred over those characterized by minimal or no phonetic information (e.g., a single phoneme or zero expression):

(1) sufficiently detailed shape > minimal or no shape

Second, it is predicted that forms which map onto individual referents or concepts and back *to the same individual forms* will be preferred over those that map onto more than one concept simultaneously, as in the case of individual Spanish fusional affixes on verbs that express tense–aspect plus person and number agreement. In addition, they will be preferred over forms whose numerous simultaneous (or coalesced) meanings are also separately and equally expressed by a number of other forms, as in the various Spanish affixes expressing first-person or present tense. These preferences are presented in (2a) and (2b), respectively:

(2) a. 1-to-1 form–meaning mapping > 1-to-many simultaneous form-to-meaning mappings
     b. 1-to-1 form–meaning mapping > 1-to-many simultaneous meaning-to-form mappings

The complex mapping procedures inherent in fusional-type affixes are a consequence of both conditions; one isolable form maps simultaneously and equally onto many meanings and each one of those meanings maps simultaneously back to a number of distinct forms (which also express another set of meanings simultaneously).

Lastly, it is predicted that individual forms that may be selected by speakers as a direct consequence of the meaning or concept to which they refer (that is, they link to entities or referents of some sort, and their selection is, therefore, semantically based) will be preferred over those that are obligatorily selected or applied as a consequence of word order (co-occurrence) restrictions or morphosyntactic rule (i.e., the concepts they represent are obligatorily expressed, and selection is, therefore, syntactically required):[17]

(3) selection optional > application/selection obligatory

These three sets of oppositions of form identification characteristics represent scalings of properties that can occur in varying degrees and combinations and, therefore, may cluster in different complementary (or potentially conflicting) ways on individual forms and form types. It is now possible to identify which form types are likely to be the most to least preferred in any borrowing situation.

Content items (words, bound roots) typically have each of the properties to the left of the arrows indicating maximal degrees of identifiability or transparency (and potential for salience) and are, therefore, always the most highly preferred form types. Fusional-type affixes, possessing every characteristic to the right of the arrows, will be the least preferred (assuming that they are, in fact, compatible with the recipient morphosyntactic system). Other bound form types (e.g., agglutinating-type inflectional affixes) will be preferred over fusional types, but less than either function items (words, bound roots) and content items. Function items (words, bound roots), which occupy medial positions on scales of borrowability and grammaticalization, will be borrowed more easily and more frequently than inflectional affixes of any type, but not as easily or frequently as content items.[18]

As a general form type, function items may possess the properties represented in (1)–(3), above, in different numbers and strengths. For example, locative (spatial and temporal) prepositions (e.g., those of Spanish or English) typically possess detailed phonetic shape (relative to inflectional affixes), 1-to-1 form–meaning mappings, and are selected as a result of the kinds of concepts (i.e., semantic relations) they express. This is in spite of the fact that they belong to a closed class and that their meanings may be considered relational in that they

---

17. For instance, in languages such as Spanish, English, or German, particular verbs (and their derived nouns or adjectives) are subcategorized for specific accompanying (obligatory) prepositions as a result of syntactic processes of phrasal organization (see, e.g., Friederici 1985: 136–139).

18. Regarding segmentability, an implicit component of complex phonetic shape, function items are typically analyzable as having word boundaries; they also take part in syntactic processes affecting the ordering of phrasal or clausal constituents. Bound grammatical forms, that are subsidiary in form even relative to function items (words and bound roots), are subject only to word formation rules. We can assume that the additional syntactic property (i.e., word as well as morpheme boundaries) acts to increase identifiability.

function to indicate relationships among other phrasal and clausal constituents. Other sorts of adpositions that are obligatorily selected for syntactic reasons are less transparent and will be preferred less in borrowing situations despite their relatively detailed phonetic form.

Other function items may be described in similar terms. For example, particular subclasses of Determiner and Pronoun may be semantically selected and have 1-to-1 mapping possibilities (others not); but, in all cases, they are typically less detailed in form than members of the open classes as a result of grammaticalization processes, which include reduction of phonological form as a result of relative frequency of occurrence. They may also be subject to processes of cliticization and so forth. All classes and subclasses of connectives share similar characteristics with respect to mapping possibilities and selection. However, with respect to auxiliary verbs, in general, some may be semantically selected (e.g., modal verbs) while others that function as markers of tense or aspect may be obligatory because of the categories they express.

In all classes of function items, various members of particular subclasses may have noticeably different configurations of the stated form identification properties (in degree or number) from members of other subclasses, and this can result in degrees of transparency even within an individual class. As a consequence, those items exhibiting the greater number and degree of properties enhancing their identifiability will be among those that are preferred in borrowing. In addition, when a particular form type has multiple functions (e.g., subclasses of Pronoun such as possessives or those with special clitic forms), salience may be affected. In one context, a form may be salient, and in another, maybe not. In one case, salience may conspire with other phonological factors to enhance overall identifiability; in the other, the lack of salience may decrease identifiability.

4.2 Semantic characteristics

The Sapirian notions of concrete versus relational concepts have been foundational in much work dealing with grammaticality, borrowing, and so on, and have provided a basis for a number of recurring ideas about meaning. Many of the characteristics that Sapir proposed can be analyzed according to two notions typically associated with descriptions of semantic bleaching. One refers to levels of generality and the other to degrees of abstractness. In each there is a set of oppositions: generality can be contrasted with specificity, and abstractness with concreteness. General terms identify types or classes of entities and so on, but specific terms provide detailed semantic information, enough to distinguish among members of particular groups. Within individual taxonomies, the meaning of a superordinate form–meaning set, a hyperonym, is always more general and inclusive of the various members than a subordinate one, or hyponym. As a consequence, the more general a term is, the greater number of contexts there will be in which it is likely to occur (e.g., *dog* versus *chihuahua*).[19]

The quality of concreteness is descriptive of entities that exist in the real world, can be actual referents, or, like *unicorn* and *Klingon*, have real (i.e., imageable) attributes but exist only in the imagination or in the realm of fiction. Being visible and tangible, actual referents possess physical properties (cues) by which mental images are obtained (see Rosch et al. 1976; Rosch and Mervis 1975; Rosch 1975). Hence, the term "imageable" refers to processes by a which a speaker assesses and analyzes features of physical objects either to secure an appropriate label or to construct a mental image (i.e., concept) that can function as the meaning in a particular form–meaning set. Abstract nouns do not point to referents that are imageable in this same sense; their referents are not physical entities that can be touched, watched, or used (de Groot 1993:41). Therefore, abstractness is characteristic of concepts that have no direct concrete existence and are not objects or entities that can be signified in a Saussurean sense.[20]

In cases of polysemic extension, in which forms representing objects are extended to refer to processes associated with those objects (e.g., to wallpaper, to carpet, to wax) or forms for actions extended to cover their results (e.g., a hit, a run, a fall) some sort of core meaning is pulled out, abstracted, and applied to a different kind of referent (object → activity, and so on). In this respect, processes of grammaticalization and derivation can both result in the emergence of concepts that are increasingly abstract and, perhaps, general (Bybee 1995:226), yet relatable to their sources. Consequently, a third property is required, based solely on degrees of grammaticalization viewed synchronically, that can screen out both (a) derived meanings that have merely become more general or abstract, and (b) meaning types that lie at different levels of generality within individual taxonomies. In each case, direct reference (i.e., a mapping of form to meaning) is maintained, albeit to different types of referents that are not necessarily more grammaticalized.

---

19. For discussion the relationships of hyponymy and hyperonymy, see, for example, Levelt 1989:201, 212–214; 1992:6ff; and Bierwisch and Schreuder 1992:36ff.

20. See Section 3.3, above, for discussion of abstractness and abstract nouns.

An opposition of meaning types based on grammaticalization is also implicit in Sapir's distinctions. It is based on characteristics that are language-specific and depends on whether the kind of meaning expressed by a particular form belongs to a broad lexical system (semantic type or subtype) or whether it belongs to a language-specific inflectional category. On the one hand, the meanings associated with some forms are members of general semantic types (e.g., concrete nouns or activity verbs) or so-called semantic fields (i.e., subtypes like nouns for body parts and motion verbs, discussed in Chapter 3) and can, as a result, be listed in a dictionary. That is, representations of clear referents and/or explanations of characteristic properties serve as definitions and can be listed alongside appropriate forms. On the other hand, the meanings expressed by inflectional affixes link to particular inflectional categories (e.g., number, tense, or gender) whose "definitions" may elude even the most proficient speakers (linguists, as well). This third opposition also reflects the fact that the topics speakers choose to discuss are not limited by a particular language grammar (i.e., morphosyntactic infrastructure) although the form types and grammatical categories they have at their disposal to express those topics may vary considerably.

4.2.1 Inflectional meanings

Much recent work has focused on the types of meanings that inflectional categories are known to express. For example, Bybee (1985) catalogs grammatical categories associated with verbs based on their occurrence in a relatively large and heterogeneous sample of languages. A cross-section of 50 languages was chosen judged to be relatively free of genetic and areal bias (cf. Carstairs-McCarthy 1992: 173) concerning the relative frequency of certain types of inflectional categories, the order in which they appear in relation to a verbal stem, and so on. They were identified according to three criteria: boundedness (the morpheme cannot be separated from a stem); obligatoriness (specific forms must appear whenever the category is applied); and predictability of meaning (the meaning is the same when applied to any verb). The list represents the kinds of categories one might expect to uncover in a particular language, though it is not assumed to be exhaustive of all the sorts of abstract, grammaticalized concepts that may occur in all of the world's languages. It does represent, however, a clear basis for a general contrast with semantic types (lexical categories).

In addition to the above, nominal inflections of number, person, gender-class, and case may also occur as a result of language-specific concord (obligatory

Table 4.2. Inflectional categories associated with verbs (according to Bybee 1985)

Category	Definition
Valence	the number and types of arguments a verb can take (e.g., causative, which affects the arguments and semantic roles taken by a specific verb)
Voice	the perspective from which the event or act described by the verb stem is taken (e.g., active and passive voice, which also affects the assignment of semantic roles)
Aspect	the way the internal temporal constituency of a situation is viewed (e.g., as an act in progressive, perfective, and so on)
Tense	the location in time of the event depicted by the verb (i.e., in relation to the moment of speech or some other point in time)
Mood	the way the speaker represents the propositional value of a statement (probable, possible, certain, etc.) — this includes evidentials and expressions of modality
Number agreement	agreement with an argument (most frequently grammatical subject) in number (e.g., singular, plural, dual, paucal…)
Person agreement	agreement with respect to first, second, third person, and so on of an argument (grammatical subject, direct object, and so on)
Gender agreement	agreement with argument with respect to gender or class (e.g., masculine or feminine gender)

patterns of agreement) on particular constituents of NPs in addition to classes of Noun, e.g., various determiners and adjectives.

As with form, the kinds of meanings that are typically expressed by function words are positioned somewhere between extremes, between those associated with content items and those of fusional affixes. For example, adpositions have no direct referents themselves but typically indicate physical relationships such as location of one entity with respect to another in space or time (Sapir 1921:89; Hopper and Traugott 1991:107). Such relational concepts are apparently restricted to the possibilities that exist in the world; in some approaches, they constitute an ontological category of their own termed relations (Clark 1993:43–49). However, this type of meaning is integral to human communication irrespective of the ways it may be expressed in an individual language. Such highly isolating-analytical languages as Vietnamese or Mandarin are obviously equipped to express temporal and spatial relationships through the use of adpositions, particles, etc. However, neither has obligatory inflectional categories indicating tense–aspect or case that may express similar, though more abstract, general, and grammaticalized, concepts (e.g., which occur in more synthetic types of languages such as German, Russian, Italian, and so on).

Other classes of function words can be contrasted cross-linguistically with differing sorts of inflectional affixes (sometimes within individual languages) in similar ways, for example, modals (which often receive tense markers and so on) versus affixes expressing mood; pronouns (in many languages indicating grammatical categories of gender and number) versus tense markers also indicating person and number agreement; and subclasses of determiner such as articles (at times marked for such grammatical categories as case and number and gender agreement) in contrast with affixes indicating definiteness. Regarding inflectional categories in a specific utterance, however, it is not very likely that a speaker/hearer is concerned with recognizing (or accessing) an abstract category of tense, person, or number. The task is to correctly identify the particular instance of any and all distinctions expressed by a discrete form (e.g., present or past tense; first, second or third person; and singular or plural). Logically, there can be no general occurrence of tense that could be significant in any specific situation; an inflectional category is neither an entity nor an imageable referent. In the case of fusional affixes, the identification of meaning requires a strategy that recognizes all such meaning possibilities simultaneously

Accordingly, in the presentation of form–meaning recognition characteristics, the factors by which kinds of meanings can be compared or contrasted (in the context of transparency versus opacity) are listed as follows in Table 4.3.

Table 4.3. Form–meaning interpretation characteristics (FMICs): Meaning

Transparency		Opacity	
(a)	concreteness: reference to distinct entities or concepts that exist	(a′)	abstract; apart from concrete or physical existence; no distinct reference
(b)	specificity: explicit; distinguishes among members of a species or type; typically occurs in a limited number of contexts	(b′)	general; applies to many (all members of a group); consequently, may occur in a larger number of contexts
(c)	grammaticalization: belongs to a broad lexical subsystem (i.e., semantic type or subtype)	(c′)	belongs to a language-specific inflectional (i.e., grammatical) category or subtype

Meaning types sharing the characteristics listed in the left-hand column, (a)–(c), are those typically represented by content items which indicate what

Sapir termed primary concepts; they designate the principal topics of discourse, e.g., persons, objects, activities, and so forth. Those types possessing all of the characteristics represented in the right-hand column, (a′)–(c′), are the meanings that belong to language particular inflectional affixes. Moreover, the various properties may cluster to identify types of meanings that occur at midpoints on scales of grammaticalization and borrowability. For instance, pronouns may represent meanings that are relatively concrete and specific based on their antecedents, but reference is made through the expression of such language particular categories as person, number, gender, and/or case. The meanings associated with auxiliary verbs (e.g., modals expressing obligation, permission, and so on), in contrast, are more abstract and general than the primary verbs with which they may occur but, nonetheless, belong to a semantic subtype of Verb.[21] Other meaning types, such as those linked to certain subclasses of connectives and determiners, appear to occupy midpoints in each respect. Even though they are relatively abstract (lack direct reference) and general (can appear in a large number of contexts), they often express semantic distinctions that are easily definable in terms of logical relations, quantities, and so on. In addition, the concepts associated with classes of connectives and determiners appear to be much more universal (i.e., typical of human discourse) than the more grammaticalized meanings of, say, tense or gender.

4.2.2 Borrowing continua of meanings

The second set of predictions, expressed implicationally in (4)–(6), below, is based on the three oppositions of meaning types outlined in the preceding portion of this section. First, it is predicted that form–meaning sets whose meanings or referents are concrete will be preferred in borrowing over those that are characterized as abstract. This should be especially evident within particular semantic domains (e.g., within occupational nomenclatures) with respect to additions to the recipient lexicon (see Subsection 1.1, above). On the one hand, concrete meanings are associated with individual or identifiable groups of persons, things, and so forth that have physical existence in reality and experience and that constitute observable entities (e.g., wind, radio waves, etc.). They include reference to close objects that have physically recognizable attributes (e.g., they are green or may become furious); consequently, they have

---

21. See Section 3.2.3, above, regarding the potential salience of modals, pronouns, and so on.

a clear definition and can be contrasted with other objects or entities on the basis of their physical properties. Objects that have physical existence can be pointed to, seen, picked up, and put to use, and, therefore, have the ability to provide the perceptually-based semantic information (e.g., shape, size, texture, material composition, etc.) necessary to establish a mental image/concept capable of being a concrete referent.[22] Other speakers will have the near identical concept (they see the same image) and receive similar amounts of exposure to its label (phonetic form).

On the other hand, abstract terms generally refer to concepts that do not have physical existence, and as a consequence, can have no physical properties of shape, texture, and so on). They may include processes, methods, ideas (truth or lie), or the results (products) of processes. They may be remote or theoretical in some sense (existing in psychological or social space) and are typically more difficult to define (or translate from L1 to L2) as a consequence (Heine et al. 1991a:41ff). Concepts associated with abstract nouns may require demonstration and illustration (e.g., how to use a particular implement) and/or conscious instruction (e.g., regarding the meanings and significance of terms commonly used within various governmental, religious, educational, or medical settings). As a consequence, the first prediction is as follows:

(4) concrete > abstract

Meanings may become more abstract either through processes of grammaticalization or through those associated with derivation. The term "abstraction" generally indicates a loss and/or change of particular semantic specifications; for example, the meaning associated with a particular form–meaning set may be reduced to its semantic core (a generalizing abstraction) or to a certain aspect of its meaning (an isolating abstraction). Metaphorical abstraction, most often linked to grammaticalization, occurs as a meaning is abstracted from one form–meaning set and applied in a more diffuse or fuzzy way to another, more grammaticalized form in discrete steps (Heine et al. 1991a:44ff; Heine et al. 1991b:160–161). It may be either structure-preserving, which does not change

---

[22]. It is also noted studies of bilingual lexical access, that concrete nouns are translated more quickly than abstract nouns, and animate nouns more quickly than inanimate (see, for example, de Groot 1993:40). One explanation is there is a greater density of conceptual features on a semantic (i.e., conceptual) level with respect to concrete versus abstract form–meaning sets. Some researchers have, therefore, proposed a "distinctly perceptual component of the semantic representation" (Kroll and de Groot 1997:189).

the word class of the affected form–meaning set, or structure-changing, which does change class membership. In the former, there is an extension of meaning and, in the latter an extension of function. Heine and his collaborators offer as examples of both the Ewe noun *ta'* "head": as structure preserving, its meaning is extended to refer to such concepts as "intellectual ability", "main issue", "group, party", and so on. As structure changing, *ta'* is used as a postposition and subordinating conjunction meaning "over", "on", etc (Heine et al. 1991a: 44–45; cf. Heine et al. 1991b: 160ff).

Concerning the second characteristic, specificity, the initial expectation may be to predict that form–meaning sets whose meanings (referents) are specific, individual entities will be preferred over those that are more general because general terms refer to kinds of entities (as opposed to individual objects) that require some sort of classificatory scheme. In preliminary fashion, therefore, the second basic prediction is set forth as follows:

(5) specific > general

However, this assumes that the most easily recognizable concepts are those that are linked to the most explicit semantic information (i.e., maximally specified concepts) because it is in some way necessary for the identification of particular referents. Perhaps, the expectation should follow by analogy from the prediction concerning phonetic detail (see Subsection 4.1.1, above), which states that form recognition is facilitated by sufficiently detailed shape in its function as a precise phonological address, allowing the speaker/hearer to access an exact and appropriate meaning (i.e., figuratively speaking, the occupant of the address). What is required for identification is an optimal, not maximal, amount of information. Hence, specificity more properly refers to the number and kind of physical features (qua semantic information) required to recognize kinds of objects and to distinguish among or between individual members of a kind or larger, more general grouping. For instance, many different types of animals have the ability to fly; however, we can distinguish among them on the basis of several other physical properties, e.g., whether or not they have feathers, wings, and so forth. Among types of birds, additional properties (i.e., more information) will be required in order to make further "category cuts" (Rosch et al. 1976).[23] As a consequence, the prediction needs to be amended somewhat in

---

23. This may evoke discussion of the naturalness of semantic types (categories). Items included or excluded from specific categories (so-called category cuts) may be open to some cross-linguistic variation based on cultural factors and/or levels of expertise. For example,

order to clarify the circumstances under which gradient levels of specificity and generality are most relevant in particular borrowing situations.

Regarding degrees of generality, Rosch et al. (1976) argue that there are semantic (conceptual) levels at which the mental representations of entities possess systematic kinds and amounts of information by which they can be differentiated and grouped. This includes a basic (entry) level which represent the most useful terms for kinds of objects, superordinate level(s) which organize objects into larger families, and additional subordinate levels which provide increased specificity of reference. Within taxonomies of common concrete nouns, they posit that basic objects are identified and named according to aggregates of physical characteristics; they have similar shapes, are identifiable from averaged shapes of other class members, and so on "in terms of cognitive economy..." (384). Within individual taxonomies, superordinate terms (hyperonyms) have a relatively small number of characteristics by which distinctions can be made, and are, as a consequence, more inclusive. Subordinate terms (hyponyms) have more attributes in common, and are more exclusive. For example, nouns such as *dog, apple, chair* are basic-level terms in English, while corresponding superordinate terms are mammal, fruit, and furniture, respectively. At a more subordinate level, one also finds such words as *chihuahua, Mackintosh,* and *kitchen chair*, respectively. Hence, while *dog* is a hyponym of *mammal*, it is also a hyperonym of *chihuahua*. However, *dog* remains the basic/entry point term.[24]

Rosch and her collaborators link abstractness, the identification of a somewhat reduced collection of characteristics that form the semantic core of a particular term (an intrinsic or non-derived kind of generalizing abstraction), with gradient levels of generality. But, for the present purposes, it is important to note that abstractness and generality are, nonetheless, distinct. For instance, the concept represented by one concrete noun may certainly be more general

---

porpoises are not fish, but share certain attributes with them; having expertise in the area of biology provides individuals with sufficient numbers and relevant kinds of attributes to enable sharper category cuts (inclusive/exclusive). See, for example, Rosch et al. 1976: 430ff. See also Lakoff 1987 (12–57) for discussion of Rosch's later work and some of the cognitive bases for categorization of meaning and perceptual types.

24. Regarding the ways object names are learned and organized during child native language acquisition, which appear to be consistent with this often cited approach, see, for example, Waxman 1994; Markman 1994, 1993, 1989; Huttenlocher and Smiley 1987; Waxman 1994; Landau 1994, 1993; and Clark 1993.

than another without any loss of concreteness, e.g. *bird* versus *sparrow*, and the concept associated with an abstract noun may be more specific than another, e.g., *psycholinguistics* versus *linguistics*. It is safe to say that processes of abstraction can lead to increased generality as a co-effect. Nevertheless, basic-level objects are those that are first sorted and named by children (cf. Clark 1993:50ff) and are the most codable (representable), most coded (represented), and most useful in an individual language (Rosch et al. 1976:382, 428). In addition, they are also the most likely to be found in cross-linguistic analyses of individual language lexicons. As a result, it is hardly surprising to find the striking resemblances among word lists in introductory foreign language texts and core vocabulary among the world's languages.

The ways levels of generality may affect borrowing patterns may vary somewhat. In the event that the recipient community is exposed to a novel entity (e.g., a specific animal, agricultural implement, and so on), there may be a number of possibilities (see Subsection 1.1, above). One is to use an already existing native form or collocation of forms and extend their range of possible referents via semantic loans or calques; another is to borrow the donor form–meaning set outright and integrate it into the recipient system (or perhaps a combination of both, so-called loan blends). When there is already an appropriate family (i.e., a semantic subtype) in the recipient lexicon to which a borrowed form–meaning set may be conceptually linked, that form can easily be assigned to that subtype. It is not in direct competition with any recipient forms — i.e., other hyponyms. However, if there is no existing semantic subtype, an entire taxonomy may be borrowed, including hyperonyms and hyponyms. This often appears to be the case regarding families of entities that are entirely new to the recipient language and culture, for instance, concepts belonging to technological fields pertinent to particular professions or industries, religious hierarchies and institutions, and so on. In this case, the most useful and basic term may be borrowed first — to provide a family name that can function as a hyperonym under which a new taxonomy will develop. Knowledge of individual form–meaning sets included within the new taxonomy will likely depend on exposure (frequency), relevance, levels of expertise, and so on.

The third and final prediction pertains to the effects of grammaticalization, that is, the synchronic status of meaning types along scales of grammaticalization. As stated in the previous sections of the present work, semantic types and subtypes (at one extreme end of a scale of meaning types) represent concepts common to all languages. However, these concepts may be gradiently concrete and/or specific. Inflectional categories (at the other end of the scale) are by definition language-specific and, as an apparent consequence, idiosyncratic with respect to the concepts they express, their functions, and restrictions on appropriate usage. Such categories are typically abstract (implying the loss or lack of concreteness) with respect to the types of meanings they express and typically general regarding their functions (implying the loss or lack of reference to specific entities). Concerning specificity, however, individual instances are more specific than the general category to which they belong; the greater the number of members in a paradigm, the more specific the meaning (or complex of meanings) expressed by each member. In addition, there is a direct correlation between specificity (as applied to occurrences of inflectional concepts) and the amount of grammatical knowledge that is required for identification within the speech stream — more so in production than in comprehension.

It is predicted, therefore, that form–meaning sets whose meanings are members of broad lexical systems (semantic types or subtypes) will be preferred in borrowing over those that are expressions, viz., specific instances, of inflectional categories. This is represented in (6), below:

(6) semantic (sub)type > inflectional category

The three sets of oppositions regarding types of meaning discussed above also represent scalings of properties that can occur in varying degrees and combinations and, consequently, may cluster in complementary (or conflicting) ways. It is now possible to identify meaning types that are most to least preferred in any borrowing situation.

Form–meaning sets whose meanings typically possess each of the properties to the left of the arrows (indicating maximal degrees of transparency and identifiability), i.e., those whose meanings belong to broad lexical categories (semantic types and subtypes) and whose referents are concrete and specific, will always be the most preferred (and most often borrowed) in any contact situation.[25] The least preferred will be those that possess all of the characteristics to the right of the arrows, that is, those that are abstract and general and

---

25. This includes the caveat that basic level categories may be preferred over either superordinate or subordinate donor categories under certain specified circumstances, i.e., depending on the prior existence of equivalent taxonomies in the recipient lexicon. It is also possible that basic level terms may be more frequently borrowed as a result of their general frequency, although those belonging to recipient core vocabulary will likely win out as a result of various social factors — in that case, recipient labels (forms) are retained as ethnic markers and so on (Field 1997b).

whose associated meanings are expressions of inflectional categories. In-between types of meaning, e.g., concepts representing gradiently concrete relations (locative, directional, and so on), modality (e.g., ability, permission, etc.), and so on (Heine et al. 1991a: 42–43), will be preferred less than members of semantic types and subtypes, but more than expressions of inflectional categories.[26]

4.2.3 Linking form and meaning

All form–meaning sets possess properties according to the six interpretation characteristics discussed above (expressed as oppositions of form and meaning). That is, every form will display (i) comparable amounts of phonetic information, (ii) different sequential and/or simultaneous mapping possibilities (1-to-1, 1-to-many, and so on), and (iii) selectional restrictions governing their occurrences; every meaning type will exhibit (iv) degrees of abstractness (e.g., from totally concrete to completely abstract), (v) specificity, and (vi) grammaticalization. In addition, these characteristics indicate properties that can cluster in various ways. For instance, forms with detailed phonetic shape often map onto individual referents (1-to-1); specificity and concreteness (and their oppositions generality and abstractness) often coincide even though they are distinguishable. Moreover, concrete concepts are usually represented by unique and segmentable forms, and inflectional meanings are typically represented by minimal phonetic shapes that are obligatorily expressed. Whenever the expression of a particular category value is required (e.g., in English, tense on finite verbs or number on count nouns), a form indicating that category is obligatorily selected and applied to the stem (or root) of a member of the syntactic (word) class to which the category applies. Even though selection of a specific instance of a category may be for stylistic reasons (e.g., the conscious choice of singular versus plural forms of generic nouns), it remains true, nonetheless, that one (and only one) member of a relevant paradigm must appear on the appropriate stem or root, even if that form is zero (see Bybee 1985: 27 and p. 202).

---

26. Perhaps, the form–meaning sets expressing such relations and attitudes belong to closed classes because there is a limit to the number of possible concepts they can signify. Their meanings are relatively specific, yet abstract; they are frequent as a result of their useful (and versatile) functions. Even though they do not belong to inflectional categories, per se, they appear to exhibit the effects of grammaticalization. We may speculate that the processes by which they emerge may lie somewhere between derivation and grammaticalization.

While form–meaning sets that exhibit the six interpretation characteristics to the highest degree (i.e., on either end of the oppositions) may provide the most obvious cues regarding identifiability, grammaticalization, and borrowability, those occupying midpoints between extremes may still be distinguished according to particular clusters of characteristics. For instance, adpositions whose semantic functions are most clearly locative (e.g., the so-called "lexical" prepositions of German and English) will be preferred over those that are subcategorized for by individual content items, so-called "grammatical prepositions" (see Friederici 1985) on the basis of form (e.g., reduced phonological form, mapping possibilities, and selectional restrictions — in the case of grammatical prepositions, they are obligatory) and on that of meaning (e.g., gradient levels of abstractness and generality and degrees of grammaticalization). Similar predictions can be made of pronominals (e.g., the full pronouns of Spanish versus reflexives that obligatorily co-occur with certain verbs), conjunctions expressing certain types of logical relations (e.g., coordinators versus subordinators), determiners expressing quantification versus definiteness, and auxiliary verbs that are semantically selected and belong to semantic subtypes of Verb (e.g., modals expressing ability or obligation) versus those expressing obligatory categories (e.g. those used in the so-called compound tenses of English), i.e., in those particular highly grammaticalized functions.

Many correlations such as these can be linked to grammaticalization and/or derivation, suggesting that each process operates concurrently on both form and meaning. However, actual outcomes cross-linguistically are mitigated by the fact that not every language will show the same degrees of grammaticalization (Bybee 1995: 228–229). Moreover, some gradable characteristics of meaning and form will be present irrespective of the extent of grammaticalization and/or derivation; they may be inherent to the individual forms and concepts themselves. Overall, form–meaning sets can, nevertheless, be compared and contrasted according to clusters of these properties. One may conclude, then, that the similarities found between grammaticalization clines (or chains) and borrowing hierarchies are each intimately linked to morphological character, that is, the ways individual languages structure their particular form–meaning sets into morphemes and words. In the case of borrowing, the morphological structuring of each language plays the critical role.

Because the establishment of property clusters may be obfuscated somewhat by the gradient character of the properties themselves, there may be a number of judgment calls with respect to the investigation of particular language data that may influence a particular prediction (e.g., A is more concrete and less specific than B, when I am the arbiter). This appears to be true when attempting to distinguish between derivational and inflectional categories in particular languages (Bybee 1985: 81; Croft 1990: 191; Heine et al. 1991a: 17). Regarding the multiplicity of gradient factors and the complexity of the issues involved in cross-linguistic comparisons of continua of forms and meanings, Sapir opined, "There are too many possibilities" (Sapir 1921: 107). Nevertheless, the number of properties that are assumed to be factors in the case of borrowability (gradient or not) can contribute to the accuracy of the predictions, especially when properties cluster in their most clearly identifiable ways.

4.3 Issues of semantic complexity

Before summing up the various predictions based on form and meaning types, one remaining issue requires discussion which concerns the relative borrowability of various major word class members (N, V, etc.). It is commonly noted that nouns are always among the first elements of a language to be borrowed, followed by other content items. It is also axiomatic in studies of language acquisition that nouns are learned before verbs. These observations have prompted a number of possible explanations suggesting that the obvious asymmetry goes beyond the mere recognition of form–meaning sets and that it is a result of the syntactic and semantic complexity of verbs relative to nouns. Numerous studies or early acquisition indicate that the ease with which verb meanings are associated onto their appropriate forms is mediated by the learner's attention to the syntactic environment (C. Fisher et al. 1994: 333; Choi and Gopnik: 96; Pinker 1996: 39ff; cf. Gleitman 1993 and Landau and Gleitman 1985). On the one hand, there is considerable evidence that nouns can be successfully identified on the basis of word-to-world mappings alone. On the other, verb meanings are apparently determined in large part by their syntactic and semantic context. This, of course, includes relationships among one to many argument and/or complement structures (and the nature of their referents) that are requisite in the phrases (VPs) in which they appear as heads. This has led to the conceptualization of verb learning as context-sensitive and involving sentence-to-world mapping procedures (Gleitman 1993: 191ff).

Implicit in this is that a rather comprehensive, prior knowledge of nouns (often representing participants in the action expressed by the verb), specifically, of those situated in the immediate context where a target verb form occurs, are prerequisites to the accurate extraction of verb meanings. The gradually accumulated and complex knowledge of verbs and their behaviors (e.g., in the creation of subcategorization frames) is drawn from inferences obtained by observing the patterns — syntactic and semantic contexts — in which they usually appear, specifically those that may restrict the kinds (semantic subtypes) and number of nouns that can participate in the expressed action, and the modifiers co-occurring within relevant phrasal and clausal boundaries. Therefore, a greater awareness of the structural (syntactic) and semantic characteristics of the language being learned or acquired is necessary for the proper identification of verbs (C. Fisher et al. 1994: 336). The more knowledge required to master a form–meaning set or structure, the more time it will take to acquire.

As discussed previously (Subsection 3.3.4), verbs exhibit a much wider range of syntactic behaviors than nouns, based on their semantic requirements. Primary verbs are syntactically the main elements of the VP and, as a consequence, are crucial to the organization of the sentence (van Hout and Muysken 1994: 55). They also assign semantic roles appropriate to their core meanings, and, therefore, entail a great deal more grammatical knowledge in performance than the simple naming of person, object, or activity. The complexity implicit in the selection process is not merely related to the number of complements but is also intrinsically related to the number and type of semantic roles. For example, a perceiver must be a concrete noun that is animate, probably human. Metaphorical extension implies some knowledge of original semantic parameters: if one says something along the lines of "That stone was just sitting there, staring at me…", it is assumed that the metaphor is accomplished by conscious choice, and presumably for literate effect (a figure of speech). The overall concreteness of the term *stone* does not change.

Regarding individual members of the word-class Verb, the number of complements may also vary depending on the intended specificity of a particular utterance. If the number of arguments were the sole determinant of syntactic or semantic complexity and, as a consequence, were decisive in respect to learnability or borrowability, then any term representing the semantic subtype give would be among the most complex (requiring three semantic roles: a recipient and a gift in addition to a giver) and the subtype modal would be among the least complex (requiring no independent roles). Based on a simple count of required arguments, modals should be learned or borrowed before giving-type verbs, and that has never been observed to be the case. Given the inherent complexity of verbs in general, the learnability or borrowability of particular verb types or subtypes undoubtedly depends on a number of other

Table 4.4. Content items according to semantic and syntactic complexity

Word class	Characteristics
Noun	
Syntactic:	Occupies syntactic slots as head of NP; may receive markers of situational number, inherent gender-class, or grammatical case; relative syntactic importance outside its own domain (NP) depends on grammatical role (subject, object, etc.); position (with respect to grammatical role) is relative to V of VP.
Semantic:	Identifies the topics of discourse (participants of processes, events, or activities specified by V of VP); generally more specific than verbs, especially those they accompany (i.e., there are more names for possible participants than there are for activities, which is reflected by sheer numbers in an individual lexicon).
Adjective	
Syntactic:	Position, function, and distribution is relative to head of NP; any syntactic process that applies to head of NP (by virtue of co-occurrence patterns) applies to Adj-modifier; dependent on head noun if marked for categories of agreement; less likely to receive nominal inflections (via agreement or concord) than head of NP; syntactic behavior more restricted relative to verbs (e.g., to the types of complements they take).
Semantic:	Meaning modifies head of NP; selection is determined by characteristics of modified noun; usually more abstract (expresses quality, not object) and general (may appear in a greater number of contexts) than noun it modifies.
Verb	
Syntactic:	As the nucleus of a clause, establishes syntactic links among clausal constituents; focal point of the greatest number of syntactic procedures; contains markers of the greatest number of inflectional and derivational categories; in many languages, must agree in number, gender-class with grammatical subject; assigns specific grammatical case in languages that mark this category.
Semantic:	Determines semantic role of its arguments, one to three places in English, with secondary roles marked by prepositions — markers resulting from semantic (and, therefore, syntactic) requirements constitute most of the significant differences among the world's languages regarding morphological structuring; relative to adpositions, assigns the greatest number of semantic roles (and case markers).

factors. General issues of complexity in acquisition or borrowing regarding classes of Noun, Verb, and Adjective are listed in Table 4.4.

In sum, there is an overall asymmetry of relationships among these three word classes. For example, there is a dependence implicit in the relationship of modifier–modified; adjectives are subsidiary in a number of aspects and characteristically respond to the syntactic and semantic categories of the nouns with which they co-occur (Hawkins 1988: 8–9). Nouns, as labels associated with the most concrete and specific of (ontological) referents, generally involve the most consistently direct, one-to-one mappings possible in a language; however, they are dependent (positionally, functionally, and distributionally) upon the head of VP and are inert with respect to the syntactic makeup of the clause. This general pattern of syntactic and semantic dependency is portrayed in (7), below (in increasing levels of semantic dependency):

(7) V (head of VP) > N (head of NP, argument of clause) > Adj (constituent of NP)

This suggests, regarding the learnability and borrowability of content items, that (primary and secondary) verbs require the most extensive knowledge of a particular language because the interpretation of every other element is directly or indirectly dependent on them (for example, recognizing the word class noun can often be accomplished only with respect to its position relative to the main verb). One would expect that nouns and adjectives would be learned or borrowed in roughly the same proportions. However, that conclusion must be tempered by the fact that the number of form–meaning sets of particular semantic sub-types assigned by an individual language to the word class Adjective may be from zero (in languages like Cree) or very few (e.g., in Igbo or the Bantu languages) to many (e.g., Dyirbal and the European languages) (Dixon 1991; cf. Waxman 1994: 249–250). In addition, adjectives are almost always subsidiary in meaning and generally less transparent than the nouns they modify. These basic semantic and syntactic contrasts are essential to the identification of content items. The numerous factors discussed above paint a picture of a dynamic process affecting learnability and/or borrowability that can only be applied to one language (or, perhaps, pair of languages) at a time.

4.4 Summary and general predictions

It is now possible to assemble the various aspects of a semantically based model of borrowing and state the predictions that naturally follow. It is apparent that languages borrow forms and form–meaning sets for a variety of reasons. Despite the inherent uniqueness of every human language relative to its particular genealogical (genetic) history and typological position on indices of synthesis and fusion, it has been suggested that all forms are borrowable, in principle, even though not every form is borrowed in practice (cf. Hudson 1980:60; Bynon 1977:255; Haugen 1950:224).[27] Nevertheless, there is a consensus in studies of bilingual/language contact phenomena that certain forms are borrowed more often and in greater numbers than others; for instance, classes of nouns are always borrowed more easily and more frequently than classes of verbs or adjectives (see, for example van Hout and Muysken 1994). Therefore, the following Hierarchy of Borrowability was developed (see Subsection 2.2.3) as a generalization of the patterns represented in the various individual borrowing hierarchies (rankings) found in the literature to date (repeated in (8), below):

(8) content item > function word > agglutinating affix > fusional affix

Considering the systematic variability of linguistic forms and the inevitable possibility of cross-linguistic mismatches, the present work has come to the conclusion that the morphological structuring of each language in a specific contact situation is a significant factor in the ultimate determination of borrowability. Moreover, the recipient system, which acts as a morphosyntactic matrix into which borrowed items are placed, plays the determining role in the assignment of donor form–meaning sets to appropriate form types and, subsequently, the distribution of such form types as content items into appropriate syntactic word classes based on semantic type or subtype. Consequently, two principles have been proposed to represent systematic limitations on borrowing inherently imposed by the matrix: (a) the Principle of System Compatibility (PSC), which defines the morphological compatibility of donor forms with a recipient system, and its correlate, (b) the Principle of System Incompatibility (PSI), which identifies a cutoff point along a scale of morpheme types beyond which forms cannot be borrowed (Section 2.3). In essence, the PSI states that no form or form–meaning set is borrowable that does not conform to the morphological possibilities of the recipient system with respect to form (i.e., morpheme) type. This is based in part on the assumption that a recipient language will always act to preserve its own morphological integrity (for the sake of continuity and intelligibility within the community of its speakers). Table 4.5 presents a synthesis of the PSC and PSI.

---

27. This is based on two assumptions. First, individual bilinguals may achieve high levels of proficiency in both (or all) languages in contact to the extent that they will have access to any form in either language. Second, form–meaning sets representative of every type portrayed in the Scale (or continuum) of Morpheme Types have, at one time or another, been borrowed by one of the world's languages.

Table 4.5. Compatibility versus incompatibility

If X is	Compatible Y-forms	Incompatible Y-forms
Isolating-analytical	words/roots (analyzed as independent words)	affixes of any kind
Agglutinating	independent words/roots + agglutinating-type affixes	only fusional-type affixes
Fusional	any Y-form borrowable, i.e., word/roots and affixes of any type	

The first general set of predictions, therefore, pertains to types of form–meaning sets. First, incompatible forms cannot and, therefore, will not be borrowed. Second, all others (i.e., compatible form–meaning sets) will be borrowed according to the rankings indicated in the Hierarchy of Borrowability. Consequently, analytical-isolating languages will not borrow affixes of any kind from any type of donor though they can freely borrow content items and function words (in each case, bound words or roots analyzed as independent words). In addition, agglutinating languages will not borrow fusional affixes, all other form types being borrowable. Fusional-type languages have the broadest range of borrowing possibilities: they can borrow any type of form–meaning set from any type of language, in principle.[28]

Even though the PSI limits the bare possibilities by identifying specific form types that must be ruled out, it does not account for the fact that, among those that are system-compatible, some are borrowed more frequently than others, and some types of morphemes are rarely, if ever, borrowed. By concluding that borrowable items are actually form–meaning sets that become words or morphemes in the recipient, the focus shifts to individual characteristics of types of form and those of types of meaning. In addition, acquisition of form–meaning sets in bilingual contexts clearly involves processes linked to simultaneous and/or sequential bilingual acquisition. Thus, it is assumed that form–meaning sets are learned in much the same way irrespective of language of origin; some sets are more difficult and take longer to learn than others because

---

28. This, however, needs to be modified to more accurately reflect actual borrowing scenarios; in all likelihood, numerous restrictions apply to form and meaning types that would restrict borrowing to areal neighbors that are genetically related as well as typologically similar (for discussion, see Section 6.1, below).

they require greater knowledge of the source language grammar. The task is, therefore, to isolate the properties that may cluster in various combinations and degrees to make form–meaning sets gradiently identifiable and learnable, and, consequently, borrowable, and that can account for hierarchies (scales or continua) of borrowability. Following the scenario that learners/acquirers assume initially that utterances within the linguistic environment are meaningful, and that their primary task is to isolate individual forms (and structures) out of the speech stream and map them onto appropriate meanings (cf. Slobin 1985), sets of interpretation characteristics (oppositions linked to degrees of identifiability) based on form have been proposed (Subsection 4.1) and, subsequently, on meaning (4.2). Form–meaning interpretation characteristics (FMICs) identified and discussed in this work are presented in Table 4.6, with those pertaining to form listed first.

Table 4.6. FMICs: Form–meaning sets

	Transparency	Opacity
SHAPE:	unique (detailed, segmentable)	minimal, no (or zero) form
MAPPING:	1-to-1 link to meaning and back to a single form	1-to-many simultaneous links to multiple meanings; return linkage of each separate meaning to many forms
SELECTION:	optionally selected on the sole basis of particular, individual meaning	obligatory; occurs in response to the requirements of language-specific grammar; gives syntactic form
CONCRETENESS:	reference to distinct entities or concepts that exist	abstract; apart from concrete or physical existence
SPECIFICITY:	explicit; distinguishes among members of a species or type; typically occurs in a limited number of contexts	general; applies to many (all members of a group); consequently may occur in a larger number of contexts
GRAMMATICALIZATION:	belongs to a broad lexical subsystem semantic type or sub-type)	belongs to a language-specific (i.e., grammatical (i.e., inflectional) category

A second set of general predictions begins with the most obvious cases. First, form–meaning sets possessing all of the characteristics in the left-hand column, typically content items, will be the most highly preferred in any borrowing situations. According to the PSC, any such donor form, irrespective of the morphological possibilities of the donor language, is borrowable into any recipient, irrespective of its morphological character, as well. In principle, content items are borrowable from any language into any (in fact, every) language. Second, form–meaning sets exhibiting all of the characteristics in the right-hand column, typically inflectional affixes of the fusional type, will be the least preferred. More specifically, the fusional affixes of one language can only be borrowed by other fusional languages — probably only by those that also have close social, genetic, and areal relationships. Implicit in the PSI is that the borrowability of any grammatical form will correspond to its relative position along the scale of morpheme types. A third general prediction follows concerning form–meaning sets with properties clustering at midpoints between the extremes (certain subclasses of function words): they will be intermediate with respect to identifiability, degrees of grammaticalization and, therefore, borrowability. More specific predictions concerning individual oppositions of form–meaning interpretation characteristics that have been proposed thus far are summarized in Table 4.7.

Table 4.7. Summary of predictions regarding FMICs

FORM:	
shape	sufficiently detailed, segmentable shape > minimal or no shape
mapping	1-to-1 form–meaning > 1-to-many simultaneous form-to-meaning; 1-to-1 form–meaning > 1-to-many simultaneous meaning-to-form
selection	selection optional > application/selection obligatory
MEANING:	
concreteness	concrete > abstract
specificity	specific > general
grammaticalization	semantic (sub)type > inflectional category

Regarding individual subclasses of content item (independent word, root), particular syntactic and semantic factors may also be powerful predictors. For example, regarding the borrowability of nouns, verbs, and adjectives, the relative semantic and syntactic complexity of verbs compared to nouns offers a tentative explanation for ratios of borrowing frequency that are reflected in various borrowing hierarchies. If these properties are combined with form–meaning characteristics and applied in individual cases, much more specific measures are obtained by which precise predictions of borrowability can be made, even within particular semantic subtypes. Regarding the relative borrowability of types of inflectional affixes, morphological criteria are available (according to the PSI), in addition to form–meaning interpretation characteristics.

Chapter 5

Borrowing patterns in modern Mexicano

Mexicano (Náhuatl) may be the most studied of the languages indigenous to the Americas. Before the advent of Spanish, it was the dominant language of Mesoamerica, the language of the ancient Toltecs, spoken also by the Aztecs, Tlaxcalans, and other peoples of Mexico and Central America. Numerous works concerning its grammatical structure (morphology, phonology, and so on) and the nature of its various dialects have been published since the latter parts of the 16th century. In addition, many teaching grammars have appeared in more recent times in such languages as Spanish, English, French, German, and so on.[1] This extensive documentation provides a rather unique backdrop against which the specific claims presented here can be examined, especially concerning the long-term effects of borrowing and certain other temporal aspects (e.g., nouns are likely to be borrowed *before* inflectional affixes).

Largely as a result of the clear, uninterrupted historical links with the so-called classical language (i.e., the language prior to the conquest and subsequent colonization of its speakers by the Spaniards) to its modern-day descendants, there has been little controversy regarding its genetic affiliation. It is traditionally classified as a member of the Uto-Aztecan family of languages, even in the face of its greatly evolved character — the rather obvious product of its intense and prolonged contact with Spanish. The tendency to stick religiously to a genealogical perspective has been referred to by some as the Adamic Model (Aarsleff 1982), and it seems to be fairly typical of linguists whose work tends toward the establishment of proto-languages, perhaps in attempts to discover evidence of an original human language (Hill and Hill 1986: 55–56). Thomason and Kaufman (1988: 1–12) devote much space to a discussion of the predispositions of mainstream historical linguists to ignore all sorts of language mixing (and their cumulative effects) which can result in the emergence of varieties not easily classed according to family lineage, that is, whose origins are not traceable to a single progenitor (evidently including pidgin and creole varieties).

---

1. See León-Portilla (1972) for an extensive bibliography of Náhuatl studies.

Maintenance of the traditional classification scheme, therefore, implies that the development of *all* modern-day varieties of Mexicano has proceeded according to the usual processes of change, which obviously puts the emphasis on language-internal processes. Surely, this betrays the biases of individual researchers more than anything else, particularly in view of the fact that modern versions of the language have changed so drastically as a result of contact with Spanish that they are no longer even the same morphological type. That is, on the basis of morphological typology, varieties of Modern Mexicano have drifted substantially away from its original polysynthetic and incorporating character towards analysis to its present point along the index of synthesis (Hill and Hill 1986:249ff.). According to grammaticalization scenarios — seen as one of a number of normal processes leading to internally motivated change — the expected direction of change is away from analysis towards synthesis, essentially the opposite of what might be expected. Regardless, borrowing is also a normal process and an obvious factor in change that is externally motivated. It is not merely some kind of linguistic oddity. The effects that it produces demonstrate its ability to interact with and, perhaps, significantly alter other normal processes of change in dynamic ways.

Judging from the results in Malinche Mexicano (the object of this study), it seems rather clear that the transmission of Classical Mexicano has been something other than according to a normal, genetic model, in which the language is passed from generation to generation fundamentally intact. As a consequence of the considerable external influence of Spanish and different kinds of borrowing, it is no longer possible to attribute all of its lexicon *and* structure to one and only one source. This includes (among other things) massive incursions of Spanish lexical items (content items and function words), the proliferation of Spanish-like prepositional phrases, and co-occurrence patterns within the noun phrase (see Subsection 5.3.2, below). According to the present gradient definition (which leans more towards qualitative rather than quantitative criteria), it can quite easily be called a contact language (see Section 1.2), leaving aside for the time being the somewhat difficult-to-define issues of genetic classification.[2] Moreover, the principle, and perhaps clearest, mechanism for the emergence of a mixed language/bilingual mixture is borrowing (Thomason 2001:158).

---

2. See Thomason 2001:158 for her definition of contact language.

Regarding the bilingual nature of such mixtures, Thomason (1997a) states that "...linguistic material from each source language is adopted wholesale, without the kind of distortion that would occur in the absence of bilingualism" (6). This is evident in Malinche Mexicano, as well, where there is very little phonological reanalysis of borrowed Spanish elements according to native (original) Mexicano phonological patterns.[3] Spanish-origin loans tend to be pronounced as they are in regional varieties of Spanish (Hill and Hill 1986:198), which is a marked change from the extensive sorts of phonological reanalysis that took place in the earliest years of contact (see Karttunen and Lockhart: 1976). In fact, older loans have become relatively infrequent in the modern, spoken language, often being replaced by newer, nonnativized forms.[4] Native Mexicano elements are pronounced as they were in its so-called classical progenitor, with phonemic contrasts among long and short vowels (e.g., ō versus o in *tōca* "to bury" and *toca* "to follow, pursue") (Hill and Hill 1986:62). Consequently, the phonemic inventory of the modern language has expanded to include a number of Spanish consonants (which appear only in Spanish borrowings) — reminiscent of the phonological characterizations of Michif (see Bakker 1997:80ff).

Mixed languages (bilingual mixtures) such as Michif, Media Lengua, Ma'a (Inner Mbugu), Pecu' (Petjo or Petjoek), Mednyj Aleut, and so on exhibit many of the same *kinds* of structural effects of contact as Mexicano, but they have not been treated in the same conservative manner regarding genetic classification. The special treatment afforded them may be due more to the circumstances surrounding their investigation (the when and where of the research) than the linguistic product might indicate. Many of these mixtures (but not all) are said to have developed within a relatively brief span of time; and, inasmuch as the emergence of many of them has been somewhat recent, each has a relatively short history. In addition, the effects of what appears to be rapid change have been systematic and extensive. As a consequence, attention has been paid in a much more contemporary context (as opposed to, say, more traditional, historical approaches) to such linguistic and social issues as the roles of primary and secondary language acquisition (e.g., native versus non-native acquisition) and code-switching in processes of change.

---

3. See Chapter 1 for discussion of the phonological adaptation of loanwords. Apparently, the kind of phonological reanalysis that occurs in Media Lengua (discussed in Muysken 1981, 1988, 1994, and 1997) is not an absolute criterion for relexification and/or language mixing.

4. At times, such nativized forms as *compālehtzīn* "co-father" and *comālehtzīn* "co-mother" (ritual kinship terms) occur alongside nonnativized forms *compadrito* and *comadrita*.

Irrespective of the special status mixed languages such as Michif and Media Lengua receive in current work in bilingualism/language contact phenomena, it seems reasonable to say that the linguistic consequences of powerful, dynamic social processes can certainly be cumulative as well as acute, accelerating perhaps at various points in the history of a particular variety. For instance, according to Thomason (1997a and 1997b), Ma'a (Inner Mbugu) arose as a result of "long-term linguistic persistence in the face of intense cultural pressure from Bantu..." (1997a: 6). The development of Malinche Mexicano appears to be similar to that of Ma'a — gradual and cumulative in a sense, but changing quite rapidly and profoundly during particular periods of time.[5] The presence of a literature tracing the historical development of an individual language certainly should not prohibit the unbiased (synchronic) assessment of its character at particular points in time. Neither should the amount of time it has taken to develop (the diachronic), for instance, whether it has emerged rather suddenly or over longer periods of time as a consequence of the social, economic, and consequent linguistic subjugation that typically accompanies colonization. Nevertheless, the knowledge garnered from studies of language mixing of various kinds, sudden or gradual, presents a challenge of some import to many traditional approaches. It offers an alternative perspective with respect to the many linguistic phenomena frequently occurring in our increasingly multilingual world (cf. Milroy and Muysken 1995:1). Such information has the potential to shed significant light on language change in general and, viewed retrospectively, on the origins of many known languages.

5.0.1 Bilingual phenomena

A number of seemingly contradictory observations have been made about the nature of Mexicano-Spanish bilingualism. On the one hand, nearly all Mexicano speakers of the Malinche region are fluent in Spanish, although the reverse is not necessarily true. In most areas where the use of Mexicano still flourishes, there remains considerable diglossia despite the massive borrowings that would indicate advancing shift towards Spanish. This suggests a fundamental asymmetry in the relationships between the two languages. On the other hand, the intense and relatively stable bilingualism characteristic of the region has led to

---

5. See 5.3.1, below, regarding a chronology of Malinche Mexicano, and 6.1.4 for discussion of Ma'a.

the description of modern forms of Mexicano, particularly that of the Malinche region, as "syncretic" by such researchers as Hill and Hill (1986:55–58). This suggests that both Spanish and Malinche Mexicano are somehow operating at the same time within the community in some kind of opposition, but that opposition is suppressed or eliminated by their simultaneous usage side by side. Inter- and intra-sentential code-switching are also normal, everyday occurrences, which is very consistent with this particular view. This indicates that both autonomous language systems are integral and active linguistic components in the construction of the social identities of individuals, and, indeed, of the community in general.

The fact that Malinche Mexicano still occupies its own social domains underscores its function as an ethnic language and marker of social identity, though this may be gradually changing as shift progresses. The purist attitudes of some older speakers place a positive value on the knowledge of *legítimo mexicano* (i.e., legitimate or "real" Mexicano) and hold perceived Mexicano forms in high esteem. Such behaviors as borrowing and types of code-switching are often considered (i.e., by purists) to be corruptions of the ancestral language (Hill and Hill 1986:99ff). Nevertheless, it may very well be that the opposing forces of shift and maintenance work against each other to establish a kind of equilibrium that actually enhances Mexicano's ultimate potential for survival (cf. Woolard 1989:355–363). It is also important to note that change may not be as easily recognized and militated against as the purists might wish. The ability to distinguish true ancestral forms from borrowed ones can be obfuscated by a number of factors, not the least of which is the basic adaptability of the language and its speakers (i.e., the ability to draw effectively from the other language as a familiar source for linguistic support). In the case of the Malinche and other regions where Mexicano is still spoken, code-mixing (borrowing) and code-switching have been part of the social fabric for nearly five centuries (Hill and Hill 1986:2).

Speakers of Mexicano appear able to borrow words and structures quite freely from Spanish. Therefore, the identification of Spanish form–meaning sets (and distinguishing Spanish forms from those of Mexicano) is a necessary part of the proficient bilingual's linguistic knowledge. It can also be assumed that highly grammaticalized elements (e.g., fusional affixes) are recognizable and interpretable by proficient bilinguals — which may not depend on any conscious ability or knowledge. However, the linguistic capabilities of proficient bilinguals (e.g., in simultaneous translation tasks) cannot be equated with the compatibility of competing languages regarding their respective morphosyntactic matrices. Even if one assumes that extensive knowledge of Spanish is characteristic of the bilingual Mexicano-Spanish speaker/hearer (who uses either language separately and independently or during various kinds of code-switching and borrowing behaviors), it is not accurate to state simply that all form–meaning sets are borrowable from Spanish into Mexicano because, in fact, morphological typology is a factor.

5.0.2 The corpus

The data base of this chapter consists of a 23,272-word portion of the oral interviews contained in the corpus (of approximately 80,000 words) gathered by Kenneth and Jane Hill of the University of Arizona. The data were collected over a ten-year period beginning in December of 1974 in the ethnographically distinct highland Malintzin (Malinche) region of central Mexico, which includes communities on the western and southwestern slopes of the Malinche Volcano in the adjacent Mexican states of Tlaxcala and Puebla.[6] At the time, the population estimates of the towns and villages in which the interviews were conducted ranged from 500 (Santiago Ayometitla) to 20,000 (San Pablo del Monte). Hill and Hill describe the region as a "particularly indigenous cultural island within the Spanish-speaking communities of Tlaxcala and Puebla" (1986:7), basing their description on such cultural factors as ritual kinship relationships and other patterns of social organization. They paint an intimate portrait of a community in the midst of enormous socio-economic pressures, whose members are being drawn by irresistible forces of modernization. The Spanish language, in opposition to the indigenous Mexicano, is the medium through which much social change finds linguistic expression. Its use has come to symbolize technological progress and economic advancement in many socially relevant areas.

Overall, sociolinguistic surveys (which included interview materials) were given to ninety-six subjects in the Tlaxcalan towns of San Pablo del Monte, San Antonio Acuamanala, Santiago Ayometitla, Santa María Acxotla del Monte, San Luis Teolocholco, San Rafael Tepatlaxco, San Felipe Cuauhtenco, and Santa Ana Chiautempan and in the Pueblan towns of San Miguel Canoa, La Resurreccion, and San Lorenzo Almecatla.[7] Each was administered by a native

---

6. The text of this survey can be found in Hill and Hill 1986, Appendix A.

7. The portion of the Hill and Hill corpus used here is from the towns of San Antonio

Mexicano speaker (a native of San Miguel Canoa)-partly to keep the conversation from drifting into Spanish, the language preferred in speaking with outsiders. Because of the interviewer's relatively young age (16 at the beginning of their research), the Hills felt that they were allowed to minimize the feeling of formality that usually accompanies such interviews. The survey itself was composed of five sections: Part A – Base Data on Speaker, in which background information of the respondent was gathered; Part B – General Conversation, containing prompts designed to elicit reports of important events, near-death experiences, and local legends; Part C – Morphology, which involved the translation of words, phrases and short sentences from Spanish to Mexicano; Part D – Language Attitudes and Self-Reports of Usage, which drew out the circumstances under which Mexicano is used by the speaker and so on; and Part E – One-Hundred Word Lexicostatistic List, used to measure knowledge of "pure" Mexicano forms. One of the purposes of the survey was to create a large enough sample to investigate correlations among attrition, the accompanying loss of functions that typically result, and the expected narrowing range of structural possibilities.

One of the many things Hill and Hill encountered was a continuum of usage which served to demonstrate a speaker's pragmatic competence and which could be linked to varying numbers of Spanish or Mexicano forms (71). In this respect, Hill and Hill disclose that the nature of the interviews appeared to bring out a relatively formal posture by the participants despite the fact that they took place in the form of visits or *visitas* (74).[8] As a result, many of the samples that they obtained (in what the participants may have perceived as somewhat official settings) may have been skewed more toward Spanish-the so-called power code-than might be expected under more normal circumstances. In more domestic settings, an increase in Mexicano forms (the purist code) was a sign of speech among intimates. The registers evident in the interviews,

---

Acuamanala (population 3,185), Santiago Ayometitla (500), and Santa María Acxotla del Monte (800), all located on or near the western slope of the volcano.

8. These visits were of four types. A casual home visit involved a chat in a kitchen area where women were generally quite comfortable. A second, more formal kind of home visit entailed sitting in the main room of the house (near a family altar), where the visitors were served food and drink by women scurrying back and forth from the kitchen. Two other contexts included informal gatherings of men (drinking the traditional pulque) on their days off or in the evenings, and during work groups-while people are mending farm equipment, shelling corn, and so on.

however, did not contain the amount of Spanish material as those typically used when the topic drifted towards politics, for example. In other words, topic and register clearly affected the ratio of Spanish or Mexicano lexical items that would occur in a particular speech event. In discourse settings at large, there was also the rather frequent occurrence of code-switching of various kinds (and, presumably, nonce borrowings). In spite of these and other potential drawbacks, the corpus contains many linguistically revealing encounters.[9] It remains true, nonetheless, that the accumulated effects of contact and the considerable skill with which these speakers manipulate their linguistic systems are remarkable.

5.0.3 Organization of this chapter

The remaining portions of this chapter deal with actual borrowing patterns found in the data. Section 5.1 begins with a brief overview of the two participant morphosyntactic systems (the donor, Spanish, and the matrix language, Mexicano) and describes the various kinds of Spanish form–meaning sets that have been borrowed into Modern Mexicano. Subsection 5.1.1 goes into some detail in describing the morphological structuring of each language. In 5.1.2., borrowing patterns are compared to various hierarchies discussed in Chapter 2, and a specific hierarchy is constructed for Mexicano. It is shown that Mexicano has, indeed, borrowed form–meaning sets from every compatible type, from content items to agglutinating-type affixes. This subsection concludes with a brief discussion of the Principle of System Compatibility (PSC) and its corollary, the Principle of System Incompatibility (PSI) and the ways the two principles delimit borrowable and unborrowable form–meaning types in this particular contact situation. The patterns found validate both: only compatible forms are borrowed, and preferences clearly follow from those depicted in the Hierarchy of Borrowability (see Subsection 2.2.3).

Section 5.2 breaks down borrowing patterns according to form–meaning interpretation characteristics (FMICs). Subsection 5.2.1 deals with the three

---

9. Hill and Hill devote considerable space to the explanation of their interview techniques and the content of the survey (67–89). Those who may be critical of any and all such techniques may benefit from reading the pages referred to. The many examples offered by the authors clearly leave one with the impression that much good and valid is obtained despite the inherent problems, especially in light of the fact that respondents often reacted to the prompts in very creative and unpredictable ways.

characteristics pertaining to form and each prediction that has been made with respect to borrowing preferences (see Subsection 4.1.3). Each prediction is upheld across the board, which is reflected quite clearly in the data. Recall that the PSI rules out any occurrence of Spanish fusional-type inflectional morphology. Form–meaning interpretation characteristics merely predict that certain types of form–meaning sets will be more or less favored in borrowing situations. 5.2.2 takes up issues of meaning and focuses on subclasses of Noun in making comparisons between concrete and abstract nouns; it then treats oppositions based on specific versus general (i.e., hyperonyms contrasted with hyponyms). Abstractness links to the lateral (horizontal) organization of the lexicon in terms of semantic types and subtypes, while specificity correlates with the hierarchical (vertical) relationships of items within those types. Borrowing patterns clearly reflect these characteristics in systematic fashion. The final prediction of this particular subsection, that form–meaning sets linked to semantic (sub)types will be preferred over those linked to inflectional meanings, is fulfilled, as well. There is a strong (though not exhaustive) correlation with characteristics of form (e.g., whether or not selection is optional or obligatory). Once again, similarities to synchronic grammaticalization clines is brought to the fore.

5.3 discusses the long-term effects of borrowing on the Mexicano matrix and, in 5.3.1, some of what can be gleaned from past studies concerning the temporal aspects of the predictions. As indicated in the work of Lockhart and Karttunen (1976), borrowing patterns have also substantially followed the predictions implied in the Hierarchy of Borrowability with respect to the order in which elements have been borrowed. In addition, there are important indications that, for nearly 300 years, Mexicano resisted structural borrowings to a great extent. Only towards the very end of the 18th and beginning parts of the 19th centuries did large numbers of borrowed function items begin to occur, at the very time a new national identity was emerging (that was not strictly associated with allegiance to the Mexicano language) and Mexico began to pull away from the colonial yoke of Spain (Wright 1992). This may be especially significant when one considers the relatively remote status of the Malinche region. Subsection 5.3.2 focuses on some of the effects various borrowings have had on Mexicano syntax, that is, on phrasal and clausal organization.

The discussion in 5.4 turns on the centrality of meaning to borrowing. Apparently, borrowing hierarchies to date have focused on form, while semantic characteristics have largely been ignored (with the possible exception of formal links to inflectional categories). Subsection 5.4.1 covers the role of form in the determination of borrowable form–meaning sets and links between borrowing hierarchies and clines of grammaticalization; it reaffirms intuitions that the more structural or grammatical an item is, the more difficult (i.e., the more time) it takes to learn/acquire and the less likely it is to be borrowed. In addition, rankings among classes of N, V, and Adj coincide with (a) predictions based on semantic and syntactic complexity and (b) the distribution of form–meaning types in Mexicano. 5.4.2 suggests that borrowing patterns reflect different kinds of meaning, and that meaning may be more significant than characteristics of form in accounting for the distribution of borrowed forms into the recipient lexicon.

5.1 Overview of the participants: Mexicano and Spanish

In general, the morphosyntactic matrix of Modern (Malinche) Mexicano retains much of the agglutinating nature of its progenitor.[10] Consequently, it is positioned higher on the index of synthesis than Spanish. It is still considered to be polysynthetic and incorporating despite losing much of the incorporating character of its classical ancestor as a result of contact (Hill and Hill 1986: 249–266). An extensive repertoire of compounds (including those incorporated into verbs) has diminished considerably as a result of the tendency to borrow Spanish forms to label new concepts (lexical strategies having replaced morphological ones). This extends to the reduction of other sorts of "adverbial" material previously incorporated into the verb, as well. As a consequence, its morphosyntactic matrix has drifted away from synthesis towards analysis. Typical of the agglutinating nature of the Uto-Aztecan family of languages, Mexicano verbal affixes generally express one, and only one individual inflectional or derivational concept.[11] In contrast, Spanish is positioned much higher on the index of fusion. Typical of the Romance languages, its verbal morphology is strictly fusional. Multiple inflectional concepts are semantically and phonologically fused together onto single, unsegmentable

---

10. For more comprehensive studies see Andrews (1975) regarding Classical Náhuatl, Karttunen and Lockhart (1976) concerning Náhuatl during the colonial period, and Hill and Hill (1986) for the particular variety spoken in the Malinche region.

11. See example (14) and its accompanying explanatory note (fn. 6), below.

forms, which results in the formation of verb paradigms (in three conjugation classes). Nevertheless, Spanish is much more analytical than Mexicano-as a general rule, it does not tend to construct extremely long, multimorphemic words typical of polysynthetic languages.

While a comprehensive treatment of Mexicano grammar goes well beyond the scope of this work, the following passage illustrates some of the characteristics of Mexicano relevant to this study. For the sake of consistency, the analysis is based on that of Hill and Hill (1986), including terminology and spelling conventions, which, in turn, is drawn to a large extent from the terminology of Andrews (1975).[12] (P signifies the interviewer, and R indicates the respondent. The top line is Mexicano; the second consists of English glosses, which is then followed by Spanish and English translations, in that order.)

P. ...ītech nīn puebloh āquin ocachi cualli yēc-laht-oa de mexicanoh.
 in this town who else well WELL-speak-TRNS of Mexicano
¿En este pueblo, quién más habla bien de mexicano?
"Who else speaks well of Mexicano in this town?"

R. poz nīn puebloh de mexicanoh poz pocos, aun miec genteh
well this town of Mexicano well some even many people
Pues, en este pueblo de mexicano, pues, poca, aun mucha gente
"Well, in this Mexicano town, well, a few, even many

tlaht-oa-h mexicanoh huān miec genteh tlaht-oa-h en castellanoh...
speak-TRNS-PL Mexicano and many people speak-TRNS-PL in castellano
habla mexicano y mucha gente habla en castellano...
speak Mexicano and many people speak in Spanish..."

huān nīn puebloh porque cada puebloh mo-patla-tīh nīn
and this town because every town REFL-change-T este
y este pueblo porque cada pueblo está cambiando este
"...and this town, because every town is changing this

para saludar para platicas...
in.order.to greet for conversations
para saludar, para platicar...
to greet (each other), to talk (have conversations)..." (S51)

---

12. Abbreviations used for the Mexicano data are essentially those of Hill and Hill 1986: ANT — anterior; IMP — imperative; APPL — applicative; T — outbound purposive; REFL — reflexive; TRNS — transitive; INTRN — intransitive; F — future; PL — plural; HON — honorific; 3P — third person; and DEF — definite.

5.1.1 Morphological structuring: The words of each language

In Spanish, nouns are inflected for gender (masculine or feminine) and number (the marked form being plural). There is also gender and number concord which spreads to other members of the individual NP. The Spanish plural marker -s is an agglutinating-type affix; when present on classes of Noun, it indicates only one concept, plural (more than one). For instance, in such form–meaning sets as *los niños* "the boys" (from *el niño* "the boy") and *las niñas* "the girls" (*la niña* "the girl"), the plural marker is added to the stem in each case. This marker (and some characteristics of Spanish number) has been borrowed into Mexicano. With respect to gender marking, both masculine and feminine are marked, usually by the suffixes -o and -a, respectively.[13] Words not overtly marked must, nonetheless, be assigned lexically to one gender or the other (e.g. *la luz* "light" is feminine, and *el pastel* "pastry" is masculine). An occasional neutral form occurs (e.g., *lo curioso* "the curious thing"), a probable remnant from Latin neuter (Corbett 1991:215). Hill and Hill (1986:266) note that Spanish gender concord, while it operates in regional forms of Spanish, does not systematically occur in Mexicano borrowings — Mexicano has no grammatical category of gender. Adjectives generally retain a masculine form, which is apparently a result of the relative frequency of such forms.

In clear contrast, nouns in Mexicano receive numerous inflectional and derivational suffixes, for instance, absolutive (i.e., non-possessed state) -*tl(i)*, plural number -*meh* or its variant -*tin*, possession (i.e., object possessed), reverential (whose forms also function as honorifics and diminutives), and pejorative.[14] For example,

(1) conē-tl   "child"
    child-ABS

(2) no-conē-h   "my child"
    my-child-POSS

---

13. See Aronoff 1994:67–74 for a revealing account of the complexities of grammatical gender in Spanish. One point that is made there concerns the inconsistency of different markers; e.g., -*o* typically marks the masculine and -*a* the feminine, but this is not always the case. Gender, then, must often be determined by looking at other members of the NP, i.e., forms of determiner and adjective.

14. The classical language (Náhuatl) marked plural only on animate nouns; as a result of contact with Spanish, plurality has spread to include classes of inanimate nouns (Karttunen and Lockhart 1976:24).

(3) justicia-tzīn   "justice"
    justice-HON

(4) ranchoh-zol   "old run-down ranch"
    ranch-PEJ

Some non-possessed nouns may be pluralized by reduplication of the initial syllable or by the suffixation of -*h*, -*meh* or -*tin*, or by the Spanish plural -*s*, as in the following examples:

(5) tlāca-tl   "man"
    man-ABS

(6) tlāca-h   "men"
    man-PL

(7) tlātlācah   "men"
    man-PL

(8) tlātlāca-meh   "men"
    men-PL

(9) yōlcā-meh   "animals"
    animal-PL

(10) múlah-tin   "mules"
     mule-PL

(11) chiquihuite-s   "baskets"
     basket-PL

Mexicano nouns also receive affixed pronominal elements (bound pronouns) to indicate possessor. When nouns are preceded by adjectives, these elements are prefixed instead to the adjective, for example

(12) no-ahuelitah   "my grandmother"
     my-grandmother

(13) to-mero mexican   "our real Mexicano"
     our-real mexicano

These bound pronominal elements may co-occur with either Mexicano or Spanish plural forms suffixed to the nominal root:

(14) no-famílíah-huān[15]
my-family-PS PL
or "my spouse and children"
no-família-s
my-family-PL

One final item which was affixed to the noun stem or root in the classical language and is increasingly rare in Malinche Mexicano usage (Hill and Hill 1986:247) was a spatial or temporal locative suffix, for instance:

(15) lunes-tica "on Monday"
Monday-LOC

In the works of Karttunen and Lockhart (1976), Hill and Hill (1986), and various other authors, these locative forms are often referred to as postpositions, irrespective of their status as bound or free morphemes.[16] For example, Sullivan (1988) writes: "The Nahuatl postposition is equivalent to the English preposition, with the difference that the postposition is a *suffix* [emphasis mine] placed after the noun or pronoun instead of before it" (107). However, Andrews (1975), in direct contradiction, states that"...relational suffixes have often been called *postpositions* [emphasis his], a name that suggests that they are prepositionlike elements that merely occur after a substantive instead of before it... The name is incorrect" (304). From the perspective taken here, they are assuredly not function words in the generally accepted sense and are rightly considered suffixes. They do not occur as free-standing elements; when they do occur, they are always affixed to a nominal stem.[17] Semantically, they indicate such relational concepts as location, direction, and instrument (cf. Sullivan, 1988:107–137). Indeed, they appear to be quite similar to form–meaning sets that are considered case markers in other Amerindian languages such as Quechua (cf. Lastra 1968:29).

---

15. This particular form may show a degree of phonological and semantic fusion, that is, of -*h* (PS) and -(*i*)*n* (PL) and of possessed-state and plural, depending on one's analysis. Both Hill and Hill (1986) and Karttunen and Lockhart (1976) merely indicate that it is "possessed form plural" (Karttunen and Lockhart 1976:20).

16. See Crystal 1991:269 for a definition of the term postposition which includes word status.

17. For some corroboration of this point, see, also Andrews (1975), which states, "...relational suffixes have often been called postpositions [emphasis his], a name that suggests that they are prepositionlike elements that merely occur after a substantive instead of before it.... The name is incorrect" (304).

The possible occurrence and ordering of morphemes relative to the noun (root) in Mexicano can, therefore, be represented as (16), below:

(16) possessor – nominal root – absolutive/object possessed, singular or plural – (or) honorific (reverentials or diminutives), pejorative – locative, etc. (case)

Spanish verbs receive individual markers (morphemes) that contain a fusion of specific category values of tense–aspect, person, and number that obligatorily agree with the grammatical subject. Hence, every tensed verb in Spanish receives a fusional-type morpheme that simultaneously encodes individual category values of (at least) three inflectional categories: tense (or aspect), person, and number (see Subsection 4.1.2, above). Mood or modality distinctions can be expressed through morphological means (i.e., subjunctive, imperative, and indicative), which involve separate paradigms which also indicate person-number values (and tense, in subjunctive), and/or through a relatively small number of modal auxiliary verbs (i.e., compared to relatively long list of modals in Germanic languages such as German, Dutch, or English). Neither Spanish verbal categories nor their individual values are borrowed into Mexicano, with two apparent exceptions: (a) a few frozen forms such as *es que* "it is that..." and (b) a small number of verbs that are treated as Mexicano modals (e.g., *debe* "must, ought to", *depende* "it depends", and *conforme* "it conforms" in the sense of "accordingly").[18]

Morphology relating to the Mexicano verb is considerably less straightforward than noun morphology (see, for example, Karttunen and Lockhart 1976:29). Here, the focus is merely on the ordering and kinds of elements that are part of the verb complex. For instance, (according to Hill and Hill 1986) Mexicano verbs receive agglutinating-type suffixes for future tense (*-z*) but are prefixed for anterior aspect (*ō-*). Individual verbal suffixes may include the following: so-called applicative objects (*-lia*) — "an object in whose favor (or against which) the action is performed" (Hill and Hill 1986:159), outbound (*-tih*) or inbound purposive, and transitive (*-oa*) or intransitive (*-(i)hui*).

---

18. Hill and Hill (1986:160) state that these forms occur with third-person, singular present tense inflection; however, in the present analysis, it appears that these are better viewed as individual form–meaning sets that cannot actually express those categories. In addition, the morphological connection between *es* and *ser* is one of drastic allomorphy (see Section 1.1, above). And, despite their relative frequency, modals seldom occur in the infinitive forms. (In Spanish, all verbs receive an infinitive marker (*-ar*, *-er*, or *-ir*) depending on conjugation class; their are no so-called base forms as in English, *to read*.)

Prefixes include imperative mood (*xi-*) and reflexive (pronominal elements such as *mo-* "you/yourself"), honorifics (*on-*, literally "away"), along with a number of derivational prefixes (such as morphemes *yēc* and *nēn* meaning "well, completely" and "badly, unfortunately", respectively). The following are but a few examples from the corpus:[19]

(17) quin-costar-oa   trabajo
 them-cost-TRNS work
 "It costs them work."

(18) costar-ihui in   nēca trabajo
 cost-INTRNS DEF that work
 "That work is costly."

(19) ti-nēch-prepar-huilī-z   cē pantzīn
 you-me-prepare-APPL-FUT one bread
 "You will fix me a piece of bread."

(20) xi-c-om-preparar-ō   in   centavos
 IMP-it-on-PREPARE-TRNS DEF money
 "Get the money ready."

(21) ō-t-c-arreglar-oh-queh   in asunto
 ANT-we-it-arrange-TRANS-PLUR the business
 "We have already arranged the business."

(22) nēn-cuatrear-oa-h
 badly-make.mistakes-TRNS-PLURAL
 "They make terrible mistakes."

(23) t-qui-mo-on-yēc-tender-hu-ilia
 you-it-REFL-on-well-understand-TRNS-APPL
 "Do you understand it well?"

(24) ye ni-c-tehtender-oh-tīh
 now I-it-understand-TRNS-T
 "Now I go along regularly understanding it."

The ordering of affixal material (morphemes) relative to the verbal root is, therefore, portrayed in (25), below.

---

19. Each of these can also be found in Hill and Hill 1986: 158–159.

(25) anterior aspect/imperative – subject marker – object marker – honorific (on-) – reflexive – derivations (e.g., "well", "badly") – verbal root – thematizing suffixes (transitive, intransitive) – applicative (/plural) – outbound/inbound purposive – future tense

The distribution of classes of Adjective in each language undoubtedly plays a role in borrowing patterns (i.e., with respect to their frequency relative to that of, say, verbs). On the one hand, Spanish has large numbers of adjectives (attributive and predicative) typical of the Romance languages. On the other, Mexicano has relatively few, as do other members of the Uto-Aztecan language family. In the classical language, modifiers were not typically free-standing. Adjectival elements were incorporated into nominal compounds, and adverbs were incorporated with verbs. Even today, Mexicano speakers use adjectives sparingly, but do, nevertheless use Spanish borrowings such as *bueno* "good", *malo* "bad", *chico* "small", and *grande* "big". There is a certain ambiguity concerning Spanish adjectives from a Mexicano perspective in that they can appear alone (e.g., as predicate nominatives) in such constructions as *es viejo* "he is old" and in nominal form as in *el viejo* ("the old one/man"). Nevertheless, independent Mexicano adjective forms may be derived by application of the suffix *-tic*; for instance, *mulatic* is glossed as "stupid" and taken from Spanish *mula* "mule". There are numerous other Spanish loans in particular subclasses of Adjective, for instance, many that can also function pronominally and/or as determiners: *algo* "some, a little", *alguno* "some", and so on.

A number of Spanish adverbs (e.g., *exacto, pronto*, etc.) have been borrowed that are used with relative frequency. However, in many traditional Náhuatl studies, a separate class of adverbs is generally not acknowledged as such, at least not in the sense that Spanish and other Indo-European languages appear to have a separate word class Adverb (cf. Andrews 1975:27–34). In general, adverbials and various other free-standing forms are referred to in the literature as particles (e.g., connectives of various sorts, exclamations, and hesitation forms). Mexicano also possesses other sorts of function words, for instance, independent determiners, pronouns, and a small number of uninflected modal verbs. In contrast, Spanish has a full complement of Indo-European sorts of independent function words/roots (pronouns, determiners, auxiliary verbs, prepositions, and conjunctions). In spite of these apparent differences, numerous Spanish loans that have fallen into the generic class of particles can be divided into either (sub)classes of content items (adverbials) or independent function words/roots based on their semantic and syntactic characteristics.

In the following tables, adverbials include those form–meaning sets which are borrowed from Spanish that function precisely as they do in their source language and that maintain the same range of conceptual meanings as their glosses and/or translations. The same criteria will apply to kinds of function words/roots. Form–meaning sets that are clearly members of more than one class (e.g., *antes* "before") are treated separately according to their functions and/or positions within phrases or clauses.[20] The number of borrowed Spanish function words is quite striking (see Table 5.2). For instance, there are numerous borrowed prepositions (e.g., *de* "of", *para* "for, in order to", *sin* "without", etc.), coordinating conjunctions (e.g., *o* "or", *pero* "but"), and subordinating conjunctions (e.g., *mas* in the sense of "even though", *hasta* "until", *porque* "because", *como* "as, since, like, how", etc.), including the complementizer *que* "that".

The examples in (26)–(30), below, illustrate the role of Spanish function words in the construction of Mexicano phrasal and clausal frames.

(26) tlacpac hasta tlatzīntlan
    above towards below
    "...(from) high to low"

(27) de huēi puebloh
    from big town
    "from the big town"

(28) pero yenon ocachi hueli in mōlli
    but that (is) more well DEF mole (kind of sauce or gravy)
    "...but it is even more delicious (or tasty) in mole"

(29) porque in tehhuān nicān to-tlahtōl   cah correcto
    because DEF we   here   our-language is correct
    "because around here, our language is correct..."

---

20. See Section 3.2, above, especially Subsections 3.2.3–3.2.5, for discussion of the formal and semantic characteristics of function words forming the basis for the distinctions made here. In addition, very frequent conversational particles such as *pues/poz* "well, then" are classified here as function words (see Hill and Hill 1986:190–194), which differs from the classification scheme of Myers-Scotton (1998 and elsewhere). This inclusion is based on the following: conversational particles (a) are semantically empty at the level of the individual form–meaning set or morpheme (i.e., their discourse-level meanings are much more abstract and general than a literal interpretation of the word, itself), (b) are members of a very small closed class, (c) and neither assign nor receive grammatical or semantic role. Consequently, they are less controversially classed as function words — not full content items (cf. Lyons 1995:65–71).

(30) poz   nēci   que   acmo   nēch-pāctiā
well (it) seems that not.yet me-pleases
"Well, it seems that I don't like it yet"

5.1.2 The borrowing hierarchy of Mexicano

To establish a borrowing hierarchy for this particular bilingual/contact situation, Spanish borrowings in the portion of the corpus treated here were analyzed according to *types* (actual borrowed form–meaning sets) and *tokens* (the number of times these individual items occurred in the text).[21] In Table 5.1, below, borrowed Spanish content items (words/roots) are displayed (with the number of tokens in parenthesis). Similarly, Table 5.2 portrays types and tokens of independent function words (or roots) and different sorts of inflectional affixes.

Table 5.1. The occurrence of Spanish content items

Nouns	570 (2,420)
Verbs	81 (268)
Adjectives	74 (332)
Adverbials	44 (411)

Table 5.2. The occurrence of Spanish function items

Function words	46 (3,221)
Agglutinating affixes	1 (164)
Fusional affixes	0 (0)

A synthesis of the two is presented in slightly different terms in Table 5.3, below. In view of the fact that function items as a whole (a) are members of closed classes (i.e., in the donor, and presumably in the recipient, as well), (b)

---

21. The ambiguity resulting from the two separate usages of the term type is, unfortunately, somewhat unavoidable. In an attempt to minimize the terminological confusion, semantic types (i.e., the classification of words according to kinds of meanings) will be referred to as semantic (sub)types. Regarding the following tables, numbers in parenthesis represent tokens to coincide with types in the more numerical sense. See Appendix II for a complete listing of borrowed form–meaning sets.

consist of various heterogeneous subclasses from independent pronoun to fusional-type affix (see, for example, Subsection 3.2.3), and (c) generally occur in discourse more frequently than individual content items, the hierarchy reflects borrowing preferences according to the number of form–meaning sets that are actually borrowed, that is, types (again, with tokens in parenthesis).

Table 5.3. The occurrence of Spanish form–meaning sets in Mexicano

Content items (N, V, Adj, Adv)	767 (3,431)
Function words (particles)	46 (3,221)
Agglutinating-type inflectional affixes	1 (164)
Fusional-type inflectional affixes	0 (0)

Clearly, borrowing patterns (in terms of types) accord with the Hierarchy of Borrowability (see Subsection 2.2.3, above), which, in turn, corresponds to the Hierarchy of Morpheme Types (2.1.3, above). The information presented in Tables 5.1–5.3 gives substance to observations such as those suggesting that the more structural (or grammaticalized) an element is, the less likely it is to be borrowed (i.e., independent of its relative frequency in either language). The striking parallels with grammaticalization clines suggest that characteristics shared by content items (whatever they might be) allow them to be borrowed quite easily, with variability among major classes of content items in all likelihood a reflection of the (a) language-particular distribution of class members in regard to form and (b) relative syntactic and semantic complexity of members of individual major classes (see Section 4.3). All things being equal (and apparently they are not), one would expect types and tokens of each individual form class to pattern out in similar (if not identical) ways-which has not been the case in any contact situation. The preferences also suggest that those characteristics which tie function items to language-specific matrices (i.e., grammatical infrastructures) make them less than ideal candidates for borrowing.

The number of *tokens* with respect to function words, however, is a sure indication that Mexicano borrowing patterns are not "normal" in a quantitative sense. Out of 23,272 words in the text, 3,221 are Spanish function words-for instance, prepositions, conjunctions of some kind, and so on. This means that 1 out of about 7.2 words (or 13.82% of the total) is an independent Spanish function word.[22] This extraordinarily high rate of occurrence undoubtedly

---

22. All percentages are rounded off to hundredths.

reflects their complete adoption into the Mexicano matrix and, consequently, their roles as integral parts of the language proper. One must, nonetheless, bear in mind that the list of potential content items is open-ended and can be expected to grow. Additional loans (types) can be expected to occur depending on such factors as topic (e.g., when the discussion shifts to politics or occupational concerns). Irrespective of these particular functional characteristics (and relative frequency), a general hierarchy representing borrowing preferences in Modern Mexicano can, nevertheless, be portrayed according to the following:

(31) content item (independent word, root) > function item (independent word, root) > inflectional affix (agglutinating-type only)

The information presented in each of the tables, above, also indicates that the morphological structuring of each participant language is certainly relevant. Mexicano has borrowed form–meaning sets from all compatible types according to the PSC. The converse is true, as well: it has not borrowed an incompatible form–meaning set. This cannot be accounted for by (a) frequency (fusional-type affixes occur on each and every tensed verb in Spanish), (b) the linguistic abilities of individual bilingual speakers (at least a subset of bilinguals will be proficient in Spanish as a result of native/first language acquisition), or (c) lack of inherent borrowability (i.e., fusional affixes have been borrowed from one fusional language to another, though this is admittedly rare). In fact, most form–meaning sets of Spanish are compatible with the morphosyntactic system of Mexicano. According to the PSI, the fusional affixes of Spanish are the only form–meaning sets that are incompatible, and, therefore, not borrowable.

Reminiscent of the situation in Media Lengua (Field 1997b; Muysken 1997), Modern Mexicano has borrowed from Spanish an inflectional affix, the plural -s, and a small number of derivational affixes-all of the agglutinating type: the diminutive -ito/ita (which function in both Mexicano and Malinche Spanish as reverentials as well as diminutives), and the agentive suffix -tero/ero.[23] A few others such as -mente, which is used in the derivation of adverbs

---

23. Malinche Spanish diminutives appear to be analyzed along the lines of native Mexicano forms. According to Myers-Scotton's distinctions between content and system morphemes (e.g., 1993:99ff; 1995:238ff), reverentials are considered system morphemes — in present terms, highly grammaticalized, while diminutives are very often considered to be derivational. Gray areas between derivational and inflectional categories are problematic for many analyses of morpheme types, and this is no exception (cf. Bybee 1985:12; Croft 1991:190f). In the present work, the diminutive *ito/ita* will be considered derivational, more as a precaution than anything else, and excluded from the tabulations of borrowed inflectional

from adjectives in Spanish, *-ado*, which creates the past participle which, in turn, can be used adjectivally, and so on, appear in the corpus on a small number of words that are probably borrowed whole, as single, unanalyzed units. This is also consistent with the occurrence of borrowed derivational affixes in Media Lengua and/or Quechua (Muysken 1997). In addition, it is possible to create double plurals and double diminutives by using both the Spanish and Mexicano forms (Hill and Hill 1986: 165 and 196).

It needs to be emphasized, however, that Spanish, in fact, possesses only a very small number of agglutinating-type affixes — most pertaining to classes of Noun and other constituents of the NP. Almost every category and category value expressible in classes of Verb are expressed via fusional-type affixes, with the only exceptions being the participial forms representing specific values of Aspect (which combine in constructions with auxiliary verbs that are marked with fusional-type affixes of tense, person, and number).[24] Therefore, Mexicano has, indeed, borrowed a significant number of compatible affixes relative to the available pool. In keeping with the PSC, one can anticipate the possible occurrence of Spanish derivational affixes, though the number of loans will most likely be relatively small compared with the number of possibilities. In spite of the depth of borrowing (the length and intensity of contact), there are no occurrences of Spanish fusional affixes, except in frozen expressions (e.g., *creo que* "I believe that") and code-switches from Spanish. They are systematically barred from inclusion and incorporation into the Mexicano morphosyntactic matrix.

5.2 The role of form–meaning interpretation characteristics (FMICs)

In Sections 4.1 and 4.2, above, characteristics associated with the ease of interpretation of various form–meaning sets were discussed in relation to their likely effects on borrowing. Within particular language contact situations involving degrees of bilingual proficiency, it is assumed that those form–meaning sets that are the most easily recognized within the speech stream will be preferred in borrowing processes over those that are the least easily recognized. This is in part due to the fact that individual members of a bilingual

---

affixes (types and tokens).

24. These individual Spanish verbal suffixes are borrowed into Media Lengua, which has, in essence, the morphosyntactic matrix of Quechua (see, for example, Muysken 1997: 385–386).

community will exhibit different degrees of fluency in each of their languages — forms that are more easily identified in the speech stream will be easier to borrow. That is, bilinguals of varying proficiency will be more familiar with those forms. For this reason, predictions pertaining to characteristics of form are argued to fall into three general areas. First, form–meaning sets that possess optimal amounts of phonetic information will be preferred over those with minimal (or zero) phonetic shape. In order to account for the rapid on-line identification that is necessary for individual words and morphemes (as form types), correlations have been made between the amount of phonetic information necessary and the number of possible associations (concepts) that must be made; motivating factors cited include the economy and efficiency of the retrieval process. Second, uniqueness of form must correspond with uniqueness of meaning; the point being that a unique phonological address must locate an equally unique concept (the inhabitant of the address). Third, because form–meaning sets are customarily classified according to their selectional possibilities, form–meaning sets that are selected optionally will be preferred in borrowing situations over those that are required by language-particular syntactic requirements of the donor variety.

It is also argued that characteristics of individual form–meaning sets can be contrasted on the basis of meaning-the other component of the form–meaning set. These characteristics also fall into three areas. Two of these, concreteness and specificity, are often mentioned in descriptions of the evolution of kinds of meaning in processes of both grammaticalization and derivation. The first, concreteness, involves the opposition of concrete versus abstract concepts and figures prominently in studies concerning the organization of the lexicon (monolingual or bilingual) and the accessibility of individual concepts. As a result of their demonstrated link to ease of access (and speed in translation), it is predicted that those meaning types that can be classed as concrete will be preferred over those considered abstract. The second, specificity is often mentioned in opposition to generality. It was initially predicted that the more semantic information associated with a particular concept (the more specific the term), the easier it would be to distinguish it from other concepts.[25]

---

25. That is, the number of perceptual features (specific physical characteristics) required to define a specific term is greater than that required for a general term. For instance, the difference between *chihuahua* and *dog*: the definition of the word *chihuahua* includes all general characteristics associated with the class of mammals known as *dog*, plus additional physical characteristics qua semantic specifications that would distinguish it from other kinds of dogs.

However, in ways analogous to amounts of phonological information required for individual form recognition, this prediction has been amended somewhat to suggest that optimal amounts of semantic information will be preferred over minimal amounts. Based on the hierarchical relationships that exist within families of terms (semantic types and subtypes), the modified prediction states that entry-level hyponyms (more specific terms), as individual members of families of terms, will be preferred over hyperonyms (general family names containing fewer semantic specifications).

The third characteristic pertaining to meaning involves associations of particular meanings with concept types, for instance, those that are linked to semantic types and subtypes (see Section 3.3) versus those associated with inflectional categories and their respective category values. Consequently, it is predicted that the kinds of meaning associated with individual semantic (sub)types which require little or no language-specific grammatical knowledge will be preferred in borrowing over those that require a much greater degree of language-particular knowledge.

5.2.1 FMICs pertaining to form

Predictions with respect to borrowing preferences according to form hold across the board, as demonstrated in the hierarchy constructed in 5.1.2 above. The comprehensive correlations that exist between the borrowing hierarchy and predictions based on FMICs pertaining to form occur irrespective of individual form-class (e.g., whether borrowed form–meaning sets are assigned to classes of Noun versus classes of Verb) or specific semantic (sub)type. This is especially significant in view of the fact that nouns, verbs, and adjectives should be borrowed in equal numbers if phonetic form were the only consideration. All classes of content items exhibit (a) sufficiently detailed shape, (b) 1-to-1 associations of form and meaning, and (c) optional selection possibilities. The tallies used to establish the hierarchy also reveal that the form–meaning sets of Spanish that typically lack these characteristics are clearly preferred *less* in borrowing processes. Of the many items available for borrowing, those that possess (a) minimal or no phonetic form (e.g., inflectional affixes in general) and (b) 1-to-many simultaneous mappings of both form to meaning and meaning to form (i.e., fusional-type affixes) are obviously not preferred.

In regard to selectional possibilities, the Spanish preposition *de* occurs numerous times in its locative function meaning "from". This is the meaning cited when the form first appeared in 1738 (Karttunen and Lockhart 1976:79).

However, *de*, which does not occur with a meaning other than locative until 1795 (i.e., *de* "of"), does appear, though very infrequently, as an obligatorily selected item in such constructions as *antes de* "before" and *después de* "after", although such an occurrence was not attested at all during the period covered by the Karttunen and Lockhart work (see Subsection 5.3.1, below). In each of these so-called complex prepositions, *de* is required; it has no independent meaning. Table 5.4, below, shows a further breakdown of borrowed form–meaning sets to include such occurrences.

Table 5.4. The occurrence of Spanish form types based on selection

Optional (N, V, Adj, etc.)	815 (6,644)
Obligatory prepositions	1 (8)
Agglutinating affixes	1 (164)

Simple tallies that merely record the occurrences of particular form types cannot make this important distinction. On the one hand, content items (i.e., open classes of N, V, Adj) are never selected on the basis of language-particular grammatical rule; they are selected for the meanings they represent. Their syntactic class may be a direct reflection of semantic characteristics (Dixon 1991) (see, also Subsection 3.3 above), but selection of individual forms is optional. Morphological marking (application of affixes appropriate to word class) and slots in which they may appear (their distribution) are, nonetheless, matters of a language-specific grammatical nature. On the other hand, inflectional affixes are, by definition, obligatorily selected on the basis of language-specific grammatical requirements. That is, while the selection of a specific form (which represents a specific category value) may be a consequence of the meaning it expresses, the expression of the general inflectional category is required. In contrast to both content items and inflectional affixes, selection of particular function items (word, roots) may be either optional (in the case of locatives, for example) or obligatory because they are subcategorized for by specific content items (in the case of so-called grammatical prepositions). For instance, the forms that obligatorily accompany *de* are clearly adverbial in nature, expressing imageable temporal and/or locative relational concepts while *de* has no independent meaning at all.

The relatively small number of obligatory function words (prepositions) and inflectional affixes that occur do illustrate two matters of importance: they are borrowable (because they are borrowed), and they are numerically far from preferred in terms of types (as opposed to tokens). Recall that fusional affixes are the only form–meaning sets that are categorically ruled out as a result of morphological incompatibility.

5.2.2   FMICs pertaining to meaning

A number of interesting issues emerge as the analysis of borrowing preferences turns to semantic characteristics. For the sake of continuity, discussion begins here with the third FMIC pertaining to meaning, that individual meanings can be associated with a range of concept types that range from those associated with semantic types and subtypes to those associated with inflectional categories. The prediction that follows from this opposition of meaning types states that meanings which belong to semantic (sub)types will be preferred in borrowing situations over those that are linked to inflectional categories. In this respect, the preceding discussion serves to make an important distinction: selectional requirements are formal requirements, and do not necessarily form comprehensive correlations with either semantic (sub)types or inflectional categories. This becomes even more obvious when investigation extends to individual languages that are isolating-analytical, that possess no obligatorily expressed inflectional categories (and, obviously, no individual category values). Functional elements (such as the noun classifiers of Vietnamese) can certainly be obligatory and not inflectional.

The semantic (sub)types discussed in Section 3.3 are direct expressions of ontological categories and represent the kinds of meanings that every language and every speaker needs to express. They identify (make reference to) topics of conversation, activities and states in which persons and objects participate, attributes (e.g., qualities and quantities) of the people and things in the environment, locations in space and time, and so on. These concept types are not dependent on any language-particular grammar, although their formal representation may vary to an extent. The kinds of independent meanings expressed by optionally selected function words are traditionally placed somewhere between extremes, according to a Sapirian perspective. Here, they are listed as RELATIONAL types of meaning according to Clark 1993 (and can, as a consequence, be properly included under the heading of semantic type or subtype).[26] In clear

---

26. See Clark (1993: 47) for her listing of ontological categories. She states the following: "Children must also make use of their ontological categories when they create meanings for adjectives that pick out properties like shape, size, or color (e.g., *round, small, red*) and for

contrast with semantic (sub)types, inflectional concepts involve abstract conceptualizations that have become obligatorily expressed in a particular language. As noted previously (see Section 4.2), the presence of general inflectional categories and the particular values they express are language-specific and, as a consequence, highly idiosyncratic (Bybee 1985).

While the data displayed in Table 5.4 (above) reflects borrowing preferences based on form, the following, Table 5.5, illustrates types of meaning:

Table 5.5. The occurrence of Spanish concept types

Semantic types	769 (3,431)
Relational meanings	46 (3,213)
No independent meanings	1 (8)
Inflectional concepts	1 (164)

FMICs regarding concreteness and specificity produce a variety of patterns within particular noun subclasses. For instance, degrees of concreteness are instrinsically associated with particular semantic types and subtypes (see Section 3.3 for discussion of groupings based on semantic characteristics). It is likely that borrowing patterns also have much to do with the identification of concepts newly introduced by Spanish speakers into the cultural and linguistic environment and that were either laterally assigned to already existing semantic subtypes or placed into newly created semantic subclasses.

For the purpose of the present study, borrowed nouns are divided into a number of different classes and subclasses of CONCRETE or ABSTRACT which represent a synthesis of the kinds of meanings developed in Dixon (1991) (discussed in Subsection 3.3.1 and listed in Appendix II) and those used by

prepositions that mark relations in space or time (e.g., *in*, *on*, *near*, or *above*). In Classical Mexicano, locative functions were expressed only via suffixation. Hence, it may be that some inflectional affixes may be viewed as possessing independent meanings associated with semantic types so characterized. However, due to the fact that such affixes also express additional, maximally grammaticalized meanings via their maximally grammaticalized forms, exact correspondences vis-à-vis individual adpositions are rare, if they occur at all. Here, one is dealing with obviously blurred and possibly shifting boundaries.

Karttunen and Lockhart (1976).[27] They include (a) CONCRETE ANIMATE (e.g., human and animal),[28] CONCRETE INANIMATE (including artifacts, materials, etc.), QUASI-CONCRETE (e.g., names of organizations, jurisdictions, etc.).[29] ABSTRACT terms consist of those types of nouns traditionally considered abstract (e.g., ideas, actions, and procedures, measurement terms, and so forth) and include ACTIVITIES (e.g., results of particular physical acts), SPEECH ACTS (e.g., question, promise, and so on), and STATES (and PROPERTIES) (e.g., embarrassment, hope, etc.). Borrowed Spanish nouns are displayed below (in Table 5.6) accordingly.

The counts in the first column represent Spanish form–meaning sets found in the portion of the Hill and Hill corpus treated here and, therefore, borrowings found in Modern Mexicano. The second and third columns are presented here for the purpose of comparison. They contain lists of borrowed items that can be presumed to be available to Malinche speakers in addition to those recorded in the spoken language of the Hill and Hill study. The counts in these columns come from two sources. The one on the far right comes from the word lists of Fray Alonso de Molina in an early Spanish-language grammar of Mexicano and an accompanying vocabulary (*Arte de la lengua mexicana y castellana* and *Vocabulario en lengua castellana y mexicana*), both published initially in 1571. These works contain the first wave of Spanish borrowings into the classical language immediately following the conquest. The middle column, designated Karttunen and Lockhart, includes word lists these authors developed from a number of texts dating as early as 1540 and continuing up to the end of the colonial period, i.e., through the end of the 18th century (Karttunen and Lockhart 1976: 52–84) (see, also Subsection 5.3.1, below).

---

27. Their terminology (traditional for Náhuatl studies) is somewhat more limited in that the kinds of nouns that needed classification appeared to refer primarily to concepts imported to Mexicano culture (cf. Karttunen and Lockhart 1976: 16ff). The more specific terms of Dixon (1991) are necessary to encompass the expanded numbers of borrowed noun types evidenced in the Modern Mexicano text. However, preserving the spirit of the earlier terminology makes these preliminary comparisons possible.

28. According to Dixon (1991), HUMAN includes subclasses of kinship terms, rank, social group, and so on. Hence, in the subclassed designated individual under QUASI-CONCRETE, characteristics pertain to such things as trades and governmental or religious function.

29. The term QUASI-CONCRETE is taken from Karttunen and Lockhart (1976) to refer to concrete referents that are distinguished by an abstract quality, for instance names for and titles of religious and governmental officials, professions, trades, and so on (e.g., terms regarding marital status). These are also considered concrete by Dixon (1991: 76).

Table 5.6. Borrowed Spanish nouns

		Hill and Hill	Karttunen and Lockhart	Molina (1571)
CONCRETE	Animate	126	54	62
	Inanimate	78	245	60
	Quasi-concrete	85	228	34
	Other	129		
	Total Concrete	418	527	156
ABSTRACT	General	77	193	45
	States (and properties)	15		
	Activities	30		
	Speech acts	30		
	Total Abstract	152	193	45

Table 5.6 shows that concreteness is, indeed, a likely factor. In the portion of the corpus analyzed here, 73.33% of borrowed nouns refer to concrete concepts of one sort or another; put differently, the ratio of concrete to abstract nouns is 2.75 to one. With the caveat that the tallies indicated in the other two columns and the ratios that can be inferred are drawn from very different sources, their similarities are, nevertheless noteworthy. The middle column shows that 73.19% of borrowed nouns occurring in the middle period also had concrete referents, as did 77.61% of the loans appearing in the Molina text. These percentages appear to have remained fairly constant.

Table 5.7, below, displays borrowed Spanish noun types according to the semantic domains in which they occur. Table 5.8 shows preferences based on specificity (entry-level hyponyms versus hyperonyms) within particular word families.[30]

The FMIC of specificity appears to be quite relevant, as well, manifesting itself in the hierarchical relationships among loans within particular word families (semantic subtypes). Of the 570 borrowed noun types occurring in the text, only 18 could be construed as possible hyperonyms (names for families of terms). That is, 96.84% of the total number of noun types were hyponyms (nearly 32 hyponyms to one hyperonym). Clearly, the patterns indicate that specificity is

---

30. Tables 5.7–5.9, below, display only counts according to types and not tokens; zeros may indicate either that specific information was unavailable or that there were zero instances. With respect to the Karttunen and Lockhart text, information concerning tokens was simply not available. At any length, relative frequency of individual nouns is not at issue here.

Table 5.7. Borrowed nouns: Semantic types

	Hill and Hill	Karttunen and Lockhart	Molina (1571)
CONCRETE ANIMATE			
human	30	–	–
rank	14	–	–
kinship terms	33	–	–
body parts	1	–	–
plants and fruits	11	17	47
animals	16	17	8
derived products	15	17	7
diseases	5	3	–
other	1	–	–
	126	54	62
CONCRETE INANIMATE			
materials (cloth, dyes, etc.)	5	25	3
artifacts (novel types)	47	162	55
physical complexes/buildings	25	58	2
other	1	–	–
	78	245	60
QUASI-CONCRETE			
individuals	67	165	24
organizations/institutions	8	31	2
places	10	8	2
other	129	24	6
	215	228	34
ABSTRACT			
general	13	–	–
religious	9	44	18
legal	7	55	–
other cultural	1	38	1
measurements	47	56	24
states (and properties)	15	–	–
activities	30	–	–
speech acts	30	–	–
	152	193	45

a factor. It may very well be that names for basic concepts (i.e., members of word families) are necessary in daily conversation for accuracy and clarity and are, therefore, apprehended and learned more frequently then general terms

Table 5.8. Borrowed nouns according to specificity: Ratios of hyponyms to hyperonyms

	hyperonym	hyponyms
CONCRETE ANIMATE		
human	gente(h) "people"	28
	persona "person"	
rank		14
kinship terms	familia(h) "family"	31
	pariente "relative"	
body parts		1
plants and fruits	frutah "fruit"	10
animals		16
derived products		15
diseases		5
other		1
	5	121
CONCRETE INANIMATE		
materials (cloth, dyes, etc.)		5
artifacts (novel types)	clothing "ropa"	45
	instrumento "instrument"	
physical complexes/buildings		25
other	cosa(h) "thing"	0
	3	75
QUASI-CONCRETE		
individuals		67
organizations/institutions/trades	trabajo "work"	6
	escuela "school"	
places		10
other		129
	2	221
ABSTRACT		
general	idea "idea"	12
religious	regelion [sic] "religion"	8
legal		7
other cultural	costumbre "custom"	0
measurements	lugar "place"	44
	tiempo(h) "time"	
	dinero "money"	
states (and properties)		15
activities		30
speech acts	idioma "language"	28
	palabra "word"	
	8	142
Totals	hyperonyms	hyponyms
	18	552

(family names). In this respect, it is also very likely that concreteness and specificity (as properties that may cluster) can and do work in concert to greatly facilitate and/or motivate borrowing.

5.3 The effects of borrowing

The extensive borrowing illustrated above has had significant effects on the nature of the Mexicano matrix system (see Subsection 6.2.4, below). First, the numbers of Spanish content items that are potentially available to bilingual Mexicano-Spanish speakers offer significant competition for the compounding and incorporating word formation processes of the classical language (see, for example, Hill and Hill 1986:249–266). As a probable result of the relatively isolating-analytical character of Spanish and its form–meaning sets, Mexicano speaker/hearers (as members of a bilingual community) may select from an almost inexhaustible store of semantically transparent content items. Second, the numerous borrowed function words create additional lexical alternatives to other, previously exclusive morphological strategies. Such a drift away from (poly)synthesis towards analysis is certainly not uncommon, especially in situations of shift and subsequent attrition (see, e.g., Mithun 1984, 1989; Romaine 1989:376).

5.3.1 A chronology of borrowing

It is generally accepted that the structural changes resulting from such borrowings accumulate gradually. In this respect, the hierarchy of (31), above, makes both quantitative and temporal claims of an implicational nature. Quantitatively, it has proved to be very revealing concerning the depth of borrowing. The texts used by Karttunen and Lockhart (1976), whose book attempts to bridge the gap between the classical language (Náhuatl) of pre-conquest times and the present (represented by the various published articles and book by such authors as the Hills), provides interesting, though at times admittedly thin, support for temporal aspects of the hierarchy, as well.

These texts came from the national archive (Archivo General de la Nación) and National Museum of Anthropology and include such documents as testaments (wills), land documentation (grants, investigations, etc.), municipal documentation (minutes from various meetings and so on), litigation, petitions, and various kinds of correspondence (including personal letters). As a language sample, the sources obviously differ from the type considered here (i.e., the spoken language of the *visitas*), but the tendencies are well worth noting for a variety of reasons. Karttunen and Lockhart report that nouns were practically the only borrowings during the 16th century and began appearing in various texts between 1540 and 1560. They state, "Since loans in almost every imaginable category put in their appearance by 1550, trends must be expressed as proportions" (16). Generally speaking, larger numbers of Spanish verbs did not begin to occur until the late 17th century, at which time a particular morphological strategy for the integration of Spanish verbs (i.e., infinitive + *oa*) began to appear (29). Borrowed adjectives are relatively sparse throughout the entire colonial period.

Appendix I in the Karttunen and Lockhart text lists all of the borrowed items that were found according to the year of their first occurrence, from the first entry dated c. 1500 to the last in 1795. From the years 1500 to 1550, only nouns were recorded with the exceptions of several titles (e.g., *don*, *doña*), the number fourteen (*catorce*), and the phrase word *etcetera*. In 1550, two words that originated as Spanish adjectives appear (*castaño* "chestnut" and *alazán* "sorrel"), both describing kinds of horses; the word *cristiano* "Christian" does not appear until 1560. One verb (*apelar* "to appeal" — in the Spanish infinitive form) appears in 1553, followed by another (*agostar* "to pasture cattle on stubble in the summer") in 1562. Clusters of verbs do not begin appearing until the beginning of the 18th century (c. 1700), and multiple occurrences of adjectives (more than two) do not occur at all during this span of nearly 300 years. The first so-called particles, the prepositions *de* "from" and *a* "to", occur in 1738-more than two hundred years after the conquest (1519). Note, too, that the only entries recorded in the final year of the sampling were function words (*de* "of", *mientras* "while", and *pero* "but"). (The authors are careful to note that words cited were in all likelihood in use prior to their first occurrences.)

At first glance, nouns are obviously the first and most frequently borrowed. Significant numbers of verbs came much later, with adjectives accumulating gradually over the entire period. While independent function words come relatively late, they apparently come into the language in numbers. Proportions of borrowed items are represented in Table 5.9, below, in terms of the dates of individual works and collections of documents in which they are first recorded, beginning with the work of Molina and followed by that of Pedro de Arenas (*Vocabulario manual de las lenguas castellana y mexicana*), a teaching text designed for Spaniards living in or visiting Mexico who wanted to become acquainted with Náhuatl, dated 1611. (Lists from the Molina volumes and that of Arenas are included in the Karttunen and Lockhart (1976) volume.) The two rows labeled Texts represent the additional collection of documents investigated by Karttunen and Lockhart (1976: 16f) and described above (in the first paragraph of this subsection); Texts (pre-1650) include those documents dated prior to that cutoff, and Texts (post-1650) were those dated 1650 and later:

Table 5.9. Spanish content items according to Karttunen and Lockhart (1976)

	nouns	verbs	adjectives	particles
Molina (1571)	201	1	0	0
Arenas (1611)	57	0	0	0
Texts (pre-1650)	496	9	7	0
Texts (post-1650)	224	24	6	10
Totals	720	33	13	10

As a consequence, the temporal nature of the proposed hierarchy appears to be substantially confirmed, as well-with one noteworthy exception.

The Spanish nominal plural marker -s seems to have been borrowed very early on, appearing in the earliest documents. Until quite recently, it only occurred on Spanish loans. If this were a general tendency (that affixes are borrowed at any time in the process), it would present a fairly serious challenge to the predictions made in the present work. However, recall that the hierarchies merely indicate preferences and not absolute barriers; the PSI has been completely accurate in that regard. It could also be true (yet unattested in texts investigated by Karttunen and Lockhart) that types of content items and function words were either borrowed prior to or *simultaneously with* the borrowed affix, therefore preserving the validity of the temporal claims implicit in the hierarchy (see Subsection 2.3.4 in reference to the timing of borrowed elements). Nevertheless, the occasional exception does require explanation. Moreover, the temptation to resort to glibness or to recklessly respond in ad hoc fashion needs to be avoided.

Consequently, the following is offered as a reasonable supposition (with the obvious caveats). First, the Spanish -s is, after all, a borrowable morpheme type and the numerical predictions hold, nonetheless (though this is less than explanatory). Second, in view of the fact that Mexicano speakers already had distinctions of number, applying the Spanish plural marker to borrowed Spanish nouns merely matches a relatively transparent, agglutinating-type affix (with one-to-one correspondence of meaning and form) of a type already known, which expresses a category value also already known, to a form recognizable as coming from the same, foreign lexical source (Spanish). An example of this very same phenomenon comes from English and illustrates the apparent ease with which a plural marker can be borrowed along with a noun form from a typologically and genetically distinct language: Some speakers of English have borrowed both the Modern Israeli Hebrew word *kibbutz* and its appropriate plural marker, *-im*. Hence, both *kibbutz*, as the singular form, and *kibbutzim* as the proper plural form, are now considered (at least by some) to be English words.[31] English already possesses the inflectional category of number and the particular category value of plural (masculine gender indicated in the particular affixal form is totally irrelevant to the speaker of English). In addition, English does not apply the borrowed affix to words of non-Hebrew origin, which is also true regarding the treatment (i.e., non-application or complete absence) of Spanish *-s* on native Mexicano forms — with extremely rare exceptions. Ultimately, explanation most likely resides in the particular bilingual/language contact situation, itself.

According to the chronology discussed above, the increased number of borrowed function items coincides with (perhaps, narrowly predating) a number of significant social changes. In considerable evidence during the first three centuries of colonization was the obvious social stratification according to ethnic and language status (i.e., European colonists and their descendants, or *criollos*, versus colonized "Indians"). The likely linguistic correlate, that language maintenance was largely responsible for the resistance of Mexicano to much structural borrowing during that time, is indicated by the careful documentation provided by the Karttunen and Lockhart text. However, many authors note such cultural changes as (a) the spread of Spanish throughout Mexico and increased bilingualism during longer periods after the conquest (e.g., Karttunen and Lockhart 1976:50), (b) the rise of a national identity that was not necessarily linked to ethnicity or language during the 19th century (e.g., Wright 1992, Berdan 1982, Vigil 1980), and (c) the rapidly accelerating emergence of a people of mixed race (i.e., mestizos) and the mixing of Spanish and indigenous cultures, also in the 19th century (see, for example, Meyer, Sherman, and Deeds 1999:209, 261, 345–355; Vigil 1980:11).

In addition, Hill and Hill (1986:104ff.) discuss the gradual decline of literate forms (and formal registers) of Mexicano and the encroachment of

---

31. A frequently cited example is *phenomenon/-a* from Greek. For the Modern Israeli Hebrew example, see Webster's New World Dictionary of American English (circa 1978), where it is the only plural listed.

Spanish into an increasing number of social domains beginning in the early parts of the 19th century, as well. They discuss these changes in terms of the social differentiation of "inside" (or in-group) versus "outside" language — terms parallel to Gumperz's (1982) distinctions of "we" and "they" codes — as Spanish was adopted by growing numbers of indigenous, Mexicano-speaking people. As a result, regional forms of Spanish have become increasingly capable of expressing social and/or ethnic status, as well. These types of socio-cultural changes surely suggest that significant language mixing has become increasingly prevalent in more recent times, bringing into question the widespread assumption that the accumulated changes in Modern Mexicano were, in fact, gradual — at least, as gradual as believed. It can be easily inferred that the many changes wrought by various kinds of borrowing have, indeed, accelerated at different times in its history.

5.3.2 Phrasal and clausal organization

The numbers (tokens) and types of borrowed Spanish function words suggest that borrowing has had far-reaching effects and that these effects provide ample evidence of significant structural changes. For example, borrowed prepositions have led to the emergence of adpositional phrases patterned after Spanish constructions that compete with applicative, purposive, and locative markers (morphological strategies). Hill and Hill (1986: 247f) state that Mexicano does have a small set of native particles which functioned like prepositions, but that received possessive prefixes (e.g., *īpan, ītech, ītzīntlan*), as in the following examples in (32):

(32) ī-pan in cama   on the bed
     it-on DEF bed
     ī-tech in no-chān   in my house
     it-in DEF my-house
     ī-tzīntlan in cama   under the bed
     it-under DEF bed

The authors also note: "Hawkins's (1980) proposals for word-order universals specify that a language such as Malinche Mexicano should exhibit prepositions" (147). That is, a language with the co-occurrence patterns of the classical language should actually have prepositions (i.e., according to other word-order characteristics associated with VSO languages) and not postpositions as often suggested in the literature. However, the bound suffixes on nouns that express locative distinctions cannot be called postpositions (see 5.1.1, above). Moreover, the fact that the so-called particles above are prefixed for possession does not necessarily rule out their status as function items (independent word, root). It seems much more reasonable to say that the locative suffixes that are apparently quite rare in the modern language (which were, however, productive in Classical Náhuatl) have essentially been replaced, and that their replacement is consistent with the implicational nature of Hawkins (1980) and his later work (e.g., Hawkins 1983, 1991).[32] In this case, it can be said that Spanish prepositions joined an already existing subclass of function items (with independent, relational meaning) and that their borrowing and subsequent effects may have been facilitated by the existence of these particles.

Additional word order changes are also reported: from Classical Mexicano Adj N to N Adj according to the Spanish co-occurrence patterns and from Gen N to N Gen with the addition of *de* to indicated possessor (Hill and Hill 1986: 237–241). These also accord with Hawkins' predictions. Change, whether gradual or acute, proceeds in an orderly, therefore, predictable fashion.

As noted in Subsection 5.1.1, above, other form–meaning sets that serve to mark phrasal and/or clausal boundaries have been integrated into the Mexicano matrix, for instance, various coordinating conjunctions (e.g., *o* "or" and the very frequent *pero* "but"), subordinating conjunctions (e.g. *como* "how", *cuando* "when", and *porque* "because"), and the complementizer *que* "that". These are further indications that lexical alternatives have replaced strategies that were once strictly morphological prior to the advent of those borrowed free-standing form–meaning sets. Taken along with the massive borrowings of individual form–meaning sets into classes of Noun, Verb, and Adjective, it is certainly not surprising that Mexicano has drifted towards analysis to its present position on the index of synthesis.

5.4 Discussion: The roles of form and meaning in borrowing

The patterns of borrowing that develop within any bilingual/contact situation will reflect the social conditions of the communities in contact and the resultant motivations of bilingual speaker/hearers of varying proficiency levels for linguistic borrowing. On the community level, particular form–meaning sets

---

32. See also Field 1994b for a discussion of implicational universals and the origins of mixed languages.

from a culturally dominant language may be borrowed into a recessive one to expand its referential capacity within specific semantic domains (e.g., those involving entities/concepts newly introduced to the community), to compensate for the loss of native forms in situations of advancing shift (as a result of attrition), and/or for social affect (Grosjean 1982). Individual, form–meaning sets from a culturally, hence, socially, economically, and institutionally dominant language variety are most often borrowed because the kinds of referents or concepts they express are an integral part of the linguistic and social milieu, and knowledge of their associated labels are required for successful reference to be made. It is also true that meanings can be borrowed without donor labels in the case of calques and semantic extensions. Conversely, donor labels (without their associated meanings) may be borrowed as a result of the perceived attractiveness of the forms, for example, for social affect when the prestige associated with the donor variety is relatively high. For example, in processes of relexification, a donor form replaces one from the recipient and presumably acquires the meaning of the corresponding recipient form–meaning set. In that event, form may at times be more important than a particular meaning, though both are intrinsically linked. Nevertheless, the role of meaning in borrowing is essential, particularly in view of the fact that the occurrence of loanwords pattern in such predictable ways.

In the case of Mexicano, initial patterns of borrowing reflected the conquered and colonized status of the community itself. Terms were borrowed en masse to represent concepts that were brought into their world having to do with the imposition of social practices (e.g. governmental, military, social, and legal organization along Spanish/European lines), religious customs (according to the spread of the Roman Catholic form of Christianity), occupational (including such aspects of business as Spanish/European monetary principles, implementation and methods of farming, and so on), and many other cultural accoutrements (e.g., clothing standards in various official and unofficial areas of life). From this perspective, there certainly seems to be some substance to the intuitions and observations of Karttunen and Lockhart (1976), who write: "We believe that there is distinct, significant diachronic and topical patterning in the Nahuatl incorporation of noun loans" (16). Most studies of similar bilingual/contact situations corroborate the premise that meaning is central, that the principal motivating factor for borrowing of such depth is the desire to express linguistically the concepts that are present physically in the social environment. It is also evident that initial limitations of a particularly linguistic nature relate to the matching of form and meaning in the respective participant languages.

5.4.1 Issues of form

The present work has proceeded along two distinct lines: according to form and according to meaning. The influence of form on borrowing in the case of Mexicano has served to illustrate that form restricts what is or is not borrowable in an absolute sense. With respect to form–meaning sets that are not borrowed, form is, perhaps, the only criterion necessary. Fusional-type affixes of Spanish have not been borrowed irrespective of the meanings they might express, as correctly stipulated in the PSI. Issues of form also provide links to formal aspects of grammaticalization clines in support of the long-reported intuitions of scholars that the more "structural" an element is (i.e., grammaticalized on scales of grammaticalization viewed synchronically), (a) the longer it will take to learn, (b) the less likely it is to be borrowed, and (c) the more difficult it will be to find a place in a language that already possesses its own full store of grammaticalized elements. In addition, form apparently interacts with function in significant, patterned ways. Among content items-which are, in principle, compatible with and borrowable by any recipient/matrix system-nouns are favored over all other types. Hence, grammatical aspects regarding the semantic and syntactic complexity of individual semantic classes and subclasses are pertinent. It has been concluded that the particular characteristics associated with classes of nouns and verbs (and adjectives, when applicable) appear to hold across language boundaries, irrespective of morphological type (i.e., with respect to position along indices of synthesis and fusion).

Mexicano has borrowed content items of all types and classes from Spanish despite the fact that inflectional morphology that applies obligatorily to each general class is not borrowed. Numerous independent function words are borrowed, as well, demonstrating that all forms are borrowable that conform to the recipient/matrix system's morphological structure. However, as strongly indicated in Mexicano, the borrowing of structural elements such as adpositions, conjunctions, auxiliary verbs, and so on will have a structural effect. Their adoption, integration, and usage indicate that the organizational patterns of Spanish (which is considerably more analytic-isolating than Mexicano) is being interwoven with those of Mexicano and its predecessor(s), a fact that reveals that the morphosyntactic matrix is undergoing changes far beyond the effects of garden-variety borrowing (e.g., the kind that merely fills lexical gaps). If the transmission of Mexicano had proceeded along normal genetic lines, one would expect that traditional syntactic strategies would suffice, and, therefore, would be maintained. Native syntax is subject to normal processes of gradual language change; the structural changes that are evident as a result of contact with Spanish are obviously distinct. Evidence of a rapidly evolving morphosyntactic matrix system immediately following the colonial period lends significant support to the claim that the resultant linguistic system constitutes a mixed language (i.e., defined on *a priori* grounds), and that grammatical aspects of two languages are being/have been intertwined.

Clusters of properties associated with form identifiability are also evidenced in Mexicano borrowing patterns (i.e., rankings according to borrowing preferences). Those forms that clearly show optimal amounts of phonetic information, one-to-one form–meaning mappings, and optional selection (content words/roots and certain independent function words/roots) are clearly preferred, while those that have minimal to zero form, one-to-many (and many-to-one) mapping possibilities, and obligatory selection requirements (specifically fusional affixes) are not borrowed at all. Various other clustering possibilities conform to the preference predictions, as well. For instance, items that have one-to-one mapping possibilities are borrowed despite the fact that they (a) have minimal phonetic form and (b) are selected obligatorily (e.g., obligatory/grammatical preposition *de* and the agglutinating-type plural noun affix *-s*); however, they are borrowed to a much lesser degree (in terms of types) than those possessing all three characteristics associated with ease of identification (e.g., content items). Typically, minimal-to-zero shape clusters with obligatory selection, and, as a consequence, can be associated with increased grammaticalization. It appears that specific aspects of form play a role with respect to borrowability as well as identifiability; it is likely that these correlations also reflect the general tendency of all languages to display certain form–meaning sets in very predictable fashion, for the same reasons, and with the same results in acquisition (some are easier to learn) and borrowing (some are easier to borrow).

5.4.2 Issues of meaning

While characteristics of form account for many of the borrowing patterns in the Mexicano data, the role that meaning plays fills out the picture in much greater detail and indicates reasons for a marbling effect in the lexicon. Veins of Spanish content items project into specific semantic subclasses representing new concepts. In fact, entire word families composed of borrowed contentive roots form coherent strands that weave their way through the entire Mexicano lexicon. It is very apparent that these form–meaning sets have diffused throughout the entire Mexicano speaking community. Hence, oppositions based on meaning may illustrate even more than general borrowability and/or overall borrowing preferences.

The strong reference for concrete over abstract nouns suggests concrete (visible and imageable) concepts are the most easily borrowed, which is supported by work indicating that they are also the fastest in translation. It can be inferred, therefore, that the semantic transparency associated with such items has its base in physical, perceptual reality. This is especially evident in the earliest borrowings noted by Molina and others, extending into current forms of the language (see Table 5.6, above). It is a very small leap to the simple conclusion that concepts formed on the basis of physical, perceptual attributes are the easiest to identify, and, as a consequence, the easiest to label-in all likelihood, this applies to any type of acquisition. Regarding the borrowability of classes of Noun, it seems that, once a concrete object is labeled, that label can be used by anyone wishing to make reference to that object.[33]

Concepts based on specificity deal with the hierarchical organization of particular semantic classes and subclasses in terms of hyperonyms and hyponyms. While it cannot be stated with absolute certainty that the relatively great amounts of semantic information provided by maximally specific hyponyms make them the most easily identifiable, it remains valid to say that entry-level sorts of terms are among the most useful, probably the most frequently used, and, hence, first learned (e.g., in native or second language acquisition) in any particular semantic domain. In addition, by virtue of their specificity and possible links to concreteness (two properties that typically cluster together), concepts that are both concrete and specific ensure very high degrees of (a) imageability and (b) uniqueness of meaning (a unique conceptual/perceptual address to correspond with a unique phonetic label). The converse, form–meaning sets associated with abstract and general concepts invoke perceptual requirements beyond the visual and tactile. They often require demonstration, explanation, and/or relative amounts of cultural knowledge in translation, which seem somewhat beyond the scope of particular entry-level terms in any language.

In the Mexicano context, abstract and general terms were necessary in dealing with Spanish colonial persons and institutions; nevertheless, they have been borrowed with less frequency because they require more effort on the part of speakers of both donor and recipient. In religious instruction, for example,

---

33. In this regard, it would be interesting to find out how many languages have borrowed the form *pizza* from Italian as a label for that uniquely Italian food.

entirely abstract principles were consciously taught through sermons and catechism books (e.g., concepts of spiritual (religious), cultural, and family organization). Mexicano speakers were taught labels representing varying degrees of importance for governmental (king, viceroy, etc.), religious (pope, cardinal, bishop, priest), and other kinds of social hierarchies (boss/chief and so on). Anecdotally, this is not merely viewing a horse and learning the label *caballo*. It is certainly no wonder, given this type of cultural context, that borrowing patterns are "topical" in the sense suggested by Karttunen and Lockhart.

Preferences for meanings based on semantic types versus those linked to language-particular inflectional categories show the clearest semantic correspondence with scales according to grammaticalization. At first glance, it seems very plausible to say that the more language-specific a concept is, the less likely it is to be borrowed. However, this points, once again, to what appears to be the inescapable conclusion that individual concepts may be language-general — that is, completely free of dependency on specific language requirements, and, therefore, universal in some sense (i.e., as types). For instance, the kinds of meanings associated with content items are (by virtue of form characteristics) borrowable by any other language irrespective of morphological typology. Certain inflectional concepts (and aggregates thereof) may be gradiently borrowable based on similar semantic criteria. In general, form–meaning identification characteristics of meaning may prove to be even more significant than those pertaining to form.

Chapter 6

Discussion

The basic nature of the proposed model is two-fold. First, the claim that anything learnable should be borrowable (i.e., from an individual speaker/hearer's perspective) has provided the appropriate starting point. Intuitively, it seems that if a speaker of X can learn/acquire relatively full proficiency in Y, then he/she should be able to enlist its resources and/or mix those resources with those of X. However, in every bilingual/contact situation studied so far, there are strong borrowing preferences for certain types of form–meaning sets, and these preferences show systematic tendencies. It has become apparent that the similarities found in various borrowing hierarchies and grammaticalization clines (viewed synchronically) are grounded in the ways individual languages construct words and other types of form–meaning sets that are relevant to both processes. Moreover, there appears to be an absolute cutoff point in particular contact situations past which certain specific form–meanings sets cannot be borrowed; that is, there is a basic systematic constraint on potentially borrowable forms based on the morphological structuring of the recipient language relative to that of the donor that goes beyond the preferences depicted in various borrowing hierarchies.

Therefore, the current formulations of the Principle of System Compatibility (PSC) and its corollary, the Principle of System Incompatibility (PSI), capture the basic intuition that restrictions on borrowing are not necessarily linked to the linguistic abilities of individual speakers, but to the inherent characteristics of the linguistic systems themselves, that is between or among specific systems in contact. Certain specifiable form–meaning sets may be blocked from borrowing because they do not conform to the morphological possibilities of the recipient with regard to morpheme types. In the specific case of Mexicano, the PSC predicts that all content items (words, roots), function words, and agglutinating-type affixes can be borrowed. And, many form–meaning sets from each of these classes are, indeed borrowed. The only form–meaning types ruled out by the PSI are fusional-type affixes; this prediction is satisfied, as well.

Second, beyond the cutoff point identified by the PSI, formal characteristics apparently cease to be relevant in an absolute sense, in that many borrowable forms are not borrowed, and those that are borrowed pattern in ways not necessarily predicted by form alone. For instance, thousands of perfectly acceptable (i.e., system compatible) Spanish nouns are not borrowed into Mexicano. At first glance, one might hazard to guess that this is for reasons that are primarily social, and this turns out to be quite feasible. Sets of social circumstances will lead to the exposure of an individual speaker/hearer to certain registers of speech, occupational nomenclatures, and so on. Those involved in maritime industries will be exposed to nautical terms, and those involved in agriculture will learn terms associated with farming implements, cultivation methods, business practices, names for agricultural products, and so forth. Thus, as a direct result of the physical characteristics and perceptual accompaniments of a socially and/or economically constructed environment, individuals, who compose social and linguistic networks, are exposed to terms associated with certain semantic domains.

6.0.1 The relevance of form–meaning interpretation characteristics (FMICs)

Regarding the three form–meaning interpretation characteristics (FMICs) pertaining to form (see Subsection 4.1), the first, sufficiently detailed phonetic shape (see Subsection 4.1.1), expresses the requirement that there is sufficient phonological substance present to make correct associations with appropriate concepts, and that borrowing preferences will favor forms with optimal (and segmentable) phonetic shape over those with minimal or no form. This is realized in the clear preference for content items (words, roots) over other more grammaticalized forms. In addition, the Spanish preposition *a* ("to"), though occurring in the text relatively infrequently, and the nominal plural suffix -*s* are borrowed; they each apparently possess sufficient phonetic form for identification and to indicate that a concept is expressed.[1] The second characteristic, which predicts a strong preference for forms with direct, one-to-one mappings of meaning and form is also fulfilled as evidenced by the total exclusion of Spanish fusional-type affixes. The third, based on selectional restrictions, is

---

1. While this is certainly consistent with observations concerning segmentability, it may call into some question claims of syllabicity (see, for example, Thomason and Kaufman 1988: 56). However, each is surely pronounceable in isolation.

likewise satisfied with the anticipated result that very few obligatory forms (i.e., donor inflectional affixes or obligatory function words) are borrowed relative to the total number of borrowed content items and independent function words (e.g., adpositions, conjunctions, etc.).

FMICs of meaning are also highly relevant to the patterning of borrowed items (see Section 4.2, above). Overall, the data reflect clear borrowing preferences for concepts that are concrete versus abstract, which can be interpreted as a preference for form–meaning sets that represent concepts easily identified on a perceptual (hence, visible, tangible) basis. However, the actual patterning corresponds also with particular semantic domains. That is, whether or not abstract form–meaning sets are borrowed at all may depend more directly on such factors as the occupational, institutional, and, perhaps, ontological domain in which they occur across semantic domains from a lateral, rather than hierarchical, perspective. For instance, with respect to religious terminology (which was consciously and deliberately taught as opposed to observed or handled in a physical environment), form–meaning sets referring to people and offices seem to be freely borrowed, along with numerous terms referring to religious (hence, abstract) concepts and processes. Within semantic groupings referring to animal and/or plant life, native forms have been preserved (and even integrated into regional varieties of Spanish), with the exception of a number of terms indicating species newly introduced or foreign to the culture (additions) and subsequently learned in a variety of settings, in the work place, school, and so on. One conclusion that can be drawn from this is that concreteness undoubtedly facilitates recognition and, therefore, enhances borrowability, but the actual motivations for borrowing are more likely to be found in areas that are primarily social, for instance, in human responses to changing social, cultural, and consequent linguistic circumstances.

This leads to preferences according to specificity. Predictions assumed to be based on processing ease or learnability associated with specific versus general types of meaning appear to require cognizance of semantic domains, as well, but this time hierarchically within specific semantic types and subtypes. Perhaps partly as a result of the fact that many borrowed items are additions, hyponyms significantly outnumber hyperonyms in terms of types and tokens; the few hyperonyms that do actually occur correlate somewhat with entire word families brought to the Mexicano culture via the colonial practices of the Spaniards. One should anticipate widespread cultural and linguistic bias towards Mexicano core vocabulary items (where relatively few Spanish borrowings are found). This attitudinal factor, even though it may be difficult to measure, is clearly present and likely functions to maintain ethnic and linguistic identity.

The third FMIC pertaining to meaning directly relates to the expected borrowing preference for kinds of meaning that can be linked to semantic (sub)types, as opposed to those associated with inflectional categories. The data overwhelmingly support this prediction. However, it should be noted that this particular characteristic, which involves oppositions of meaning types, is not coterminous with formal selectional possibilities, particularly in view of the fact that numerous forms are obligatorily selected that are not markers of inflectional categories. Nevertheless, only one Spanish agglutinating-type inflectional affix is borrowed; and, while numerous Spanish adpositions are borrowed, those that are obligatory as a consequence of language-particular syntactic requirements (e.g., as a result of subcategorization frames of particular content items) are quite rare — in fact, restricted to the infrequent occurrence of obligatory *de* (see Subsection 5.2.1, above).[2]

6.0.2 The organization of this chapter

The remaining portions of this concluding chapter include a number of generalizations that can be made based on the various borrowing patterns in Modern Mexicano with a look at other language contact phenomena that seem to be related to borrowing. The departure point in Section 6.1 is the extension of the Hierarchy of Borrowability, the PSI, and predicted preferences based on FMICs to the entire range of bilingual/language contact situations and the possibilities that present themselves in regard to morphological typology. Subsection 6.1.1 treats the types of patterns expected to occur in contact situations involving languages that are typologically similar; 6.1.2 and 6.1.3 deal with languages which differ along the indices of fusion and synthesis, respectively. 6.2 takes a look at the types of analyses that follow from the PSI if applied to apparent exceptions, that is, to situations that appear to push borrowing to its limits and/or exhibit violations of the PSI.

---

2. See Jake and Myers-Scotton (1988) for a current and much refined version of the MLF Hypothesis in which similar distinctions of morpheme types are made on the basis of whether or not they are *conceptually activated*, which is similar to distinctions made here in terms of semantic types, and their participation in *Theta-role* assignment, which coincides in many respects with formal selectional possibilities. this new work from a psycholinguistic perspective suggests that comparisons with the approach followed here may yield many more parallels.

Next, in 6.3, discussion moves on to some of the connections that can be established among a number of different bilingual/language contact phenomena, for instance, among various kinds of code-switching and borrowing (6.3.1). This is done especially with respect to what these seemingly disparate processes may have in common and what they may reveal about lexical representation in the bilingual lexicon. Convergence and the possibility of the emergence of a composite language matrix are discussed in 6.3.2 in a context of externally motivated language change.

In Section 6.4, discussion proceeds to a topic for future research, a logical outgrowth of morphological compatibility: the role of the most grammaticalized *types of meaning* in borrowing and their relevance to the general borrowability of inflectional categories (i.e., as opposed to individual category values or exponents). While some earlier researchers have claimed that inflectional categories are never borrowed, most note (in apparent contradiction) that individual inflectional markers are indeed adopted in specific situations characterized by intense language contact. Some of the conflict over this particular issue may very well be terminological in nature. By unraveling some of the confusion of terms and briefly discussing the nature of inflectional categories, in general (in 6.4.1 and 6.4.2), a significant generalization is proposed: categories as such are not borrowed, but individual category values may be borrowed under certain specified conditions. This generalization is tentatively stated in the Principle of Categorial Compatibility (PCC) and its correlate, the Principle of Categorial Incompatibility (PCI) in Subsection 6.4.3, which are patterned along the lines of the PSI and its correlate, the PSC (see Section 2.3, above). It may just be that meaning types will figure just as prominently (perhaps more so) in our understanding of the patterns of borrowing as types of form.

Finally, a few measured conclusions are offered in 6.5 concerning the light that borrowing and other contact phenomena can shed on the language faculty itself, and what the programmatic nature of this particular work may suggest as fruitful areas of future research.

6.1 The PSI, FMICs, and other contact situations

While the constraints proposed in the PSI and the preferences outlined according to FMICs successfully account for the borrowing patterns of Modern Mexicano, a number of other patterns are expected to follow in other contact situations. As in the case of Mexicano, the first step in the assessment of borrowability in a formal sense involves the morphological typology of the participating languages relative to each other (see Section 2.3, above). As an opening move, this approach has the ability to deal with the complete range of possibilities (perhaps in a qualitative sense) and, as a consequence, to make immediate sense of the apparent chaos in various contact situations. A sweeping claim that inflectional affixes are never borrowed and are, therefore, not borrowable is more than an overgeneralization; it is empirically false. The opposite claim, that there are no restrictions at all to borrowability may need some modification, however slight it may seem at first glance. The fact remains that sometimes inflectional affixes are borrowed, and sometimes they are not. This cannot always be linked to social conditions (e.g., length and intensity of contact). A comprehensive model of borrowing and borrowability needs to account for such inconsistencies and suspected anomalies outside of the kinds of preferences (and scales) reported in the early literature on contact. Apparently, the only way to get there is to look at both/all languages in contact and the direction in which borrowing occurs. A second step is to assess the sorts of preferences one expects based on FMICs (in a more quantitative sense), which assumes only that items in a language can be classed and placed on a scale of borrowability (according to gradations of form and meaning), from prototypical content items (words or roots) to function words/roots, and on to inflectional affixes when applicable.[3]

It would appear that a system of (universal) constraints is not possible, that is, unless it can be adapted to (or specified in) particular contexts. The PSI represents precisely that. At times, clear constraints are needed to account for the absolute unborrowability of specific form–meaning sets (e.g., particular types of inflectional affixes in certain contexts). At other times, however, typological limits simply do not hold. In such situations, FMICs merely predict preferences (only) — recall that just because an item is borrowable in principle does not mean that it will be borrowed in fact. Particular FMICs such as concreteness and specificity also point to the likelihood that individual and community-wide social patterns may result in clusters of loanwords within specific semantic domains. (Knowledge of such patterns may allow us, nonetheless, to predict fairly accurately in which semantic domains loanwords are most likely to occur.)

The typological barriers indicated by the PSI pertain specifically to situations in which morphological structuring differs significantly in a donor and

---

3. Blurred boundaries among classes (e.g., among certain classes of adverbs, prepositions, and conjunctions), items with multiple or overlapping membership, and so on, are similarly anticipated.

recipient along either index of synthesis or fusion (see Subsection 2.1.1). For instance, when the recipient is (a) strictly isolating-analytical, it cannot borrow inflectional affixes of any kind (neither agglutinating- nor fusional-types) from a synthetic language; when the recipient is (b) an agglutinating-type language (and, as a consequence, it is positioned relatively high along the index of synthesis), it cannot borrow fusional-type inflectional affixes from a language positioned significantly higher on the (other) index of fusion. These barriers are one-way. Typological constraints are irrelevant if the patterns are the reverse (e.g., when a synthetic language is the recipient and the donor is agglutinating or isolating-analytical). In the event that participant languages are similar with respect to morphological structuring, no absolute limits hold. Borrowing patterns, then, will be the consequence of the dynamic interplay among various social factors and borrowing preferences based on language-specific characteristics, not on absolute (universal) constraints.

6.1.1 Typologically similar languages

When participant varieties are typologically similar (i.e., positioned similarly along indices of synthesis and/or fusion), one can anticipate the relatively unencumbered flow of form–meaning sets from one to the other, at least without typological constraints. This may occur in borderland areas where languages in contact are also genetically related (see 6.2.3, below). Borrowing patterns will, nevertheless, demonstrate preferences according to FMICs, which will reflect degrees of grammaticalization (for instance, content items will be preferred over function words, and so on) and such factors as semantic and/or syntactic complexity (e.g., nouns will be preferred over verbs). Consequently, in terms of types, nouns will be preferred over verbs and/or adjectives, which will be preferred over function words and inflectional affixes of any type (when relevant), in that order. In addition, regarding subclasses of Noun, which are borrowable in any bilingual contact situation irrespective of morphological typology, concreteness and specificity will be relevant, accounting for the distribution of borrowed form–meaning sets laterally, into semantic (sub)classes, and vertically, according to the proven strong preference for hyponyms over hyperonyms.

To illustrate the ease with which typologically similar languages appear to be able to borrow from each other, Heath (1981) discusses situations among Australian languages, all positioned high on the index of synthesis but low on that of fusion. They apparently have borrowed agglutinating-type affixes quite freely even though some of the varieties involved are not genetically related. Large numbers of borrowed content items (types) are also found; one expects that they would pattern along the lines established by FMICs (and degrees of grammaticalization) and according to semantic and syntactic complexity (nouns being the most frequently borrowed content items). Another well-known situation involving fusional-type languages occurs in bordering areas of northern Uruguay and southern Brazil, where "bilingual" varieties (putative dialects) have arisen (so-called *fronterizo*) in which elements from both Spanish and Portuguese are mixed in various combinations. Some varieties appear to be Spanish-based while others appear to be Portuguese-based (Elizaincín 1976: 127; see also Hensey 1975 and 1993; Elizaincín, Behares, and Barrios 1987; Elizaincín and Behares 1981; and Rona 1965).

With respect to pairs of isolating-analytical languages, barriers imposed by morphological typology are simply not there. As a consequence, borrowing patterns will reflect primarily semantic and syntactic complexity and the various FMICs — exemplified by the massive borrowing from Chinese into Thai, which, in past studies, has led to proposals (later rejected) of possible genetic relationships among these typologically similar languages (cf. Hock and Joseph 1996: 478; W. Lehmann 1992: 86). In fact, the establishment of genetic relationships among such typologically similar languages which are also in close areal contact may be quite problematic. Comparisons among clusters of Indo-European languages based on inflectional morphology apparently have facilitated the organization of these languages into (handy) family trees; however, the establishment of genetic relationships among isolating-analytical languages may not be so easily based on this sort of method alone. What appears to be left are comparisons of other grammatical characteristics (e.g., noun classifier systems, tone systems, and so on) and perhaps those based on core vocabulary (cf. Wang and Lien 1993).

6.1.2   Along the index of fusion: Agglutinating versus fusional types

Perhaps, the more intriguing cases of borrowing involve language pairs that clearly differ in morphological typology. In the event that the typological asymmetry were the reverse of the situation in Mexicano-Spanish — and the dominant, hence, donor variety were an agglutinating-type language and the recipient were fusional — no typological limitations hold. This appears to be the case involving particular dialects of Asia Minor Greek which have borrowed Turkish agglutinating noun morphology (Thomason 2001: 63; cf. Thomason and Kaufman 1988: 18ff). In addition, the fact that the inflectional categories (in this specific instance of case and number) already existed in the borrowing (Greek) system may also be seen as a facilitating factor (from a semantic point of view). In this kind of contact situation, patterns may indeed differ in a number of respects from those in which morphological compatibility is a clear factor. First, donor inflectional paradigms (associated with fusional-type inflectional morphology) are not at issue; fusional-type affixes are simply absent as candidates and their borrowability is moot. Consequently, the entire repertoire of the most highly grammaticalized donor form–meaning sets would be available for borrowing, particularly on the grounds of sufficient (segmentable) phonetic shape and (one-to-one) mapping possibilities. Second, key inhibiting factors would, therefore, turn on selectional possibilities (optionally selected sets being preferred over those that are obligatory) and links to inflectional categories (members of semantic types clearly preferred over those expressing inflectional category values). Semantic and/or syntactic complexity will play likely roles with respect to the particular patterning of content items, as will such characteristics as concreteness and specificity in subclasses of Noun. Unlike the PSI, which establishes inviolable typological barriers in particular contexts, all of these potential factors merely predict preferences and not absolute cutoff points. Apparent exceptions to the preferences predicted, therefore, do not constitute typological anomalies of any kind. On the contrary, exceptions can be expected to occur, (but) rarely, and possibly due to extralinguistic factors (see 6.1.4, below).

6.1.3 Along the index of synthesis: Isolating-analytical versus synthetic types

Situations in which isolating-analytical languages come in contact with those higher on the index of synthesis, either agglutinating or fusional-types, will show the same kinds of asymmetrical patterning as those regarding agglutinating versus fusional language types, with typological restrictions applying to the participant language that is isolating-analytical and not to the more synthetic variety. For instance, in western China, Mongolian languages (e.g., Baonan) have been in long-standing contact with Chinese and have borrowed extensively with little structural effect at all (Thomason and Kaufman 1988: 90). Japanese, which at various points in its history has been under heavy cultural and linguistic pressure from Chinese (i.e., via highly literate genres), has borrowed thousands of Chinese words with relatively minor resultant structural changes

(Miller 1967), none affecting morphological typology. As stated in previous sections, Chinese languages remain fundamentally isolating-analytical despite intense areal contact with more synthetic languages along most of its frontiers.

6.2 The analysis of apparent exceptions

Claims have been made about the origins of a small number of languages which show the obvious effects of deep contact and bilingual acquisition and which appear to either stretch the limits of borrowability (testing the creativity and resourcefulness of the speakers) or contradict the principles and preferences discussed here (and the intuitions of linguists, as well). Accounts seem at times to be contradictory in a number of respects. Honest inquiry often includes attempts to reconcile differing accounts; perhaps current, accumulated knowledge is still insufficient in specific cases. Irrespective of the final outcome, the principles and preferences discussed here point to the kinds of information that would be most relevant to the discussion, from historical, social, and linguistic perspectives (whichever may be the clearest or most available), especially concerning an individual bilingual mixture and its emergence. For instance, in the presence of clear linguistic evidence of a morphosyntactic matrix system (e.g., Quechua in Media Lengua), one might search for plausible, corroborating evidence from a historical viewpoint — the account that "best fits the attested data and which requires the smallest number of unattested steps is to be preferred" (Thomason and Kaufman 1988:181). This assumption certainly includes the great likelihood that portions of the *lexicon* are more prone to change and/or replacement than (say) inflectional morphology, and, hence, morphological typology.

6.2.1 Ma'a

This kind of combined approach has been taken with interesting but somewhat conflicting results in the case of Ma'a (also called Inner Mbugu by Mous 1994), the mixed variety spoken in parts of Tanzania. Ma'a is described in various studies of language contact as a Cushitic language that has borrowed complex Bantu nominal and verbal *inflectional morphology* while retaining a primarily Cushitic core vocabulary, in apparent violation of all previously known borrowing hierarchies. For one thing, current work brings into question its status as an independent language (Mous 1994; Mous forthcoming, and Thomason 1997b).

Mous considers it to be a register of (Normal) Mbugu, a Bantu language, functioning as a marker of ethnic identity. Contrary to the earlier and perhaps better-known analyses reported in Thomason and Kaufman (1988:223–228), Hudson (1980:60), and Bynon (1977:253–254), Mous (1994, forthcoming) surmises that it has a clear Bantu (rather than Cushitic) morphosyntactic matrix that appears to have kept Cushitic lexical items, not a Cushitic matrix that has borrowed Bantu morphology — the result of gradual "Bantuization" over several centuries (Thomason 1997b:470).

To account for this particular mixture, Myers-Scotton (1998) hypothesizes that there was a complete turnover (changeover) of the morphosyntactic matrix (301, 306–310) from one language to the other. Each of these alternative analyses concludes, based on various historical accounts, that members of the community (most being multilingual in at least one other Bantu variety and Swahili, the national language) were most likely originally speakers of a (possibly Southern) Cushitic language who reluctantly adopted Mbugu (which is also intelligible to Bantu speakers, though Ma'a is not), and which consequently became the new morphosyntactic matrix framing lexical items associated with their particular ethnic identity (retained largely en masse). In essence, Ma'a speakers became proficient and presumably native-acquirers of Bantu varieties and copied lexical entries from their original language into the newly adopted one, thereby preserving significant markers of ethnic identity. The ends look basically the same, but the means differ. This kind of phenomenon is also seen in various versions or dialects of Romani (see Boretzky and Igla 1994), where a particular core of lexical items are retained and inserted into different matrices, as in the well-known example of Angloromani. In the scenarios proposed by Mous and Myers-Scotton, there is no typological anomaly.

Joseph Greenberg, a typologist and Africanist of considerable repute, creates a different scenario in a paper published in 1999 (in which he discusses both Ma'a and Mednyj Aleut). He asserts that Ma'a, "known in the earlier literature as Mbugu" (627), is clearly a Cushitic language, lexically *and* grammatically. He raises an important issue, that the attachment of Bantu noun-classifier prefixes was an "affectation," that is, a contrived strategy to make the lexical items appear more Bantu-like (629), a point with which Mous (1994:199) essentially agrees in principle, at least to the extent that Ma'a was consciously created, though the reasons for its development were the reverse: it was to set Ma'a speakers *apart* from their Bantu-speaking neighbors. Greenberg concludes that the most plausible scenario is that Ma'a is a Southern Cushitic language "which underwent considerable and, in certain respects, remarkable changes induced by contact with Bantu languages" (630), a point that Thomason also has argued (1997b: 477ff).

Key to the discussion here is morphological compatibility and not whether grammatical morphemes can be borrowed, for clearly, they are. The anomaly or apparent exception seems to be focused on the complete borrowing and integration of a noun classifier system by proficient bilinguals in their affectation of Bantu-like speech, if that is indeed the case; even that may be somewhat questionable for its inconsistency of application (according to Greenberg). Morphologically, these classifiers are semantically transparent with a basic one-to-one form–meaning correspondence, making them compatible with Cushitic morphology. Cushitic gender distinctions have disappeared, if they were indeed there in the first place, apparently replaced by a distinct and greatly expanded Bantu classifier system, ostensibly taken from Bantu languages learned natively by the same Ma'a speakers. Clearly, this pushes the envelope of borrowing but violates no formal principle. As a consequence, the present work leans towards to the approaches of Mous and Myers-Scotton, but cannot rule out Greenberg's latter scenario.

6.2.2 Mednyj (Copper Island) Aleut

A much discussed language in the literature on contact is Mednyj Aleut, another apparent exception, which is claimed to have borrowed Russian fusional-type verbal morphology (entire paradigms) and essentially preserving its Aleut lexicon and primarily agglutinating-type morphological system (cf. Thomason 2001:11 and Thomason 1997b:450; Thomason and Kaufman: 233–238). Significantly, little is known of its actual history (Golovko 1994:113), and any real conclusions are tentative, at best (Thomason 1997b:463). Among the hypotheses of its origins is that it emerged as the linguistic product of mixed marriages, among the offspring (so-called creoles) of Russian seal hunters and Aleut women, with the Aleut women presumably bilingual in Russian as a result of educational practices brought to their island and concomitant socioeconomic pressures. As a consequence, the children were of mixed ethnic and, therefore, social status, creating a language of their own (along the lines of Michif).

From its structural description, including Russian intonation contours, some kinship terms, and mixed word order, it seems possible that it was the language of the fathers relexified to some extent by Aleut vocabulary, making use of local lexical items in spoken registers and in order to accommodate the women. According to Golovko (1994), the Aleut lexical portion is reduced, and the Russian component is greatly simplified (117). In fact, Golovko hypothesizes that it was constructed by adults. From a relexification standpoint, it seems a relatively simple task to pick out lexical items necessary (which may have had some currency within the seal hunting trade) and insert them into a primarily Russian (verbal) grammatical matrix. This could in turn form the input necessary for acquisition by the children, whose mixed heritage resulted in their social exclusion from both groups. It is also important to note that the unique mixed population was most likely quite small (estimates vary) and composed mostly of proficient bilinguals, so linguistic accommodation could be accomplished quite rapidly (cf. Thomason 1997b). If we take the middle of the 18th century as an approximate starting point, then more than two centuries passed until the language was under serious investigation (Thomason 1997b: 461). Considerable Aleut (areal) influence can accrue in that amount of time, obfuscating much of the linguistic evidence. The possibility that it could have been a (mostly) relexified variety of Russian (with considerable Aleut grammatical influence) is not directly mentioned in the literature; and, there could be a variety of social reasons for this, for example, establishing a social distance by Russian scholars by simply ignoring its existence.[4] In the absence of sufficient historical evidence, not much can be said with complete confidence.

Greenberg describes verbs in the mixed variety as follows, which he analyzes according to Menovshchikov (1968, 1969):

> Here also, except for obvious Russian loans, the vocabulary is Aleut. In the verb, however, in the indicative tenses, the present has the Russian endings -*ju*/-*is*/-*it*/-*im*/-*iti*/-*jut* and the past has the Russian form in -*l* derived, of course, from a Slavic participle and agreeing in Russian with the subject in number and gender but not in person. To indicate the persons, in this tense Mednyj Aleut uses the Russian nominative pronouns, but nowhere else. Menovshchikov here mentions no Aleut feminine, or neuter forms but he does cite a plural form *aguli* 'they built'. Moreover in the listing of categories of the verb he includes number, but not gender. Aleut does not have the category of gender. It is likely that the verb inflections cited above all reflect the Russian first conjugation probably the most frequent one.

This clearly suggests a reanalysis of sorts, the type of morphological reanalysis in the direction of compatibility expected in such a situation, as discussed in 2.3.3, above.

---

4. This has been one of the problems in investigating so-called Afro-Hispanic varieties of Spanish; scholars within the Spanish-language studies have been very reluctant to admit that such varieties exist or that they are worth studying (see, e.g., Schwegler forthcoming).

Similar to the situation referred to above in Ma'a, Golovko (1994) hypothesizes that a kind of "code-mixing game" could have played an important role in the development of this particular mixed variety (118f). This once again brings up the possibility that it was the product of conscious behavior by proficient bilinguals, and that the mixed code subsequently served to indicate special or separate social and/or ethnic status, as in the case of Ma'a, Michif, and various other mixed varieties. Much more needs to be known of this kind of conscious language (lexical) manipulation, especially considering the possibility that such linguistic acts may push borrowing to its limits, perhaps violating or temporarily suspending the principles of systematic language interaction.

6.2.3 Wutun

Similar approaches may be quite revealing for other apparent contact varieties, as well. Take, for example, Wutun, spoken in western China. According to Li (1983), Wutun is a Chinese language which has borrowed some of the word order patterns and affixes of Anduo, called Amdo in Thomason 2001 (86), the local Tibetan language (see Thomason and Kaufman 1988: 92). Even though its lexicon is mostly of Chinese origin, it also has significant numbers of Anduo words. Its speakers, often bilingual in both, are descendants of Chinese immigrants who were apparently compelled to assimilate into the surrounding Tibetan culture and to learn its language; few now know another Chinese language. However, Wutun, as Anduo, lacks a tone system (atypical of Chinese languages), has non-Chinese consonant clusters, and only one noun classifier (a total reduction from the kinds of classifier systems typical of Chinese languages), most likely the results of long-standing areal contact and convergence within a particular Sprachbund in Western China (Thomason 2001:98).[5]

If it is true that an isolating-analytical language has, in fact, borrowed affixal morphology (of any kind), there is an apparent typological anomaly. In the case of Chinese languages, various clitics carry highly grammaticalized meanings. Consequently, discussion of the borrowing or copying of foreign agglutinating-type affixes into such languages enters a potentially gray area. Blurred lines that are primarily phonological in nature may go beyond the present discussion, but may need to be addressed eventually nonetheless.[6] The present work strongly

---

5. See also Slater (forthcoming) for a comprehensive treatment of this particular variety and the long-term effects of contact.

6. See Subsection 2.3.2, above, regarding morphological reanalysis.

suggests, however, that additional historical information is needed to prove or disprove Li's original analysis. On the linguistic evidence alone, it seems quite possible that there was a community-wide changeover to Anduo as the matrix language in a context of extensive bilingualism. That is, Wutun speakers adopted Anduo as their community language (under intense cultural pressure or out of necessity) and have retained large numbers of Chinese lexical items to index special or separate ethnic status, thereby giving this particular contact variety its distinctive character. Consistent with views that language mixture is a gradient phenomenon (cf. Thomason 1997a: 3–4), Wutun may, indeed, show degrees of mixing and the intertwining of two or more systems.[7]

6.2.4 Family trees with crooked branches

Perhaps the main issue raised in Greenberg's article is the genetic origins of such mixed languages; he concludes that there are *no* mixed languages because transmission has been continuous (presumably with a few bumps in the road), a position obviously not taken here. So, links from a particular variety to its direct (or distant) antecedent may show a few twists and turns, but they remain essentially intact. His observations about continuous transmission should not be dismissed out of hand, however. It is true that Mednyj Aleut could only arise among Aleut speakers, and that Ma'a emerged among speakers of a Cushitic language. Extending this merely to Media Lengua and Michif, the same sort of continuous transmission claims can be made, in that Media Lengua arose among Quechua speakers and Michif among Cree speakers.

Referring back to an earlier analogy (suspension versus mixture), the question seems to be clearly a matter of one's point of view. If we were to take a liquid such as milk, for instance, and add chocolate syrup to it, we create a kind of mixture. All things being equal, one drop may not make much difference; it may not change the color nor the flavor that much. It may not even be noticeable to the milk drinker. But, over time, the composition of the mixture would gradually change. One could certainly say that it has never stopped being milk (of some kind) despite the admixture, but one could with equal logic say that its composition as 100% milk has stopped. Gradually, as the amount of chocolate increases, the characteristics of the mixture will change, to the point,

---

7. See 2.1.3, above, for discussion of the likelihood that an isolating-analytical language will develop inflectional morphology of any kind as a result of contact, i.e., external, rather than internal forces of language change.

presumably, that it is more chocolate than milk. Does it then stop being a kind of milk and become a kind of chocolate? If the entire process were reversed, and milk were added to chocolate, the characteristics of the mixture would be quite different, and the same question of genetic origins would hold, at least until its component parts were precisely equal. However, it is still possible to say that at the point of admixture, purity is lost. In the case of language mixture, genetic links considered to be more or less identical with pure and unadulterated (*normal*) transmission are halted/discontinued. Nevertheless, it is equally reasonable to say that the mixture is related to both. On the other side of this issue, it is also reasonable to say that *genetic* affiliation lies in the order in which elements mix: in the first case, it is a type of milk with chocolate added to it, and in the second case, it is a kind of chocolate with milk added to it.

Two points seem relevant here: one, these bilingual mixes are generally unintelligible to monolingual speakers of either component variety; and two, even to the trained linguist, genetic origins may be controversial. All of these authors emphasize, intentionally or unintentionally, the inherent difficulties in defining the term *mixed language*. With respect to both Ma'a and Mednyj Aleut, quantitative measures fail. Neither is an exact fit with Bakker's earlier definition in a strict sense. In addition, if we accept that language mixing is borrowing (and the reverse, that borrowing is language mixing), then there are a number of ramifications. Borrowing progresses incrementally, so it is by definition gradual.[8] It cannot, therefore, halt or arrest continuous transmission. Moreover, direct transmission of a language in pure and unadulterated form may simply be a myth — or wishful thinking (see Mufwene 2001:15ff). One may certainly add that not all continuous transmission is *normal* (according to the family tree model), as has been the purported case with many modern-day languages. Questions can certainly be raised regarding nearly *all* modern languages, say, all varieties of English or Spanish, Romanian, Japanese, and Vietnamese, just to name a few.

6.3 Connecting borrowing and various contact phenomena

Wherever there is intense language contact, members of a single community acquire/learn and use two or more languages on a daily basis. Those who

---

8. The null hypothesis would be, of course, that borrowing is neither language mixing nor gradual.

become proficient in both (or all, in the case of multilingualism) may develop skills to translate utterances spontaneously from one language to the other, to alternate from one to another depending on the situation (i.e., in inter-sentential code-switching), and borrow from the resources of both at various levels of grammar. Many may be quite adept at switching from one language to the other intra-sententially, that is, at points in a single utterance within clausal and/or phrasal boundaries. Throughout this work, the concept of a morphosyntactic matrix is held to be at the heart of various bilingual/language contact phenomena. As a result, there are clear links to language acquisition and such matters as individual and/or community bilingual acquisition history (e.g., simultaneous or sequential), levels of proficiency in each language in the bilingual's linguistic repertoire, and so on. It should not be surprising, then, to find similarities among various contact phenomena such as borrowing and code-switching. Since both kinds of phenomena involve the alternation of elements from two languages in some way, we might expect that the lines separating the two would appear somewhat blurred at times.[9]

To account for the full range of these linguistic behaviors, it has been proposed that bilinguals are continually faced with a continuum of situation types that call forth particular language modes: a bilingual mode, in which both languages are activated (in the psycholinguistic sense), and a monolingual mode for each language, used when speaking with monolinguals of the particular language (cf. Grosjean 1995: 259). At one extreme, they are interacting with speaker/hearers of one language. At the other end, they are speaking with other bilinguals who share their two languages and with whom they are free to use either or both (i.e., in various types of code-switching and borrowing). At first glance, it would seem that speakers in a bilingual mode would be able to (perhaps even be inclined to) engage in code-switching of various kinds. All of the required on-line operations and processing can be accomplished rapidly and efficiently because all aspects of both languages are at the ready, capable of being accessed simultaneously.

In this view, speakers may also find themselves at points between extremes depending on such matters as the dynamics of the situation, personal choice, and degree of proficiency in one of the languages. Some may appear to be in a perpetual bilingual state, for instance, those living in close-knit bilingual

---

9. Muysken 2000 (1–34) provides a thorough overview of approaches to code-switching viewed as insertional, alternational, and so on. He later contrasts code-switching and borrowing (69–73).

communities where conversational code-switching and language mixing are the norm (such as the one depicted in the Mexicano data). Others, who are not part of such an environment, who disdain switching and mixing behaviors, and/or who have not acquired conversational code-switching behaviors (Penfield and Ornstein-Galicia 1985: 14), may rarely leave a monolingual mode (irrespective of proficiency in each language). As a consequence, it is not difficult to see how actual data can be interpreted in different ways. It may be quite problematic deciding from which mode a particular utterance has originated in the absence of comprehensive background information of all participants in the particular speech event. The occurrence of a single form–meaning set from a donor in a recipient/matrix language may be the consequence of either code-switching or borrowing. Perhaps, one of the few clues as to which process has occurred is the degree of integration into the recipient system and the extent to which the specific elements (i.e., morphemes, words, and/or phrases) have diffused into the borrowing language and have been accepted and conventionalized throughout its community of speakers.

In this regard, one significant issue pertains to possible connections between separate linguistic systems, for instance, in the ways lexical items in two (or more) languages are represented and accessed in the mind/brain of the bilingual, who may have degrees of proficiency in each. More-or-less equivalent form–meaning sets in each language (so-called translation pairs) appear to be closely linked, which is particularly evident in the simultaneous translation abilities of many proficient bilinguals (see Section 1.1, above). Much recent research suggests that bilingual representation may not merely be a question of one system or two (see, for example, Kroll and de Groot 1997; Poulisse 1997, Paradis 1997). On the one hand, the bilingual lexicon seems to be a unitary store of forms and meanings (with parallel levels of activation a possibility); on the other, it appears to contain two distinct components (one for each language), which can be selectively and/or accidentally activated and, therefore, put to use (Poulisse 1997: 206–208, 219f).

De Groot (1993) proposes that the degree of similarity of the conceptual meanings associated with translation pairs may ultimately determine their representation.[10] In the case of sequential second language learning, form–meaning sets from the individual emerging bilingual's mental lexicon are conceptually linked and initially stored compoundly (i.e., one meaning, two

---

10. See, also, de Groot 1992, in regard to cognate status of such translation pairs.

forms): "It [the bilingual lexicon] is parsimonious where it is justified to be so; representational space is not wasted by storing the same meaning twice, once for the word in each language" (46). This is based in part on the assumption that a second language learner often assumes, based on prior knowledge, that the referent of an L2 concrete noun form is identical to that of an L1 form already known, which is often the case based on experience. They are very likely to share numerous physical or perceptual properties and possess overlaps of meaning based on physical appearance (in terms of numbers and kinds of properties). More abstract concepts have fewer or fuzzier perceptual properties and/or conceptual overlaps. As proficiency in the second language progresses, there is an increasing ability to represent form–meaning sets in each language in more independent (optimal) ways (Kroll and de Groot 1997). This developmental tendency illustrates one way in which degrees of proficiency figure in various language contact phenomena, including borrowing, code-switching, and other types of language mixing.

6.3.1 Distinguishing code-switching and borrowing

From numerous observations concerning types of code-switching and types of borrowing, it seems reasonable to assume that there is not only a continuum of situation types, but of phenomena, as well (for various social and psychological reasons). These phenomena may manifest themselves naturally during a proficient bilingual's on-line speech production, from clear instances of inter-sentential code-switching at one extreme to obvious cases of borrowing at the other. One issue that is particularly relevant here is whether or not code-switching is always insertional, in which elements from one language are dropped into the morphosyntactic matrix of another, or strictly alternational, in which the speaker moves from one language system to another, however seemlessly it might appear (Muysken 2000:3). Consequently, in a continuum of situation types, exact distinctions may be somewhat difficult to make in each and every instance, especially in view of the fact that similar looking phenomena may be products of very different underlying processes. Nevertheless, it is one matter when a proficient bilingual switches from X to Y spontaneously to "borrow" an individual form (in its more literal sense), whether or not it is consciously or unconsciously adapted on-line to X phonologically and/or morphologically. It is quite another when a unilingual speaker/hearer of X uses that identical form from Y because it has diffused permanently into the community of X speakers.

A number of generalizations have been made that point to the more obvious differences (see, for example, Poplack and Sankoff 1984; Muysken 1995). For instance, when the use of forms from different languages proceeds along phrasal or clausal lines (i.e., a phrase or clause in language X followed by a phrase or clause in language Y), it may be a relatively simple task to recognize this as code-switching, although phrasal-like borrowings such as idioms, ritualized greetings, and so on are also distinct possibilities (e.g., from French into English: *fait accompli* "a thing accomplished" and *faux pas* "false step"). In cases that are not so clear-cut, in what the literature often refers to as nonce borrowings, single-item code-switches, or lexical transfer (van Hout and Muysken 1994: 40; Romaine 1995: 229), a precise definition of borrowing such as the one proposed here may help make sharper distinctions (e.g., by pointing out what cannot be borrowed).

In separating the two processes, another issue to be discussed is the level of grammatical analysis. Borrowing involves the analysis of donor form–meaning sets in the process of complete integration into the recipient system (see Subsection 3.0.1).[11] Borrowed elements are (re)analyzed according to the morphological structuring of the recipient system; word class of a borrowed form–meaning set is in all likelihood assigned by analogy, based on the semantic characteristics of other similar form–meaning sets in the recipient. Word or morpheme type is, therefore, epiphenomenal. In addition, lexical borrowing typically involves the permanent adoption of individual constituents of phrases or clauses (i.e., words or morphemes) from a foreign system, which are, in turn, used to build up exclusively recipient frames (i.e., phrases and clauses). Hence, structural units are assembled from material analyzed as belonging to the recipient, that are subject to the rules and processes of its grammatical system. Indeed, morphological structuring is always essential to the discussion of borrowing while the construction of syntactic frames may not be particularly relevant, except, perhaps, to illustrate the ways syntax and morphology interface in the final product. This is true whether we consider long- or short-term borrowing.

In contrast, code-switching involves running syntactic analyses. In production, it involves the establishment of entry and exit points in the linear speech stream, so-called switch points at which the language not in use is deactivated

---

11. Muysken 1995 (190f) notes that the integrative processes of borrowing bear striking resemblances to those involved in derivation. According to the position presented here, the only actual difference is the source lexicon of individual form–meaning sets. See also Chapter 3, above, especially Subsections 3.0.1. and 3.2.6.

to an extent. These analyses mark syntactic boundaries between phrasal and/or clausal constituents of two separate language systems (see, for example, Grosjean 1995:261; Muysken 1995:177ff; Myers-Scotton 1995:235). Such boundaries may merely serve to indicate one-word constituents (e.g., an NP consisting of a proper noun or pronoun or a VP consisting of a single verb). In other words, code-switching entails the identification and construction of phrasal and clausal frames whose individual (or collocations of) constituents may originate in either language (cf. Muysken 1995:191). Occasionally, these frames may appear to be mixed, consisting of elements of both an embedded and matrix (or base) language.[12]

Another factor to consider is recognition and control of a matrix and awareness of non-matrix (i.e., foreign) material (Hill and Hill 1986:345). A speaker/hearer must discern whether there are two (or perhaps more) autonomous language systems being employed in particular utterances. This may be a matter of degrees, as well, and depend on such factors as the level of proficiency in each language. For example, when a speaker is significantly more proficient in only one of the two languages whose elements occur in a single utterance, it is likely that the dominant (according to proficiency) will play a greater role in the determination of such linguistic characteristics as phonology (including prosody and so on), word order, and other grammatical characteristics (e.g., application of inflectional categories and their associated values). Code-switching necessarily involves the recognition of separate, autonomous systems whether or not a clear matrix language responsible for setting phrasal or clausal frames can be unambiguously established in each specific case. In borrowing, there is no question that only the recipient system is relevant to the utterance. As a consequence, morphological integration may be the only other criterion (in addition to the form's conventionalization and acceptance within the community) that can be used to distinguish borrowed from switched forms in specific instances (cf, Hill and Hill 1986:346), though it is not completely foolproof.[13] Attending to morphosyntactic characteristics — that is, the

---

12. This point is consistent with most major views of code-switching viewed as alternational, insertional, or some combination of the two. See Muysken 2000 and 1995 for discussion.

13. See Hill and Hill 1986, Chapter VII, for a thorough discussion of the kinds of problems that exist in telling code-switching and borrowing apart in Modern Mexicano. For the most part, we take the position here that code-switching is much more likely to have a temporary effect, and that borrowing necessarily involves full morphosyntactic integration of form–meaning sets.

degree to which particular form–meaning sets are (re)analyzed and integrated into the recipient morphosyntactic matrix — is likely to yield evidence of permanent borrowing. However, we have learned by now to anticipate numerous gray areas where identification is made more on intuitive (the intuition of the individual researcher) rather than strictly linguistic grounds.

Links are certainly there between code-switching and borrowing, but it may not be possible to establish clearly and unequivocally that they are relationships of cause-and-effect (Field 1999b). For instance, those who frequently use borrowed forms in the speech stream are very likely to code-switch, as well. Nevertheless, the reverse is equally true: those who engage in conversational code-switching are also likely to use numerous borrowed forms. (The fact of extensive borrowing in a socially non-dominant variety may even encourage, in a sense, frequent code-switching.) It is also important to note that individuals may code-switch between or among community languages in situations characterized by neither convergence nor change, within so-called stable bilingual communities. Despite this, it seems that each phenomenon (in various strengths and degrees) are easily associated with particular segments of the community that engage in both, for example, a subset of individual bilinguals with the resources and required proficiency levels to be conduits of borrowing. In cases of deep structural borrowing (including processes, co-occurrence patterns, and so on), code-switching may play a role similar to the one it likely plays in lexical borrowing, in increasing the frequency of donor form–meaning sets and structures in the actual speech patterns of fluent bilinguals. Rather than *causing* borrowing (a community-wide phenomenon), code-switching (as an individual behavior) may be seen more accurately as *facilitating* the establishment of community norms. Extensive societal bilingualism, simultaneous bilingual acquisition scenarios, and community-wide attitudes of acceptance towards various mixing behaviors — which, according to Grosjean (1997a:228) includes borrowing and code-switching — may very well constitute a set of underlying conditions, predisposing factors, that can lead to a variety of bilingual phenomena. Hence, widespread bilingualism and code-switching may be precursors of externally motivated change (Field 1999b).

Claims that intra-sentential code-switching plays a direct role in the formation of a mixed language (Bakker 1997:21ff; cf. Slabbert and Myers-Scotton 1997) require careful formulation to explain just how code-switching, conversational styles of code-switching notwithstanding, can congeal into a single, coherent code that operates under only one predictable set of morphosyntactic procedures (processes or rules) and constraints, however mixed it might appear. Positing a separate process (or amalgam of processes) needs to be carefully done. The appearance of lexical items with co-occurrence patterns (i.e., word order) of two languages, along with a blending (or alternation) of phonological and syntactic characteristics attributable to both linguistic systems is easily traceable to intense lexical and structural borrowing. The environment in which such extensive borrowing occurs is certainly likely to include code-switching, but that does not necessarily imply that code-switching is a cause — it may merely be another manifestation of similar underlying conditions.

6.3.2 Convergence and a composite matrix

Convergence in bilingual/contact situations is typically referred to as an assortment of processes by which two languages or varieties of the same language become more alike in specific areas of grammar, or when one language or dialect becomes more like another.[14] Both borrowing (the copying and integration of forms from one variety into the other) and transfer (the affects of a native language, or NL, in the acquisition of a second/subsequent language, or SL) play significant roles. Assuming that one language is dominant within the community in particular social domains, speakers of another, culturally subordinate or recessive variety (who have become bilingual in both) are very likely to borrow forms from the dominant one, especially in cases of advancing shift. As a consequence, their original, native language may become more and more like the dominant (within the morphological parameters delimited by the PSC and PSI); this is illustrated in the long term effects of borrowing of Mexicano from Spanish. The other side of convergence, transfer, can have an affect in the other direction; evidence (traces) of native (recessive) language processes and strategies may be found as the socially dominant language is acquired/learned non-natively by a relatively homogeneous community (see Subsections 1.2.2 and 1.2.3, above).

In the case of the Malinche region, Spanish was the language of interlopers, a conquering people. At first, it was learned sequentially as a secondary language, and was most likely spoken in varying degrees of proficiency. Up until the early parts of the 19th century, maintenance of Mexicano was the rule; massive lexical borrowings and those of a more structural nature were a later development. As Spanish gained in currency in the Malinche region and

---

14. See, e.g., Gumperz and Wilson, 1971 for their classic study of convergence.

elsewhere, the effects of transfer have become increasingly evident (cf. Lipski 1994: 279f). These effects may surface on individual and community levels and in all areas of grammar, from phonology to syntax to pragmatic areas of discourse. For instance, Hill and Hill (1986) discuss the Mexicano "accent" in Spanish (198ff),[15] the numbers of Mexicano loanwords in regional Spanish (99, 143), and even morphological/semantic adaptation of Spanish diminutives for honorific usage resembling that of Mexicano (196). Spanish sounds, form–meaning sets, and even discourse-level characteristics (e.g., particles) have been interpreted according to native forms. As a direct consequence, the Spanish of the Malinche region has become more like Mexicano. In essence, each language has moved towards the other in numerous ways (cf. Silva-Corvalán 1994: 4–5, 166).

The concept of a morphosyntactic matrix that is a blend of two separate language systems is certainly a possibility and consistent with views of convergence. As a product of processes associated with language *internal* change, the morphosyntactic matrix of a particular language will gradually evolve from one generation of speakers to the next.[16] In bilingual/contact situations, the matrix of each language may also change as the result of *external* factors (evidenced in patterns of convergence). In some instances, there is an interaction among apparently disparate processes, for example, when structural borrowing (from outside) affects grammaticalization (on the inside). As a result of the interaction of internal and/or external processes of change, the morphosyntactic system of an individual language may show an assortment of changes, each proceeding in its own direction, in discrete steps. In addition, it can be assumed that the matrix of each individual speaker exists as a part of a community-wide network of individual systems, with overlaps (certain changes taking place more or less simultaneously from speaker to speaker) and layering (changes primarily occurring in particular areas of grammar, for example, phonology) producing a variety of effects in dynamic ways.

Jake (1998) argues that individual interlanguages, or ILs (discrete steps along the process of SL acquisition), represent the gradual development of a speaker's SL (L2) matrix and evidence of the simultaneous operation of more than one system (i.e., native language/L1 and L2). Hence, the emerging second

---

15. See, also, Gimate-Welsh 1980: 33–35, and Lipski 1994.

16. See, for example, Labov 1972: 160ff for discussion of sociolinguistic factors of change and W. Lehmann 1992: 9–14 and Hock and Joseph 1996: 3–17 for aspects of language known to be subject to internal change.

language system can be viewed as a *composite* of L1 and L2 phonological and morphosyntactic characteristics (in ways that may appear quite similar to those associated with pidginization and creolization). Numerous researchers have reported observations of spontaneous child language mixing (i.e., code-switching and borrowing of various sorts) in the simultaneous acquisition of two (or more) languages and different kinds of mixing in the speech of adults (e.g., Grosjean 1995:263) in which a clear, unitary matrix does not appear to be consistently exhibited in uninterrupted fashion.[17] Individual structures are traceable to separate systems. In the development of an individual or community-wide interlanguage (qua dialect), *fossilization* (the gradual slowing and eventual arresting of SL acquisition processes) may result in a composite matrix becoming the conventionalized, regional norm, while spontaneous mixing in child or adult speech may have a number of effects within a bilingual speech community. Social pressure towards proficiency in the separate autonomous language systems is very likely to affect the teasing apart of a child's mixed language. In any event, the incidence of various language contact phenomena like spontaneous borrowing and code-switching generally tends to increase the numbers of potential candidates for borrowing (inclusive of form–meaning sets, structures, and even processes). Lexical borrowing may increase to include additions and substitutions based on frequency (from the perspective of the individual speaker/hearer) in either or both languages, most likely within specific semantic domains.

In summing up the conclusions of her study of Los Angeles Spanish, Silva-Corvalán (1994) states that "in language-contact situations bilinguals develop strategies aimed at lightening the cognitive load of having to remember and use two different linguistic systems" (206). While it may be inferred from such comments that bilingual speakers employ their various strategies for the purpose of economy, in order to make perception and production, and, hence, learning easier, it may be more accurate to turn the inference around. The implicit goals (in Silva-Corvalán's view) of the strategies bilingual speakers employ appear to be the natural consequences of rather normal processes. In fact, there may be few other options available. By using prior (i.e., L1) linguistic knowledge (see, for example, Corder 1993; Zobl 1993), learning is facilitated; it is a means, not an end. Any reliance on first language experience to bootstrap

---

17. See, e.g., Grosjean 1997b, regarding simultaneous the acquisition of two (or more) languages; Hoffmann 1991:75–79 (cf. Relinger and Park 1980 and Volterra and Taeschner 1978.

into a second or subsequent language will always entail an amount of first language influence — that is, transfer (cf. Sharwood-Smith 1994:13).

6.4 The borrowability of inflectional categories

In Chapter 2, issues of formal compatibility were discussed with the resultant formulation of the PSI and PSC. Based on formal, morphological characteristics, it was proposed that morphological constraints on borrowing hold under specifiable conditions and that these proposed barriers are unidirectional, applying only to specific situations of contact and to particular language pairs. Assuming that various types of borrowing and other contact phenomena reported to date constitute a reasonably broad and sufficient sample from which such generalizations and predictions can be formed, the following observation is also made concerning the roles that semantic characteristics play in processes of borrowing: *entire* inflectional categories such as Tense or Aspect associated with various (sub)classes of verbs or Gender, Number, and Agreement on nouns are not borrowed in language contact situations.

Despite the fact that knowledge of such inflectional categories (and the distinctions they make) of an encroaching, culturally dominant language cannot and do not go beyond the linguistic abilities of speakers of the subordinate (recessive) variety. It may become an integral part of an emerging bilingual's skill and usage in that language. Obviously, this kind of linguistic knowledge is typically available in *normal* bilingual/contact situations. Despite the fact that there are no definitive instances in which entire inflectional categories have been borrowed, particular *distinctions*, that is, category values of a type already present in the recipient language, expressed by morphologically compatible grammatical markers have, in fact, been taken.[18] For instance, the borrowed Spanish plural marker -*s* (which expresses one and only one category value) into Mexicano and Media Lengua is permitted because the recipient in each case already makes distinctions of number (also singular and plural), and, therefore, possesses the inflectional category of Number. The relevance of this particular subsection should become apparent when considering precisely what *kinds* of inflectional materials are in fact borrowable within specific contact situations.

---

18. See Heath (1981) for numerous examples of borrowed inflectional affixes among typologically (though not genetically) related Australian languages.

6.4.1 The emergence of category values

To provide a context for this observation, we turn, once again, to the kinds of issues that are typically treated in studies of grammaticalization. Particularly relevant are observations of the semantic nature of general inflectional categories such as Tense or Aspect.[19] Individual inflectional markers express category values that provide distinctions or oppositions (e.g., between present and past, or first and second person). Therefore, it is not feasible that a language would have only one instantiation or value of Tense, say past. Every action would obligatorily receive a marker for past (or perhaps an unmarked form indicating this one-member category). Because the usual function of a past tense marker is to indicate that the action depicted by the verbal element to which it is affixed has occurred at some point in time in the past, then all so-called finite or tensed verbs would express events or occurrences located in the past. Surely, such a language cannot exist. Moreover, the complete absence of tense distinctions (i.e., a category with no members) in a language cannot be construed as indicating that the language possesses, say present tense as a sort of default or category with one and only one value. In that case, every finite verb would obligatorily depict an action or state that is present and/or located in present time. This concept of inflectional categories applies to all other categories, as well, for instance, in regard to nominal markers of Gender or Number (Croft, 1990:65). A language cannot have only one value for grammatical gender (say, masculine); the absence of distinctions is surely an indication of the absence of the category.

In addition, languages can quite capably indicate reference to time (past, present, future) without the inflectional category of Tense by means of particular adverbials and so on (Comrie 1985:4). Any language is quite capable of indicating natural gender and specifying number without the existence of inflectional categories of Gender or Number. The presence of plural markers despite the absence of singular markers in a particular language shows clear evidence that some items are counted (and/or countable) and that distinctions between individual and groups of items are grammaticalized in that language. The reverse is also a possibility, though relatively rare crosslinguistically, where singular is the marked form and plural unmarked (Croft 1990:66). The existence of a plural marker, then, implies that there is a way to indicate singularity even

---

19. See Comrie 1976 and 1985 for the definitive works on the meanings and forms associated with Aspect and Tense, respectively, across languages.

if that necessarily presumes an unmarked form (i.e., one that has zero expression). A language cannot have an inflectional category for Number with only one category value, say singular. This would imply that every object is countable, and there is only one in every instance. Of course, a language may indicate semantic number or amount and countability without an inflectional category for its expression. For instance, Vietnamese employs various noun classifiers/determiners for this purpose without marking plural number on nouns.

Even if one takes a primarily Indo-European language perspective, individual values within each general inflectional category may differ significantly from language to language within a family proper. However, the emergence of entirely new categories is quite rare (e.g., Tense, Aspect, and Mood on classes of V and Number, Gender, and Case on N), though in some languages, entire categories have, in fact, disappeared (e.g., Gender in English). What is known indicates the following:

a. individual markers and the meanings or values they express gradually emerge, most likely in the expansion of the referential and expressive capacity of a language and, of course, its speakers (see, for example, Bybee 1985:137–9; 1995:226–227; Traugott 1982, 1988; Traugott and König 1991; Herring 1991; Hopper 1991; Hopper and Traugott 1993; Heine et al. 1991a and 1991b); Lichtenberk 1991.
b. individual category values come about as contrasts, even if one of a set of oppositions has no expressed form (see, for example Bybee 1995:228 and 1985:191ff; Matthews 1991:39; Croft 1990:64ff; Comrie 1985:9; Lyons 1968:270–273; Sapir 1921:105–109).

6.4.2 The inheritance of categories and category values

Another problem area concerning inflectional categories in individual languages is that their existence in modern-day varieties, in the vast majority of cases, is a consequence of historical lineage. That is, they are generally inherited from common progenitors. For instance, the occurrences of Number and Gender distinctions on nouns in the Romance languages are matters of inheritance from Latin; they have not been created out of nothing (ex nihilo) in each language in the same sense that individual markers and their associated values may have developed. To illustrate, regarding the often cited example of the historical development of Spanish future "tense" markers, it is seldom, if ever, mentioned that Spanish already possessed the inflectional category of Tense, which it inherited from Latin. This development is portrayed once again in (1), below:

(1) Vulgar Latin *amare habeo > Spanish amaré

The specific emergence of a future marker/tense distinction in the Romance languages involved the development of an additional category value, viz., an abstract, grammatical distinction that contrasted with present and so on. This new value augmented an already existing store; it was certainly not the development of the category of Tense by any means. Moreover, particular distinctions of Person and Number and, in this case, their obligatory expression via agreement, are semantically and phonologically fused with the emerging future distinction — a result clearly allowable by the morphological structuring of the morphosyntactic matrix.[20] These are values of inherited inflectional categories, as well.

In stark contrast, if an individual inflectional marker is *borrowed*, then it does not necessarily imply that both the general category and the specific value it expresses are borrowed. That is to say, where there is no general category, there can be no specific value. Moreover, it would not be possible for a language to borrow a tense marker (hence, a particular value or exponent) if the category and the kinds of values it expresses were not already present in that language. Logically, either the category is already present (setting up the possibility for the borrowing of an equivalent or additional value), or the entire category is borrowed — which does not occur. It is quite possible that the effects of contact will facilitate the emergence of a particular category value if the category already exists, for instance, the development of future in a language which previously had only present (or non-past) and past.

One of the cornerstones of grammaticalization theory is that the progression from one concept type to another is in discrete steps in the direction of increased grammaticalization (cf. Hopper and Traugott 1993: 207f; Heine et al. 1991a: 112–113; Heine et al. 1991b: 161ff). However, the transition of postposition directly to case affix has not been documented in languages of the isolating-analytic type (which have no affixes of any kind), suggesting that language internal processes of change are not likely to motivate the spontaneous development of either inflectional categories or inflectional morphology. An intermediate stage is required in which previously free-standing elements become cliticized and the concepts that map onto them (a) become gradiently

---

20. Note that it is clearly the case that Tense is obligatory in Spanish, and not specifically "future". Individual category values are selected on the basis of meaning, for example, as the speaker locates the event depicted by the verb at a place in time.

more abstract and general, (b) develop categorial distinctions (category values), and (c) eventually become obligatorily marked. It seems unlikely that borrowing (as an instance of external language change) will lead to the sudden development of entirely new cognitively based semantic domains where internal processes of change are gradual, generally imperceptible (because of the time depth involved), and based on the accumulation of favorable conditions (e.g., word to clitic prior to the development of an affix). This would suggest that borrowing can accomplish overnight what grammaticalization scenarios cannot do over much longer periods of time, for instance, skipping over intermediate stages of cliticization.

6.4.3 Limits on types of borrowable meanings/concepts

The point at which the grammaticalization processes stop in an individual language also appear to be determined by the *kinds* of meanings that are expressible in that language (see Bybee 1995: 227–229). That is, typological limits that restrict the development of particular types of form–meaning sets appear to reflect constraints on grammaticalized meanings, as well. As indicated in indices of synthesis and fusion, inflectional categories and the distinctions they express can be analyzed along two distinct lines analogous to those of their corresponding forms. One is according to the type of meaning (e.g., those linked to inflectional categories), and the second is according to the number of meanings expressed by a single form. As a consequence, the inflectional concepts expressed individually by agglutinating-type affixes can be distinguished from those that are semantically fused onto individual fusional-type affixes. In the former, form–meaning sets involve the mapping of a single category value onto one, segmentable form (a single representational unit or type) and, consequently, maintain a 1-to-1 correspondence of meaning to form (and back, from form to meaning). In the latter, multiple distinctions coalesce onto one form that is not segmentable according to individual category values. Therefore, not only are types of individual meanings relevant (i.e., categories and their values), the *number* of coalesced meanings present on one form is relevant, as well. In each case, there is one form/affix.

As a consequence, a set of principles can be proposed that are analogous to the PSC and PSI formulated in Chapter 2. The first, the Principle of Categorial Compatibility (or PCC), identifies the types of meanings that are compatible with those of a recipient/matrix system:

(2) The Principle of Categorial Compatibility (PCC):
Any concept or fusion of concepts is borrowable from a donor language if it conforms to the semantic possibilities of the recipient language with regard to conceptual types (e.g., semantic types and/or inflectional categories) and inherent fusional possibilities.

In essence, this states that borrowed concepts will conform to matrix requirements regarding (a) meaning (or conceptual) types of the recipient and (b) the number of concepts that can be simultaneously expressed by one, discrete form. So, isolating-analytical languages can borrow any concept codable by content items and independent function words. Agglutinating-type languages may borrow these and individual grammatical concepts, as long as they already possess types of concepts (categories and category values) that are equivalent in some discernable ways (e.g., for purposes of translation), and that a 1-to-1 correspondence of meaning to form is maintained.[21] Consequently, the morphological and semantic integrity of the matrix language is preserved. Fusional type languages can borrow any meaning (i.e., category value) represented by any other synthetic language (from agglutinating to fusional type) with the same kinds of semantic and formal constraints: for a category value to be borrowed, the category must be already present.

Its corollary, the Principle of Categorial Incompatibility (or PCI) can be expressed in (3), below:

(3) The Principle of Categorial Incompatibility (PCI):
No concept or fusion of concepts is borrowable from a donor language if it does not conform to the semantic possibilities of the recipient language with regard to conceptual types and inherent fusional possibilities.

Consequently, an isolating-analytical language can borrow neither the individual, isolable inflectional meaning types of agglutinating languages nor the multiple, simultaneously expressed category values associated with fusional-type languages (and fusional-type affixes). For instance, such highly isolating-analytical languages as Vietnamese cannot borrow inflectional markers of any kind because they do not have inflectional categories. Strictly agglutinating languages (e.g., Mexicano) may, indeed, borrow inflectional markers, but only

---

21. Note, too, the caveat concerning the crosslinguistic equivalence of inflectional categories, which is especially problematic (see Croft 1990: 11ff).

in cases where they have at least an equivalent general category (i.e., a category that already consists of two values). In the same ways that agglutinating languages are constrained from borrowing fusional affixes as a result of formal mismatch, they are also blocked from borrowing the multiple simultaneous distinctions (inflectional concepts) represented by fusional affixes — they neither fuse forms (through phonological bonding or fusion) nor fuse meanings (as a result of the coalescence of multiple meanings onto a single form). Support for this comes from the case of Mexicano, which has not borrowed any of the fusional affixes of Spanish.[22] For an agglutinating language to borrow an affix from a fusional-type language, that affix would have to undergo semantic reanalysis: only one concept will map onto one form.

Fusional languages offer special, multifaceted challenges because types of affixes are generally restricted to the types of category values that they can express (see, for example, Blake 1994:106). For instance, classes of nouns may express category values of Gender/Class, Number, and/or Case, but only certain combinations (coalescences) occur in the languages of the world. On verbs, only certain categories find appropriate expression. The kinds of meanings that can coalesce in a single affix appear to be restricted in similar ways (e.g., on nominals and/or verbals). With respect to form, a fusional-type language can borrow any affix from any other language of similar morphological structuring — in principle. However, according to the PCC, above, it cannot borrow a nominal affix (without some sort of morphological reanalysis) which represents a coalescence of particular values of Number and Gender, for example, when it has no category of Gender. A verbal affix which expresses a coalescence of Tense, Person, and Number category values (which can be phonetically minimal irrespective of the number and types of distinctions it makes) cannot be borrowed into a language that does not have any *one* of those inflectional categories. Ultimately, semantic barriers may provide the most significant constraints to the borrowing of individual category values and entire categories themselves.

While it goes well beyond the scope of this book to argue which inflectional meanings go with which others, it should suffice to say that the borrowing of

---

22. In the present context, it is more likely to say that, ultimately, the reasons for the complete lack of borrowed fusional affixes are based on both (a) morphological structuring and (b) conceptual (i.e., semantic) representation. Obviously, either serves to constrain borrowing. However, as proposed in the ensuing discussion, arguments for semantic barriers may be even more persuasive.

inflectional categories and associated category values would be a considerably complex and problematic task with respect to types, numbers, and specific combinations of meanings expressed in fusional-type languages. It will depend both on meaning type (e.g., which category is represented and the values it expresses) and number of simultaneously expressed concepts. This provides support for the observation that the only circumstances under which fusional-type affixes can be borrowed are those in situations of intense social and linguistic contact where the participant languages are close areal neighbors, are genetically related, and close typological fits. For instance, this might occur in borderland areas where each variety may be considered a dialect of the other (i.e., at one time), though it is likely to be infrequent for reasons of national, socio-cultural, linguistic, and/or ethnic identity (which may be under some degree of conscious control).

One would be remiss not to mention a set of related possibilities. The first involves the special relationships that exist between putative standard and nonstandard varieties of an individual language (see fn. 64), for example, with respect to reported influence of so-called Standard Serbo-Croatian (now Serbian and/or Croatian) on nonstandard dialects (Thomason and Kaufman 1988:30–31). The other is the influence of a superstrate (acrolect or standard) on its respective mesolects and/or basilects within communities of creole speakers. However, it should be noted that in both cases, there is some degree of pressure exerted (top-down) on individual varieties that systematically diverge from their "standards" via the conscious, institutionalized practices enforced and reinforced through the educational systems of their respective communities (see, for example, Gillman 1993; Rickford 1988; cf. Romaine 1988:195–197 and Alleyne 1980:15).[23] In such cases, one would expect a variety of linguistic and social consequences.

6.5 Conclusions

As illustrated in the case of Mexicano, borrowing plays the primary role in processes of externally motivated change. Whenever intense language contact

---

23. This is in addition to, perhaps, the less conscious pressures that accompany the desire to speak a prestige dialect or to have a wider potential communication network, for instance, in the case of speakers of regional or social dialects of limited or marked membership (see Milroy 1987; cf. Milroy and Wei 1995:137ff).

occurs, lexical borrowings are to be expected, and when contact situations become protracted as a consequence of particular sets of social conditions, borrowing will likely increase, even to the point that fundamental changes will become evident in the recipient language system, both in terms of lexicon and in terms of structure. As a result of intense and prolonged contact with Spanish, lexical borrowing has resulted in a typological drift from polysynthesis to analysis, a process not uncommon in such contact situations. In addition, the wholesale borrowing of Spanish function words has resulted in significant structural changes. It seems likely that (a) the borrowing of such function items as prepositions and various types of conjunctions and (b) word order changes (e.g., co-occurrence patterns within the NP) show the effects of change at much deeper levels of grammar. The nature of borrowing is a kind of imitation (Haugen 1950:212). It progressively manifests itself as speaker/hearers of a recipient language employ (to the best of their abilities) the forms and strategies of another (the donor) to augment, and, in more extreme cases, to eventually replace the forms and strategies of their own. To the degree that this is an accurate description of such situations, structural borrowing (copying the ways proficient bilingual speakers string together certain forms and concepts in the culturally dominant language) may necessarily entail the copying (borrowing) of constructions, i.e., phrasal or clausal patterns, along with their associated forms. In this case, form accompanies function.

It has also been shown that borrowing processes can interact with language-internal processes of change, especially grammaticalization. As one obvious motivating factor in the drift from a (poly)synthetic and incorporating character to one that is more highly analytical and isolating, borrowing provides evidence that the normal, single direction from analysis to synthesis assumed to be integral to grammaticalization can be reversed. This includes borrowing of a more grammaticalized nature, which is evidenced by the thorough incorporation of Spanish function words into the Mexicano matrix and resultant typological changes. The resemblances borrowing has with normal, language-internal derivational processes also demonstrates that borrowing is, in fact, an equally normal process, one that speaker/hearers of a language can utilize to their linguistic advantage (e.g., to increase expressive and referential power).

Without a comprehensive knowledge of such social conditions as the extent and effects of community-wide bilingualism, it may be impossible to measure the real impact of borrowing of any kind — not all of the its effects are apparent at first glance. In the case of the inhabitants of the Malinche region, the addition into Mexicano of entire semantic domains from Spanish in the wake of cultural domination is the cognitive equivalent of adopting whole sub-systems of thought. It involved sweeping changes in the ways the people viewed themselves and their roles in the cosmos and in society. There have been far-reaching cultural consequences in accepting foundational concepts associated with religious and, hence, spiritual terms (including official mandates of right and wrong behavior, marriage and family, faith, spiritual salvation, and so on), social organization (from personal naming practices to institutional nomenclatures associated with education, politics, ethnicity, etc.), temporal and spatial measurement (teleological conceptualizations of time, e.g., counting millennia, centuries and years before and after the common era — i.e., AD or BC, and employing European standards of measurement), and so forth.

While the adoption of form–meaning sets representing such concepts are mere *additions*, and not *substitutions* or relexification in a technical sense, they represent the fact that age-old practices and ways of *thinking* are being replaced; these changes will surface linguistically, as well. As a result of contact and intense cultural pressure, traditional behaviors may disappear almost entirely, or continue to co-exist within a new composite cultural framework, possibly to be subsumed within the newer European-style systems. This has been characteristic of the Spanish conquest in various parts of the world.[24] "Borrowing" hardly seems an adequate term to describe these sorts of cultural and cognitive changes, particularly as linguistic expression will emerge inevitably as a result of profound cultural/cognitive change. This is true wither the new concepts maintained Spanish forms or acquired native ones as calques of different sorts.

Connections among borrowing and other language contact phenomena also illustrate a number of interesting things. For instance, the relationships between different types of code-switching and types of borrowing may show a logical progression, one that, in all likelihood serves as an indicator of impending shift and/or language death. Both code-switching and borrowing have the ability to reflect patterns of language acquisition and usage, including acquisition histories (e.g., simultaneous or sequential). However, borrowing is a much more reliable indicator of the state of a language. While both types of phenomena involve the interaction of social and psychological conditions (i.e., in the activation of different bilingual or monolingual modes), borrowing of different sorts is the more accurate predictor of the extent and direction of change.

---

24. See, for example, Wright (1992: 150) for ways cultural domination manifested itself in Mexico during the colonial era. It is also true that traditional concepts may find expression in the colonial language via a kind of transfer, in this case, regional forms of Spanish.

Moreover, the spread of form–meaning sets among members of a bilingual community reflects social structure, from individuals to networks of individuals and onto the community at large (cf. Milroy and Wei 1995 and Milroy and Magrain 1980). The evidence provided by the Mexicano data shows the extent to which borrowing can spread and points to a potentially challenging topic for future research: the roles of social and linguistic networks in borrowing and subsequent externally motivated language change.

This study has provided considerable evidence that linguistic borrowing is not at all random. It is systematic because each language participating is systematic, particularly in the ways that form–meaning sets are structured (morphological structuring). Issues of compatibility are firmly grounded in this fact. In this regard, the concept of matrix language (with its obvious links to acquisition) is crucial; the similarities (and differences) among bilingual mixtures, on the one hand, and pidgin and creole languages on the other also serve to illustrate the systematicity that always accompanies the emergence of new language varieties. Its clear presence in contact languages provides significant, observable support for approaches to pidginization and creolistics that assume (and, hence, search for) evidence of substrate languages. In this sense, both pidgins and creoles clearly link to language contact, even if original (substrate) varieties can only be inferred.

One issue merely broached in this final chapter deserves additional attention and requires future research: the roles of types of meaning in diverse bilingual contact phenomena. For instance, to what extent do various types of meanings determine the character of borrowing? Can this be extended to code-switching? Can it be applied pidgin and creole genesis and more generally to externally motivated language change?

In sum, extensive lexical and structural borrowing, even though it is often neglected as a specific area of study, has the ability to shed significant light on the language faculty, on differences among various kinds of form–meaning sets (e.g., organization of the bilingual lexicon), and particularly on ways different language systems can interact in the mind/brain of the individual bilingual speaker/hearer and in the emergence of entirely new contact varieties.

Appendix A
Additional Mexicano text

One additional text from the data is presented below. While other portions of the Mexicano text may show considerably greater numbers of Spanish loans, this particular exchange is, nevertheless, illustrative of many of the characteristics of the content of the interviews. It was uttered by an elderly man in Acxotla in response to the translation section of the questionnaire (Hill and Hill 1986:120–121). Those familiar with Spanish will note the ways borrowed content items and function words are fully integrated into the sentences and appropriately used according to American Spanish norms. The first version in (1) appears as transcribed in the corpus. The line below the Mexicano text (in small caps) contains Spanish words that are generally word-by-word translations. However, they obviously do not represent exact morpheme-by-morpheme glosses. The same portion of text as it appears in Hill and Hill (1986) immediately follows in (2) with its English translation.

(1) R. tnamiquih ce tlacatzintli, huan quihtoa in tla cualcan
    ENCONTRAMOS A UN SEÑOR Y DICE SI ES LA MAÑANA
"quen otonmixtonaltih, cox timopaquiltihtica" in tla tlahcah,
    COMO AMANECI SI ESTA UD CONTENTO SI ES EN EL DIA
"cualli itlah cahtzin Dios quen omitzmomaquilih, cox timezticah
    BUEN DIA DE DIOS COMO LE DIO SI ESTA USTED
contento? quemah, tla canin tmoica nican nioh ica in notrabajo,
    CONTENTO SI DONDE VA UD ACA VOY CON MI TRABAJO
niah itech monte, niah itech trabajo de campo, niah itech
    VOY EN EL MONTE VOY EN TRABAJO DE CAMPO VOY EN
trabajo de tronco de mezontetl nicuilihua, yenon oficio.
    TRABAJO DE TRONCO DE MAGUEY ARRANCO ESE ES EL OFICIO
huan yahui quihtoa poz buenoh ximoicatehua ximoicatehua,
    Y VA DICE PUES BUENO VAYA UD VAYA UD
oncan thualmonamiquih tiotlac, thualmanamiquih, yenon panoa,
    AHI NOS ENCONTRAMOS EN LA TARDE NOS ENCONTRAMOS YA ESO PASA
can tmoica poz niah nican ninemitih nican niah nicyehualotih
    DONDE VA UD PUES VOY ACA A CAMINAR ACA VOY A DAR UNA VUELTA
in noaxca canin xamo cox panoa in milli, nozo amo panoa
    EL MIO DONDE SI NO SE PASA LA MILPA O NO PASA
milli, yenonic de campo, mh, yenon, yenon totlahtol, huan tla ye…
    LA MILPA POR ESO DE CAMPO MH, YA ESO ES NUESTRO IDIOMA Y SI ES

poz orale poz in cualcan   tiahzqueh ica in yunta ttlapehuatihua,
PUES ORALE PUES EN LA MAÑANA VAMOS A IR CON LA YUNTA VAMOS A ARRAR
xtlalican ce tlaquehual ome tlaquehual yeyi tlaquehual para
PONGAN UN PEON   DOS PEONES   TRES PEONES   PARA
ctzinmelahuatih in milli, cpetlahuatih   in milli campa repente
QUE ENDERECEN LA MILPA VAN A DESTAPAR LA MILPA DONDE DE REPENTE
pachitoc   ica tlalli, mixpetlahua para   mozcaltia, yecah, poz
ESTA TAPADO CON TIERRA SE DESTAPA   PARA QUE CREZCA   YA ESTA PUES
xmaca in tlalli, xtlalhui, xictzatzacua   campa yahui in atl
DALE   LA TIERRA PONLE   TIERRA CIERRA DONDE VA   EL AGUA
den zanja   de atl   xtlali zanja de tlalli,   apamitl, para huitz
DE LA ZANJA DE AGUA PON   ZANJA DE TIERRA ZANJA   PARA QUE VENGA
in atl   ctzacuilia, eh? ye non, ye non tlahtol ticpiah   in tehhuan, amo de
EL AGUA LO ATAJE   EH YA ESO YA ESO IDIOMA TENEMOS NOSOTROS NO DE
ocachi mas itlah…
MAS   MAS ALGO…

(2)

Tnāmiquih cē tlācatzīntli (Mhm), huān quihtoa, in tlā cualcān. "¿Quēn ōtonmīxtōnaltih? ¿Cox timopāqulihticah? (Mhm.) In tlā, tlā tlahcah, ¿Cualli ītlahcahtzīn Dios? ¿Quēn ōmitzmomaquilih? Cox timetzticah contento?" "Quēmah. Tlā cualtzīn in tehhuātzin. ¿Cānin tmoica?"

"Nicān nioh īca in notrabajo. Nioh ītech monte, nioh ītech trabajo de campo, nioh ītech trabajo de campo, nioh ītech trabajo de trongo de metzontetl nicuilēhua." Ye nōn oficio. (Mhm) Hmm?

Huān yahui, quihtoa, "Pos buenos, ximoīcatēhua, ximoīcatēhua." Oncan thuālmonāmiquih tiōtlac (Aha), thuālmonāmiquih, ye nōn panoa…"¿Cān tmoīca?" "Pos nioh nicān ninemitīh nicān, nioh nicān nicyehualōtih in no-, no- noāxca, cānin, xāmo cox panoa in mīlli, nozo āmo panoa in mīlli." Ye nōn ic, de campo. (Mhm.) ¿Hmm? Ye nōn totlahtōl.

We meet a gentleman (Mhm), and he says, if it is morning, "How did you greet the day? Are you happy?" (Mhm.) If, if it is noon, "God's noon is good. How did he reward you? Are you happy?"

"Yes. Surely you are well. Where are you going?" "I'm going here for my work. I am going to the countryside, I am going to the fieldwork, I am going to the work of pulling out an old maguey plant." That is work. (Mhm.) Hmm?

And when he goes, he says, "Well, good [day], be going, be going, be going." Then we come meeting in the afternoon we come meeting, now he passes by… "Where are you going?" "Well, I am going to walk about here, I am going here to take a turn round my, my my property, where, perhaps the corn is coming along, or the corn is not coming along." That's it, about the fields. (Mhm.) Hmm? That's it, that's our language. Eh?

Huān tlā ye cah, "Pos, pos órale. Pos in cualcan tiāzqueh īca in yunta ttlapēhuatīhueh." (Aha.) ¿Hmm? "Xtlālīcān ōme tlāquēhual, tlāquēhual para quimelātīh in mīlli." ¿Eh? (Mm.) "Para cmelāhuatīh in mīlli, cāmpa de repente pachihtoc īca tlālli, mīxpetlāhua para mozcaltia." ¿Hmm? Ye cah, "Pos, xmaca in tlālli, xtlāhuī, xictzatzacua cāmpa yahui in ātl den zanja de ātl. Xtlālī zanja de tlālli, āpāmitl, para huītz in ātl ctzacuilia." ¿Hmm? Ye nōn, ye nōn tlahtōl ticpiah in tehhuān. Amo de ocachi más ītlah.

And if that's done, "Well, well let's go. Well in the morning we will go with the ox team to plow." (Aha.) Hmm? "Put on two laborers, laborers to straighten the corn plants." Eh? "To straighten the corn plants, where they have just been covered with earth [by the cultivator in the "second plowing"], they get uncovered in order to grow." Hmm? That being done, "Well, give it earth, put it there, block it up where the water runs in the water ditch. Put in a ditch of earth, an irrigation ditch, so that when the water comes it blocks it off." Hmm? that's it, that's the language we have. It's nothing more than that. (S76)

Appendix B
Spanish borrowings in the data

Spanish borrowings found in the data are presented in the following order: I – Nouns: concrete animate; II – Nouns: concrete inanimate; III – Nouns: quasi-concrete; IV – Proper nouns; V – Abstract nouns; VI – Verbs; VII – Adjectives; VIII – Adverbials; IX – Independent function words and affixes. The final section, X – Word counts by village, lists the participants/subjects by number and amount of text attributed to each. Different semantic (sub)types of nouns are listed according to the classifications used in Chapter 5 (see Subsection 5.2.2). Proper nouns (names of individuals), which generally have visible and tangible referents, are listed separately, here, to illustrate the cultural impact of Spanish and its speakers on Mexicano culture.[1] In nearly every instance, inhabitants of the Malinche area have adopted surnames of Spanish origin, and, presumably through the influence of the Roman Catholic church, Christian forenames (and so on). Place names, on the other hand, are often referred to by either the original Mexicano toponym or by the name of the locale's patron saint (Hill and Hill 1986:11), and frequently both, as in San Antonio Acuamanala.

Under the heading of Function words, Spanish numerals appearing in the text are also listed. In the literature on the classical language (Náhuatl), native numerals are referred to variously as a subclass of substantives (e.g., Noun) and/or quantitative pronominals (see Andrews 1975:143, 183ff). In such languages as English and Spanish, such words are typically included as a subclass of Determiner (i.e., function words). As a consequence, whether or not borrowed Spanish numerals are rightly classed as content items or function words could not be determined with complete certainty in every instance. Hence, they were not counted as members of either class. Obviously, word counts may be slightly affected, specifically regarding the ratios of content items to function words.

In fact, the occurrence of native numerals was quite rare in the text (i.e., beyond *ce* "one" and *ome* "two"). The wholesale adoption of Spanish/European naming practices and contemporary lack of native Mexicano numeracy skills (i.e., knowledge of the ancient vigesimal system of calculating) prompted Hill and Hill (1986) to comment," ...the concern of many people about the fact that their names are not legítimo mexicano 'genuine Mexicano', and the concern that they cannot count correctly in the language can be seen as

---

1. Proper nouns were tabulated under QUASI-CONCRETE, OTHER in Table 5.7 for the sake of convenience; they represent names for individuals, organizations, and places. Irrespective of status as proper versus common noun, proper nouns adopted from the Spanish language and culture certainly have concrete referrents and are necessarily included in the word counts.

a remarkable continuity of resistance to the resymbolization of their social universe in Christian, Occidental terms" (49). The impact of colonization is clearly felt in these two particular domains.

Next to each entry is an English gloss, with the number of tokens in parenthesis. Hyphens before or after the form indicate that the item typically occurs with either a Mexicano prefix or suffix. Thus, Verbs depicts fully integrated Spanish verbal roots. Verbal loans that normally occur without accompanying Mexicano morphology (or ambiguously with apparent inflection) are listed separately. Such forms as the latter seem to occupy the frontier between code-switching and borrowing; however, their occurrence is always within a totally Mexicano context (no other Spanish forms co-occur). In these and similar cases, it is assumed that the items are borrowed; this is also in view of the fact that little additional linguistic evidence exists that two separate, autonomous systems are being used alternately in code-switching.

I — Nouns: Concrete animate

1. HUMAN
   alma "soul" (1)
   amiga "female friend" (1)
   amigo "male friend" (2)
   amiguitos "friends hon" (1)
   ancianitas "old women" (3)
   ancianito- "old man" (1)
   ancianoh- "old person" (4)
   antiguanos "ancient ones" (1)
   antiguitos "ancient persons" (4)
   auxilio "aid, assistance" (2)
   bandas "bands" (1)
   chiquitos "children, boys" (1)
   -conocidoh "acquaintance" (3)
   difunto "corpse" (1)
   dijundito "dead body hon" (2)
   dijunto (var. of difunto) (1)
   finadito "deceased hon" (4)
   gente(h) "people" (24)
   gobiernoh "government" (2)
   hombre "man" (2)
   joven "youth, young man" (5)
   jovencito "youth" (2)
   juvenazos "juveniles pej" (1)
   muchacho "boy" (4)
   mulatoh "mulatto" (1)
   niña "girl" (1)

niñoh "boy" (5)
pendejitos "pubic hair PEJ" (1)
persona(h) "person" (15)
pobre- "poor" (1)

2. RANK
   dama "lady" (1)
   don (title of respect, m.) (32)
   doña (title of respect, f.) (9)
   padre (priest, father) (14)
   -padrecito (priest, father) (1)
   -pastor "pastor, shepherd" (2)
   -patronas "patrons, saints, f." (3)
   patrón "patron, saint, m." (3)
   presidentah "president, f." (3)
   presidente "president, m." (1)
   principe "leader" (1)
   señor "mister, lord" (17)
   -señora (at Madam) (8)
   teniente "lieutenant" (1)

3. KINSHIP TERMS
   -a(b)uelitoh "grandmother" (7)
   -ahijada "goddaughter" (4)
   -ahijado "godchild" (5)
   -comadre "godmother" (1)
   -comalehtzin (older var. of comadre) "godmother" (2)
   -compadre "godfather" (3)
   -compadrito "godfather" (7)
   -compalehtzin (older var. of compadre) "godfather" (2)
   -cuñado "brother-in-law (4)
   -familiah- "family" (20)
   -hermano- "brother" (4)
   -jefa- "chief, wife" (1)
   -jefe- "chief, husband" (1)
   -madreh "mother" (4)
   -mamacita "mother" (1)
   -mamá "mother, mom" (17)
   -papacito "father, dad" (4)
   -papá "father, dad" (41)
   -primoh "cousin" (8)
   -suegrah "mother-in-law" (3)
   -tiah "aunt" (2)
   -tioh- "uncle" (2)
   -viudoh "widower" (1)
   abuelos "grandparents" (1)

comadrita(h) "godmother" (35)
confianza "fiancŽe" (1)
cuñadah "sister-in-law" (3)
hermana "sister" (1)
hija "daughter" (1)
hijo "son" (1)
parejah "couple, pair" (1)
pariente(h) "parent, relative" (3)
viudah "widow" (1)

4. BODY PARTS
puño "fist" (1)

5. FRUITS AND VEGETABLES
ajo "garlic" (2)
arrocito "rice" (1)
azucar "sugar" (1)
brijolitoh (from frijolitos) "beans" (1)
cebada "barley" (2)
cebollah "onion" (1)
chavacano "type of apricot" (1)
cilantroh "coriander" (2)
frutah "fruit" (2)
mangoh "mango" (1)
plátanoh "plantain" (2)

6. ANIMALS
animales "animals" (1)
-axnoh "donkey" (1)
burrito "burro dim" (6)
burro(h) "burro" (6)
caballo "horse" (1)
cabrón "goat" (usage PEJ) (4)
camarón "shrimp" (1)
carpah "carp" (1)
lechón "suckling pig" (pej)(2)
pajarito "bird" (1)
-palomax- "dove" (1)
pavitoh "turkey" (1)
toritoh "bull" (1)
toroh "bull (12)
vacada "cattle" (1)
vacas "cows" (1)

7. DERIVED PRODUCTS
abonoh "fertilizer" (1)
alcohol "alcohol" (1)
cachitos "bull horns" (1)

chitoh "beef" (2)
cigarros "cigarettes" (2)
comidah "food, meal (1)
manteca- "butter" (1)
pan-tzin "bread" (4)
producto "product" (1)
puntal "snack" (1)
refresco "drink" (1)
sopah "soup" (1)
toroh-nacatl "bull meat" (2)
tortah "round cake" (1)
-tortillah "tortilla" (2)

8. DISEASES
   enfermedad "infirmity" (4)
   inyección "injection, shot" (2)
   pastillas "pills" (1)
   pulmonía "pneumonia" (1)
   remedio "remedy" (2)

10. OTHER
    -vida(h) "life" (50)

II — Nouns: Concrete inanimate

1. MATERIALS
   hilo "thread, string" (1)
   ladrillo "brick (1)
   maderas "wood" (1)
   teja "tile" (1)
   vigah "beam, rafter" (2)

2. ARTIFACTS
   alambique "still" (1)
   arado "plow (1)
   bacinica "chamber pot" (1)
   bolsa "bag" (2)
   cajas "boxes" (1)
   cajetitos "boxes, packets" (1)
   calzoncilloh "men's shorts" (1)
   calzón "trousers" (2)
   cama "bed" (1)
   camión "truck" (1)
   camixah- "shirt" (3)
   coche "car, auto" (1)
   copa "cup" (4)

diarioh "daily paper" (2)
escopeta "shotgun" (2)
escuperas "cuspidor" (1)
espuelas "spurs" (1)
garrote "club, stick" (1)
gropecia (from gropos?) "special dyed cloth?" (1)
-hacha "ax, hatchet" (2)
hornoh "oven, furnace" (1)
instrumento "instrument" (1)
iscuadrah "carpenter's square" (2)
lozo "kind of crockery ?" (2)
-machete "machete, knife" (1)
macna (var. of mߥquina) "machine" (1)
máquina "machine" (1)
mesa "table" (2)
palah "stick" (3)
pantalón "pants" (2)
periodico "newspaper" (1)
pistola "gun, pistol" (4)
popoño-tzin (from puñal) "dagger, sharp point" (1)
-puerta "door" (4)
retrato "portrait, photo" (1)
ropa "clothing" (1)
silla "chair" (1)
sombreritos "hats" (1)
sombrero(h) "hat" (4)
-tapetes "rug" (1)
tocadisco "record player" (2)
tren "train" (1)
tronco "trunk, log" (1)
vestido(-v) "dress, garment" (1)
xaloh (var. of jarro) "jar" (1)
yunta "yoke of oxen" (10)
zapatos "shoes" (1)

3. PHYSICAL COMPLEXES/BUILDINGS
calle(h) "street" (2)
carretera "highway" (2)
cárcel "jail, prison" (3)
cementerio "cemetery" (2)
cocina "kitchen" (1)
corral "corral" (1)
cuartito "room" (1)
cuarto "room" (1)
establo "stable" (1)

fabricah "factory" (3)
hospital "hospital" (1)
iglesia "church" (3)
juzgado(h) "court" (27)
mercado(h) "market" (14)
oficio "office, position" (9)
pasillo "corridor" (1)
patioh(-p) "patio" (2)
plaza "plaza, town square" (3)
pozo "well, shaft" (1)
sección "section of town" (14)
temploh "temple" (1)
tienda(h) "shop" (19)
troje "barn, granary" (1)
xahuen (from jagüey) "reservoir, pool" (1)
zanja "ditch" (2)

4. OTHER
cosa(h) "thing" (20)

III — Nouns: Quasi-concrete

1. INDIVIDUALS
agente "agente" (2)
albañil "mason" (2)
arrieros "muleteer" (1)
barboncito "bearded person" (1)
-boyeroh "cowsherd" (4)
campesino "peasant, farmer" (1)
campista "herdsman" (2)
candidato "candidate" 1)
cantor "singer" (3)
carceleños "prisoners" (1)
catequistas "catechists" (4)
comercianteh "merchant" (2)
costurah "seamstress, sewing" (2)
criada "maid" (1)
cuatrero "horse-thief" (3)
-cuchilero "cutler" (1)
cura(h) "priest, curate" (4)
Dios "God" (27)
director "director" (1)
doctor "doctor" (2)
doctorah "doctor, f." (2)

eclesiastico "eclesiastic" (1)
escribano "secretary" (2)
figurah "figure" (2)
-fiscal "church steward" (9)
gobernador "governor" (2)
guardah "guard" (1)
huerah "blond" (1)
inocente "innocent" (2)
jornalero "journalist" (1)
juez "judge" (1)
juntah "council" (1)
-lavandera "laundress" (2)
lepero "leper ?" (1)
limosnero "beggar" (1)
maestra "teacher, f." (1)
maestroh "teacher, m." (10)
maldades "wicked persons" (1)
malditos "accursed persons" (1)
marchanteh "merchant" (1)
mayor "mayor" (1)
mayora "mayor, f.â (1)
mayordomo "steward, major-domo" (6)
mexicanera (Mex. speaker) (9)
mexicanistas (pro Mexicano) (6)
músico "musician" (1)
obreroh "worker" (1)
paisanos "countrymen" (1)
pistolero "gunman, gangster" (1)
pixcal (var. of fiscal) (2)
-politica "politcal person" (3)
portería "work of a porter" (1)
portrero "doorman, porter" (2)
presidenta "president, f." (1)
presidente(h) "president, m." (2)
presos "prisoners" (1)
profesora- "professor, f." (2)
revolucionarioh "revolutionary" (3)
sancristan "sacristan" (1)
señoritas "young ladies" (1)
servidor "server" (1)
terrenos "lands, terrain" (1)
trabajador "worker" (1)
-trabajo "work, job" (29)
-vecinoh- "neighbor" (22)

vigueroh "one who works with beams, lumber" (2)
zapatistas "poltical group named after Zapata" (3)

2. ORGANIZATIONS AND INSTITUTIONS
colegio "high school" (3)
escuela(h) "school" (47)
gradoh "grade level" (1)
hermandad "brotherhood" (4)
mayordom'a "estate" (1)
primaria "primary school" (3)
regelion "religion" (1)
secundaria "secondary school" (1)

3. PLACES
barrio "neighborhood" (13)
campo(h) "field" (17)
cerro "hill" (1)
ciudan/h "city" (5)
estado "state" (1)
loma "small hill" (1)
monte "mount, mountain" (1)
mundo "world" (1)
-pueblo(h) "town" (181)
vecindad "neighborhood" (1)

IV — Proper Nouns

1a. INDIVIDUALS
Abrahán (1)
Abrahán Sanchez (2)
Alberto Zepeda Serrano (3)
Albino Lunah (4)
Antonio (1)
Antonio Corte (1)
Aparicio (1)
Ascensión Manzana (1)
Carlos (2)
Carmentzinco (1)
Carnaciónah (2)
Chucha (1)
Concepción (1)
Cruz (7)
Dominguez (2)
Esperanza (1)
Eufemia (1)

Eufemia Rojas (1)
Eugenio Zepeda (1)
Faustino (1)
Felipeh (5)
Fidencia Flores (1)
Fidencio (2)
Florencio (1)
Franciscah (1)
Grabiel (2)
Graciela (1)
Guadalupena (1)
Gutierrez (1)
Hernán Cortez (1)
Ismael (1)
Jesús (2)
Josefa (1)
José (2)
Juan (1)
Juan Luna (1)
Juan Roldán (1)
Juana (2)
Juanita (2)
Leonardo Rojas (1)
Luis (1)
Lunah (1)
Lupe (1)
Manuel (1)
Marcela (1)
Mariana Meza (1)
María (3)
Martinez (1)
Máximo (2)
Miguel (2)
Milio (1)
Murilleroh (1)
Pedro (4)
Pedro Flores (2)
Pepencita (1)
Perez (1)
Petra Serrano (1)
Polonia (3)
Ramos (4)
Reyes Sanchez (1)
Rosah (3)
Rosalía (1)

Rosalía Sánchez (1)
Rosario (1)
Sánchez (3)
Señor Santiago (1)
Silvia (1)
Silvia de Gutierrez (1)
Teodora (1)
Tiburcia (2)
Tomás (1)
Vicente (1)
Victor (1)
Yolanda (1)

1b. RELIGIOUS FUNCTIONARIES
(in) Señor de Canoa "the Lord of Canoa" (1)
(Señor de San Isidro "the Lord of San Isidro" (1)
(in) Señor de San Pablo "the Lord of San Pablo" (1)
El señor de quinto viernes "the Lord of the Fifth Friday (of Lent)" (1)
Jesús Santa Mariahtzin "Jesus and Holy Mary" (1)
Judas "Judas" (1)
La Purisma "the Blessed Virgin (i.e., Mary, mother of Jesus Christ)" (1)
María de Pilar "Mary of Pilar" (1)
María Santisma "Most Holy Mary" (2)
Sagrado Corazón "Sacred Heart (of Jesus)" (1)
Santisma Trinidad "Holy Trinity" (1)
Virgen "the Virgen (Mary)" (1)
Virgen de Carmen "Virgen of Carmen" (3)
Virgen de Guadalupe "the Virgin of Guadalupe" (7)
(in) Virgen del Rosario "the Virgin of the Rosary" (1)
Virguemaría "Virgin Mary" (1)

2. ORGANIZATIONS
Acción Católica "Catholic Action (association)" (4)
Associación "Association" (4)
Associación Acción Católica "Catholic Action Association" (1)
Federación "Federation" (1)

3. PLACES
del Monte "(San Pablo) of the Mountain" (1)
españa "Spain" (1)
Estados Unidos "the United States" (3)
Madalenah (4)
Muñoztla (1)
Puebla(h) (15)
San Antonito (5)
San Bartoloh (4)
San Bernaldino (2)

San Cosme (4)
San Crisol (1)
San Diego (1)
San Estabán (2)
San Francisco (14)
San Isidro (13)
San Juan (1)
San Juañeros (1)
San Luis (11)
San Marco (4)
San Martín (2)
San Miguel (9)
San Miguel Canoa (2)
San Pablito (1)
San Pablo del Monte (7)
San Pedreños (2)
San Pedritoh (1)
San Pedro (5)
San Simón (2)
Santa Ana (5)
Santa Catarinah (5)
Santa Cruz (5)
Santa Inés (1)
Santa Isabel (3)
Santa María (3)
Santiago(h) (4)

V — Abstract nouns

1. GENERAL
   carga "load" (2)
   cargo(h) "charge, duty" (18)
   caso "case, instance" (3)
   contenidoh(-c) "contents" (1)
   contrario "contrary" (2)
   eje(m)plo "example" (8)
   estilo(h) "style" (1)
   idea "idea" (1)
   juventud "youth" (1)
   limpieza "cleanliness" (2)
   -modo "way, style" (12)
   punto/a "point" (2)
   suerte "luck" (1)

2. RELIGION
   bautismo "baptism" (2)
   confesión (w/var. confisi — n) "confession" (2)
   doctrina "doctrine, teaching" (2)
   fé "faith" (1)
   milagroh "miracle" (5)
   misah "mass, church service" (3)
   -sacramentado "sacrament" (1)
   -sacramento "sacrament" (1)
   santo- "saint, holy person" (1)

3. LEGAL
   causa "case, cause" (1)
   justicia "justice" (5)
   ley "law" (4)
   pleito(h) "lawsuit, case" (4)
   -pleitista "plaintiff, quarelsome person" (1)
   registro "registration" (1)
   seguro "insurance" (1)

4. OTHER CULTURAL
   costumbre "custom" (1)

5. MEASUREMENTS
   almon (from almud) "grain measure (5)
   anterior- "front, previous" (3)
   año "year" (12)
   base "base, foundation" (1)
   centavito "cent, part of peso" (1)
   centavo(h) "cent" (12)
   clase "class, kind" (1)
   cobro "charges, price" (1)
   dia "day" (4)
   dinero "money" (1)
   domingo "Sunday" (1)
   edad "age" (9)
   falta(h) "lack" (11)
   fecha "date" (2)
   fin "end" (1)
   gastoh "expense" (1)
   hora(h) "hour" (13)
   igual "equal, the same" (1)
   julio "July" (1)
   junio "June" (1)
   kiloh "kilogram" (6)
   lado(h) "side" (8)
   litroh "liter" (1)

lugar- "place" (10)
lugarcito "place" (1)
lultimo "last one, thing" (4)
lunes "Monday" (1)
mayor(-m) "major part" (3)
mayoria "majority" (5)
martes "Tuesday" (1)
medio "half, means" (5)
parte(h) "part" (12)
pasado "past" (1)
pedacito "piece" (1)
pedazo "piece" (1)
pesoh "monetary unit" (8)
precio "price" (1)
presente "present" (1)
principio "beginning, source" (1)
rato "short time, while" (2)
rumboh "direction, route" (1)
semana "week" (4)
sur "south" (2)
tarde "afternoon, late" (1)
tiempo(h) "time" (39)
tomín (a coin) "money" (4)
veces "times, occasions" (2)

6. STATES (and PROPERTIES)
alegría "joy, mirth" (1)
ansias "anxiety" (1)
borrachera "drunkenness" (1)
esperanza "hope" (1)
gracia "grace" (2)
gustoh "pleasure" (3)
necesidad (w/var. necesidan) "necessity" (3)
novedad- "novelty" (2)
perjuicio "prejudice" (1)
picardía "mischievousness" (1)
respeto "respect" (3)
sabiduria "wisdom" (1)
tontito "foolishness" (1)
verguenzah "shame" (1)
vicio(-v) "vice, defect" (2)

7. ACTIVITIES
accidente(h) "accident" (15)
acuerdo "accord, agreement" (2)
borracho- "drunk" (1)

briagos "drunks" (1)
cooperación "cooperation" (1)
cuidado "care, charge" (2)
cuidar "care, charge" (1)
-demanda "demand" (2)
dificultad "difficulty" (2)
educación "education" (2)
elección "election" (2)
estudio(h) "study" (9)
favor "favor" (1)
gana "appetite, desire, will" (1)
guerra "war" (1)
-herencia "inheritance" (1)
-luchah "fight, battle" (1)
mandado "order, command" (1)
movimiento "movement" (1)
nacimiento "birth" (1)
patada "kick" (1)
probeza "trial" (1)
razón "reason" (2)
recaudo "safeguard, precaution" (1)
revolución "revolution" (3)
risa "laughter" (1)
traguitoh "gulp" (1)
visitah "visit" (2)
votación "vote" (2)
vueltah "turn, return" (1)

8. SPEECH ACTS
burla "mockery, jest (2)
calunia "slander" (2)
castella (var. of castilla" (1)
castellano(h) "Castilian Spanish" (100)
castilla(h) "Spanish" (49)
castillano (var. of castellano) (27)
claración(-c) "claim" (1)
cuenta(h) "account, story" (2)
cuento(h) "story, tale" (19)
cuestión "question, query" (1)
español "Spanish" (6)
grosería "rude remark" (3)
historias "history, account" (3)
idioma "language" (31)
Inglés "English" (4)
intonación "intonation" (1)

letrah "letter (of alphabet)" (3)
leyenda "legend" (4)
licción "lesson" (var. of lecci — n) (1)
mentirah "lie, falsehood" (2)
nombramiento "naming, nomination" (1)
nombre "name" (1)
oracion- "prayer, speech" (1)
palabra(h) "word" (20)
perdón "pardon, forgiveness" (1)
platica(h) "conversation" (3)
repaso "revision, re-examination" (1)
señas "signs, gestures" (2)
-tono "inflection, tone" (2)
-voz "voice" (2)

VI — Verbs

1. FULLY INCORPORATED VERBS
   -adivinaroah "divine, guess" (5)
   -aguantar- "endure" (1)
   -apaciguar- "pacify" (1)
   -apenar- "grieve, afflict" (1)
   -apuraroa "exhaust, drain" (6)
   -arreglar- "arrange, put in order" (3)
   -atender- "understand" (1)
   -cambiar- "change" (7)
   -castigar- "punish" (2)
   -cayer- "fall" (1)
   -cenaroah "have dinner" (2)
   -chotear- "fool around" (1)
   -coliaroa "shake, wag" (1)
   -comprender- "understand" (2)
   -confesar- "confess" (1)
   -consentiraoa "consent, agree" (2)
   -contar- "count, recount" (1)
   -contestar- "ask a question" (1)
   -convenir- "agree, assemble" (1)
   -costumbrar "become accustomed to" (w/refl) (2)
   -crer- "believe" (1)
   -cuatrear- "make mistakes" (2)
   -cumplir- "fulfill, carry out" (1)
   -defender- "defend" (2)
   -depender- "depend" (1)

-desconoceroah "fail to recognize" (1)
-despensar- "grant, distribute" (1)
-dirihgiroh "direct, regulate" (1)
-encamar- "be put in bed" (1)
-encontrar- "meet, find" (1)
-estudiar- "study" (24)
-invitar- "invite" (2)
-justicah- "judge, condemn" (1)
-juzgar- "judge, decide" (1)
-leer- "read" (1)
-linih- (from llenar) "fill" (1)
-maldecir- "speak ill of s.o." (1)
-mandar- "order, send" (2)
-mencionar "mention" (1)
-negaroz "deny, refuse" (1)
-nes(z)tar- (from necesitar) "need, be necessary" (2)
-nombrar- "name, nominate" (1)
-ntrigor- (from entregar) "surrender, deliver" (1)
-obligar- "compel, obligate" (2)
-ofrecer- "offer, promise" (1)
-osar- (from usar) "use" (2)
-padecer- (from parecer) "seem" (3)
-paroa "stop, stand" (1)
-paxialo- (from pasar) "happen, pass" (1)
-pensar- "think" (3)
-perdonar- "pardon, forgive" (1)
-persiguir "persecute, pursue" (1)
-planchar- "iron, smooth out" (1)
-quehjar- "complain" (1)
-quivocaroa "be miskaken" (2)
-recibiroa "receive" (1)
-reclamaroa "complain, protest" (4)
-regañaroah "grumble" (1)
-rehgistrar- "register, inspect" (1)
-reinar "rule, prevail" (1)
-resolveroa "resolve, decide" (1)
-respetaroh "respect" (1)
-responder "answer, respond" (1)
-revolver- "revolve, mix up" (1)
-rezar- "pray, recite" (12)
-salvaroz "save (rescue)" (1)
-señalar- "point out, signal" (1)
-serviroa "serve, be of use" (1)
-su(h)frir- "suffer, allow" (5)
-suhjetar "subject, subdue" (1)

-tender- "understand" (58)
-tocar- "touch, play (musical instrument)" (3)
-tomar- "drink, take" (1)
-torearoah (from corretear) "to chase" (1)
-tratar- "treat, handle" (1)
-vivir- "live" (25)
-votar- "vote" (25)
-zpiraroh (from espiar) "spy" (1)

2. MISCELLANEOUS
depende (var. of -depender) "depends" (1)
es que "it is that" (4)
parece (var. of -padecer-) "seems" (3)

VII — Adjectives

acostumbrados (1)
ajena "another's, alien" (2)
anciano "ancient" (1)
antigua/o "ancient, old" (4)
atrasado "backward, slow" (1)
baraturah "cheap, inexpensive" (2)
borrachito "drunk" (1)
borracho(h) "drunk, intoxicated" (3)
bueno "good" (8)
capaz "capable" (1)
cargadoh "loaded (with)" (1)
cayendo "falling" (1)
cercano "near, neighboring" (1)
civilizados "civilized" (1)
clemente "merciful" (1)
colado "strained, sifted" (1)
completoh "complete" (2)
contento(h) "happy" (13)
correcto "correct" (1)
criada "created, made" (1)
cualquier "whatever" (3)
cumplimiento "fulfilled, completed" (1)
dicho "said" (1)
diferente "different" (3)
divino "divine" (2)
feliz "happy, lucky" (2)
feo "ugly" (3)
finado "deceased" (1)

grosero "rude, impolite" (3)
huero "blond" (2)
igual "same, equal" (52)
impuesto "accustomed to" (2)
jodido "ruined" (1)
joven "young" (1)
juerteh (from fuerte) "strong" (3)
leg'timo "legitimate, true" (5)
libre "free, liberated" (1)
listo "ready" (2)
maloh "bad" (5)
mayor "major" (1)
mediano[2] "middle" (1)
medio/a "half, middle" (4)
mejor "better" (21)
-mero "real, true" (12)
mezclado(h) "mixed" (1)
mismo "same" (16)
moderno "modern" (1)
nuevo "new" (2)
ordeñada "milked" (1)
pare(h)jo "both, same" (6)
pior (var. of peor) "worse" (1)
-pobre "poor" (5)
poco "little bit" (4)
poquito "very little bit" (1)
posible "possible" (1)
practicado "practiced" (2)
preferible "preferible" (2)
preparado "prepared" (1)
prohibido "prohibited" (1)
-proprioh "proper, one's own" (2)
puro "pure" (64)
raro "rare" (2)
rempujada "shoved, pushed" (1)
respetoso "respectful" (1)
rudo "rude, coarse" (1)
santa "holy" (2)
solo "only" (26)
suelta "paralyzed" (1)
tonto "stupid, foolish" (2)

---

2. Spoken by S49, a female, in reference to herself; this illustrates the lack of gender agreement in borrowed forms.

tranquilo "peaceful, quiet" (1)
tristeh "sad" (3)
útil "useful" (2)
verdadero "real, true" (1)
verde "green" (1)

VIII — Adverbials

abajo "below" (1)
adentro "within" (1)
ahí "there" (1)
ahorita "now" (40)
algo "somewhat" (3)
allá "there" (3)
anteriormente "previously" (3)
antes "before" (12)
aparte "apart, aside" (2)
apenas "hardly, barely" (1)
apoco "hardly, unlikely" (4)
bastante "a lot, plenty" (2)
bien "well, good" (4)
cazi (from casi) "almost" (11)
cerca "around, nearby" (11)
ciertamente "certainly" (1)
comoquiera "however" (8)
completamente "completely" (1)
debajo "underneath" (1)
después "afterwards" (3)
dondequiera "wherever" (3)
entonces (w/var. tonces, tonz, toz) "then, at that time" (20)
exactamente "exactly" (1)
fueras "outside" (1)
fuerza "hardly" (3)
más "more" (44)
menos "less" (4)
muy "very" (13)
no "no, not" (75)
principalmente "principally" (1)
pronto "soon, quickly" (3)
(de) repente "suddenly" (10)
siempre "always" (13)
sí "yes" (4)
solamente "only" (14)

solo "only" (11)
tal vez "perhaps" (2)
también "also, as well" (43)
tampoco "either" (3)
tanto "so much" (9)
(al) tiro "a lot" (2)
todavia "yet" (8)
unicamente "only" (9)
ya "already" (2)

IX — Independent function words and affixes

1a. PREPOSITIONS (optional)
a "to, at" (17)
antes "before" (16)
cerca(h) "near" (9)
con "with" (5)
de (w/var. den)[3] "of, from" (1,273)
desde "since, from" (10)
despues "after" (7)
en "in, on" (28)
entre "between" (1)
hasta "until, towards, until" (56)
para "for, towards" (179)
por "for, by, through" (65)
segun "according to" (4)
sin "without" (3)

1b. PREPOSITIONS (obligatory)
(cargo) de (3)
(cerca) de (2)
(después) de (1)
(fin) de (1)
(según) den (1)

2. COORDINATING CONJUNCTIONS
niōn (from ni aun) "not even, neither" (28)
o "or" (200)
pero "but" (289)
y "and" (9)

---

3. The variant *den* appears to be the Spanish preposition *de* with cliticized Mexicano *in* (DEF).

3. SUBORDINATING CONJUNCTIONS
como "like, how" (52)
cual "which" (1)
cuando "when" (76)
donde "where" (4)
lo que "that which" (1)
mas "though, even though" (22)
mazcamo (mazqui + amo) "though not" (1)
mazque/i (from mas que) "even though, though" (7)
para (pa') que "so that" (6)
porque "because" (97)
que (complementizer) "that" (75)
quien "who" (3)
quera (var. of siquiera) "if only, even if" (2)
si "if" (15)
siquiera "if only, even if" (2)

4. MISCELLANEOUS
cada (det) "each" (16)
eso (det) "that" (9)
nada (pro) "nothing" (6)
toda (det) "all" (7)

5. CONVERSATIONAL PARTICLES (by frequency)
pues (w. var. poz) "well" (392)
este (lit. "this") "uh" (as hesitation form) (79)
bueno "well" (43)
vaya(h) (pres. subjunctive form of ir "to go") "I mean…" (25)
ándale(h) "absolutely" (21)
aver (from a ver, lit. "to see") "let's see, hmm" (20)
verda(d) "true/truth" (19)
claro(h) "of course, clear" (11)
órale "right on!" (2)

8. NUMERALS
cinco "five" (1)
cincuenta "fifty" (3)
cincuenta y nueve "twenty-five" (1)
cuarenta "forty" (1)
cuarenta y cinco "forty-five" (1)
cuatro "four" (12)
diez y seis "sixteen" (4)
doce "twelve" (6)
dos "two" (1)
dosientos "two hundred" (1)
nueve "nine" (3)
ochenta "eighty" (2)

ochenta y cinco "eighty-four" (1)
ocho "eight" (4)
primero "first" (3)
quince "fifteen" (1)
quinto "fifth" (1)
segunda "second" (3)
sesenta "seventy" (1)
sesenta y dos "sixty-two" (1)
sesenta y seis "sixty-six" (2)
setenta y cinco "seventy-five" (1)
sexta "sixth" (4)
trece "thirteen" (1)
treinta seis "thiry-six" (1)
treinta "thirty" (1)
treinta y nueve "thirty-nine" (1)
tres "three" (3)
veinte "twenty" (2)
veinteicinco "twenty-five" (3)

9a. AFFIXES: DERIVATIONAL (by frequency)
-ito "dim and hon" (118)
-a/ido "past participial suffix used to derive Adj" (32)
-ero[4] "agentive" (24)
-mente "derives Adv from Adj-akin to Eng. -ly" (23)
(c)ión "derives N from V" (18)
-ista "agentive" (12)
-dad "derives N from types of Adj-akin to Eng. -ity" (10)
-a/ente "derives N from types of Adj" (6)
-miento "N from types of V-akin to Engl. -ment" (5)
-ador "agentive" (4)
-arioh "derives Adj or N-akin to Eng. -ary" (3)
-eños "agentive" (2)
-ible "derives Adj from V" (2)
-oso "agentive" (1)
en- "causative" (1)

9b. AFFIXES: INFLECTIONAL
-s "plu" (164)

10. MISCELLANEOUS PHRASES (not included in counts of individual items)
adiós "goodbye" (1)
¡arréh! "rise (as from the dead)" (3)
buenos dias "hello, good day" (7)
buenos tardes "hello, good afternoon" (4)

---

4. Also appears on native Mexicano forms, e.g., *cuah-tero* "wood-cutter".

¿cómo no? "why not" (19)
de acuerdo "in agreement" (1)
de veras "truly, really" (7)
más o menos "more or less" (2)
¡ojalá! (lit. Would to Allah!") "God grant!; I hope so!" (2)
por eso "for that reason" (13)
por ejemplo "for example" (9)
¿quién sabe? "who knows?" (5)

X — Word Counts by Village

1. Ayometitla

S42	661
S43	1,624
S44	1,285
S45	727
S46	1,301
sub (1)	5,598

2. Acuamanala

S47	915
S48	550
S49	732
S50	1,139
S51	988
S52	868
sub (2)	5,192
	10,790

3. Acxotla

S74	988
S75	1,522
S76	3,487
S77	2,057
S78	3,852
S79	576
sub (3)	12,482
	10,790
	23,272

References

Aarsleff, H. 1972. *From Locke to Saussure: Essays on the Study of Language and Intellectual History*. Minneapolis, MN: University of Minnesota Press.
Albó, X. 1970. Social constraints on Cochambamba Quechua. Doctoral dissertation, Cornell University.
Alleyne, M.C. 1980. "Introduction: Theoretical Orientations in Creole Studies". In *Theoretical Orientations in Creole Studies*, A. Valdman and A. Highfield (eds), 1–17. New York: Academic Press.
Alleyne, M.C. 1986. "Substratum Influences: Guilty until Proven Innocent". In *Substrata versus Universals in Creole Languages*, P. Muysken and N. Smith (eds), 301–315. Amsterdam: John Benjamins.
Andersen, R.W. 1989. "The "up" and "down" staircase in secondary language development". In *Investigating obsolescence: Studies in language contraction and death*, N.C. Dorian (ed.), 385–394. Cambridge: Cambridge University Press.
Anderson, S.R. 1992. *A-Morphous Morphology*. Cambridge University Press.
Andrews, J.R. 1975. *Introduction to Classical Náhuatl*. Austin: University of Texas Press.
Ard, J. and T. Homberg. 1993. "Verification of Language Transfer". In *Language Transfer in Language Learning*, S.M. Gass and L. Selinker (eds.), 47–70. Amsterdam/Philadelphia: John Benjamins.
Arenas, P. de. 1611. *Vocabulario manual de las lenguas castellana y mexicana* [edition by C. Romey, Paris, 1862].
Aronoff, M. 1994. *Morphology by Itself*. Cambridge, Mass.: The MIT Press.
Bakker, P. and M. Mous (eds). 1994a. *Mixed Languages: 15 Case Studies in Language Intertwining*. Amsterdam: IFOTT.
Bakker, P. and M. Mous. 1994b. "Introduction". In *Mixed Languages: 15 Case Studies in Language Intertwining*, P. Bakker and M. Mous (eds), 1–11. Amsterdam: IFOTT.
Bakker, P. and R.A. Papen. 1997. "Michif: A Mixed Language Based on Cree and French". In *Contact Languages: A Wider Perspective*, S.G. Thomason (ed.), 295–363. New York and Amsterdam: John Benjamins.
Bakker, P. 1988. "Relexification: The case of Métif (French-Cree)". In *Vielfalt der Kontakte: Beiträge zum 5. Essener Kolloquium über "Grammatikalisierung: Natürlichkeit und Systemömkonomie"*, 119–137. Essen: Universitätsverlag Dr. N. Brockmeyer.
Bakker, P. 1994. "Michif, the Cree-French mixed language of the Métis buffalo hunters in Canada". In *Mixed Languages: 15 Case Studies in Language Intertwining*, P. Bakker and M. Mous (eds), 13–33. Amsterdam: IFOTT.
Bakker, P. 1997. *A Language of Our Own: The Genesis of Michif, the Mixed Cree-French Language of the Canadian Métis*. Oxford: Oxford University Press.

Bakker, P. 1998. "Some future challenges for pidgin and creole studies," paper presented January 9, 1998 at the annual joint meeting of the Society for Pidgin and Creole Linguistics with the Linguistic Society of America (LSA) at the Grand Hyatt in New York, N.Y.

Bavin, E. "Some lexical and morphological changes in Warlpiri". In *Investigating obsolescence: Studies in language contraction and death*, N.C. Dorian (ed.), 267–286. Cambridge: Cambridge University Press.

Beard, R. 1981. *The Indo-European Lexicon: A Full Synchronic Theory*. Amsterdam: North Holland.

Berdan, F.F. 1982. *The Aztecs of Central Mexico: An Imperial Society* [Case Studies in Cultural Anthropology]. New York: Harcourt Brace.

Bickerton, D. 1981. *Roots of Language*. Ann Arbor: Karoma.

Bickerton, D. 1984. "The language bioprogram hypothesis". *The Behavioral and Brain Sciences* 7: 173–221.

Bickerton, D. 1987. "The language bioprogram hypothesis and second language acquisition". In *Language Universals and Second Language Acquisition*, W. Rutherford (ed.), 141–161. Amsterdam/Philadelphia: John Benjamins.

Bierwisch, M. and R. Schreuder. 1992. "From Concepts to Names". In *Lexical Access in Speech Production*, W.J.M. Levelt (ed.), 23–60. Cambridge, MA: Blackwell.

Blake, B.J. 1994. *Case*. Cambridge: Cambridge University Press.

Bloomfield, L. 1933. *Language*. New York: Henry Holt.

Boretzky, N. and B. Igla. 1994. "Romani Mixed Dialects". In *Mixed Languages: 15 Case Studies in Language Intertwining*, P. Bakker and M. Mous (eds), 35–68. Amsterdam: IFOTT.

Butterworth, B. 1992. "Disorders of Phonological Encoding". In *Lexical Access in Speech Production*, W.J.M. Levelt (ed.), 261–286. Cambridge, MA: Blackwell.

Bybee, J. and W. Pagliuca. 1985. "Cross-linguistic comparison an the development of grammatical meaning". In *Historical Semantics and Historical Word Formation*, J. Fisiak (ed.), 59–83. Berlin: de Gruyter.

Bybee, J. 1985. *Morphology*. Amsterdam/Philadelphia: John Benjamins.

Bybee, J. 1995. "Diachronic and typological properties of morphology and their implications for representation". In *Morphological aspects of language processing*, L.B. Feldman (ed.), 225–246. Hillsdale, NJ: Lawrence Erlbaum Associates.

Bynon, T. 1977. *Historical Linguistics*. New York: Cambridge University Press.

Campbell, L. and M.C. Muntzel. 1989. "The structural consequences of language death". In *Investigating obsolescence: Studies in language contraction and death*, N.C. Dorian (ed.), 197–210. Cambridge: Cambridge University Press.

Caplan, D. 1992. *Language: structure, processing, and disorders*. Cambridge, Mass.: The MIT Press.

Carr, P. 1993. *Phonology*. New York: St. Martin's Press.

Carstairs-McCarthy, A. 1992. *Current Morphology*. New York, N.Y.: Routledge.

Choi, S. and A. Gopnik. 1993. "Nouns Are Not Always Learned Before Verbs: An Early Verb Spurt in Korean". In *The Proceedings of the Twenty-fifth annual child Language Research Forum*, E.V. Clark (ed.), 96–105. Stanford University: Center for the Study of Language and Information.

Clark, E. V. 1993. *The Lexicon in Acquisition*. Cambridge: Cambridge University Press.
Clark, E. V. 1997. "Conceptual Perspective and Lexical Choice in Acquisition". *Cognition* 64: 1–37.
Comrie, B. 1976. *Aspect*. Cambridge: Cambridge University Press.
Comrie, B. 1985. *Tense*. Cambridge: Cambridge University Press.
Comrie, B. 1989. *Language Universals and Linguistic Typology*. Chicago: University of Chicago Press.
Corbett, G. 1991. *Gender*. New York: Cambridge University Press.
Corder, S. P. 1993. "A Role for the Mother Tongue". In *Language Transfer in Language Learning*, S. M. Gass and L. Selinker (eds), 18–31. Amsterdam/Philadelphia: John Benjamins.
Croft, W. 1990. *Typology and Universals*. Cambridge: Cambridge University Press.
Crystal, D. 1991. *A Dictionary of Linguistics and Phonetics*. London: Blackwell.
Cutler, A. 1989. "Auditory Lexical Access: Where Do We Start?" In *Lexical representation and process*, W. D. Marlsen-Wilson (ed.), 341–356. Cambridge, Mass.: The MIT Press.
Cutler, A. 1994. "Segmentation problems, rhythmic solutions". In *The Acquisition of the Lexicon*, L. Gleitman and B. Landau (eds), 81–104. Cambridge, Mass.: The MIT Press.
DeGraaf, M. 1999a. "Creolization, Language change, and Language Acquisition: A Prolegomenon". In *Language Creation and Language Change: Creolization, Diachrony, and Development*, M. DeGraaf (ed.), 1–46. Cambridge, Mass.: The MIT Press.
DeGraaf, M. 1999a. "Creolization, Language change, and Language Acquisition: An Epilogue". In *Language Creation and Language Change: Creolization, Diachrony, and Development*, M. DeGraaf (ed.), 473–543. Cambridge, Mass.: The MIT Press.
De Groot, A. M. B. 1992. "Determinants of word translation". *Journal of Experimental Psychology: Learning, Memory, and Cognition* 18: 1001–1008.
De Groot, A. M. B. 1993. "Word-Type Effects in Bilingual Processing Tasks: Support for a Mixed-Representational System". In *The Bilingual Lexicon*, R. Schreuder and B. Weltens (eds), 27–52. Amsterdam/Philadelphia: John Benjamins.
De Gruiter, M. 1994. "Javindo, a contact language in pre-war Semarang". In *Mixed Languages: 15 Case Studies in Language Intertwining*, P. Bakker and M. Mous (eds), 151–159. Amsterdam: IFOTT.
Di Sciullo, A. M. and E. Williams. 1987. *On the Definition of Word*. Cambridge, Mass.: The MIT Press.
Dixon, R. M. W. 1991. *A New Approach to English Grammar, on Semantic Principles*. New York: Oxford University Press.
Dorian, N. 1989. "Introduction". In *Investigating obsolescence: Studies in language contraction and death*, N. C. Dorian (ed.), 1–10. Cambridge: Cambridge University Press.
Field, F. 1994a. "Caught in the Middle: the Case of Pocho and the Mixed Language Continuum". *General Linguistics*, 34 (2): 85–105. Binghamton, N. Y.: Medieval & Renaissance Texts & Studies, State University of New York.
Field, F. 1994b. "Implicational Universals and the Origins of Mixed-codes: When Languages Combine". Presented at the 10th Biennial Conference of the Society for Caribbean Linguistics/Society for Pidgin and Creole Linguistics at the University of Guyana, Turkeyen, August 26, 1994.

Field, F. 1995. "When Languages Combine: Morphology and Language Mixing". Paper presented at the Annual Joint Meeting of the Linguistic Society of America and The Society for Pidgin and Creole Linguistics in New Orleans, Louisiana, on January 7, 1995.

Field, F. 1997a. Review of P. Bakker and M. Mous (eds.), *Mixed Languages: 15 Case Studies in Language Intertwining* (Amsterdam: IFOTT). *Journal of Pidgin and Creole Languages* 12 (2): 403–408.

Field, F. 1997b. "Mixed systems: the determining role of a matrix (substrate) system". Paper presented January 10, 1997 at the annual joint meeting of the Society for Pidgin and Creole Linguistics with the Linguistic Society of America at the Sheraton Chicago Hotel and Towers in Chicago, IL.

Field, F. 1997c. "Patterns in language mixing: the effects of a matrix system". Paper presented June 28, 1997 at the annual meeting of the Society for Pidgin and Creole Linguistics at the University of Westminister in London, England.

Field, F. 1998. "Revealing contrasts: Function words and inflectional categories in modern Mexicano and Palenquero". Paper presented January 10, 1998 at the annual joint meeting of the Society for Pidgin and Creole Linguistics with the Linguistic Society of America at the Grand Hyatt in New York, N.Y.

Field, F. 1999a. "Language Mixing: the Effects of a Matrix System." *Southwest Journal of Linguistics* 18 (2): 47–78.

Field, F. 1999b. "Long-term effects of code-switching: keys to structural borrowing". Paper presented April 17, 1999 at the 2nd International Symposium on Bilingualism, University of Newcastle upon Tyne, U.K.

Field, F. 1999c. "A quantitative look at borrowing patterns in Malinche Mexicano." In *Volume 9: Proceedings from the second Workshop on American Indigenous Languages*, 42–52. Santa Barbara, CA: Santa Barbara Papers in Linguistics.

Field, F. 2001. "Second Language Acquisition and the emergence of a creole". Paper presented April 18, 2001 at the 3rd International Symposium on Bilingualism, University of West England, U.K.

Field, F. Forthcoming. "On massive borrowing and the genesis of mixed languages." In *University of Aarhus Working Papers Volume on Language Mixing*, P. Bakker and F. Field (eds).

Fisher, C., D.G. Hall, S. Rakowitz, and L. Gleitman. 1994. "When it is better to receive than to give: Syntactic and perceptual restraints on vocabulary growth". In *The Acquisition of the Lexicon*, L. Gleitman and B. Landau (eds), 333–375. Cambridge Mass.: the MIT Press.

Fortescue, M. and L.L. Olsen. 1992. "The Acquisition of West Greenlandic". In *The Crosslinguistic Study of Language Acquisition, Volume 3*, Dan I. Slobin (ed.), 111–219. Hillsdale, N.J.: Lawrence Erlbaum.

Frauenfelder, U.H. and R. Schreuder. 1992. "Constraining Psycholinguistic Models of Morphological Processing and Representation". In *Yearbook of Morphology 1991*, G. Booij and J. van Marle (eds), 165–183. The Netherlands: Kluwer.

Frazier, L. and C. Clifton, Jr. 1996. *Construal.* Cambridge, Mass.: The MIT Press.

Friederici, A. 1985. "Levels of processing and vocabulary types: Evidence from on-line comprehension in normals and agrammatics". *Cognition* 19: 133–66.

Gal, S. 1989. "Lexical innovation and loss: The use and value of restricted Hungarian". In *Investigating obsolescence: Studies in language contraction and death*, N.C. Dorian (ed.), 313–331. Cambridge: Cambridge University Press.

Gass, S.M. and L. Selinker. 1993. "Afterword". In *Language Transfer in Language Learning*. S.M. Gass and L. Selinker (eds), 233–236. Amsterdam/Philadelphia: John Benjamins.

Gass, S.M. 1995. "Universals, SLA, and language pedagogy: 1984 revisited". In *The Current State of Interlanguage: Studies in Honor of W.E. Rutherford*, L. Eubank, L. Selinker, and M.S. Smith (eds), 31–42. Amsterdam/Philadelphia: John Benjamins.

Gillman, C. 1993. "Black Identity, Homeostasis, and Survival: African and Metropolitan Speech Varieties in the New World". In *Africanisms in Afro-American Language Varieties*, S.S. Mufwene (ed.), 388–402. Athens, Ga.: University of Georgia Press.

Gimate-Welsh, A. 1980. *Lenguaje y Sociedad*. Puebla, México: Universidad Autónoma de Puebla.

Gleitman, L. 1993. "The Structural Sources of Verb Meanings". In *Language Acquisition: core readings*, P. Bloom (ed.), 174–221. Cambridge, Mass.: The MIT Press [First MIT Press edition 1994].

Golovko, E. 1994. "Mednyj Aleut or Copper Island Aleut: an Aleut-Russian mixed language". In *Mixed Languages: 15 Case Studies in Language Intertwining*, P. Bakker and M. Mous (eds), 113–121. Amsterdam: IFOTT.

Green, D.W. 1993. "Towards a Model of L2 Comprehension and Production". In *The Bilingual Lexicon*. R. Schreuder and B. Weltens (eds), 249–278. Amsterdam/Philadelphia: John Benjamins.

Greenberg, J.H. 1966. "Some Universals of Grammar with Particular Reference to the Order of Meaningful Elements". In *Universals of Language*, J.H. Greenberg (ed.), 73–113. Cambridge, Mass.: MIT Press.

Greenberg, J.H. 1974. *Language Typology: A Historical and Analytic Overview*. The Hague: Mouton.

Greenberg, J. 1991. "The last stages of grammatical elements; contractive and expansive desemanticization". In *Approaches to Grammaticalization, Volume 1*, E.C. Traugott and B. Heine (eds), 301–314. Amsterdam/Philadelphia: John Benjamins.

Greenberg, J. 1999. "Are there mixed languages?" In *Essays in Poetics, Literary History and Linguistics. Presented to Viacheslav Vsevolodovich Ivanov on the Occasion of His Seventieth Birthday*. Moscow: OGI.

Grosjean, F. and J.P. Gee. 1987. "Prosodic structure and spoken word recognition". In *Cognition*, 25: 135–155.

Grosjean, F. 1982. *Life with Two Languages: An Introduction to Bilingualism*. Cambridge, Mass.: Harvard University Press.

Grosjean, F. 1995. "A Psycholinguistic Approach to Code-switching: the recognition of guest words by bilinguals". In *One speaker, two languages: Cross-disciplinary perspectives on code-switching*. L. Milroy and P. Muysken (eds), 259–275. New York: Cambridge University Press.

Grosjean, F. 1997a. "Processing Mixed Language: Issues, Findings, and Models". In *Tutorials in Bilingualism: Psycholinguistic Perspectives*. A.M.B. de Groot and J.F. Kroll (eds), 225–254. Mahwah, New Jersey: Lawrence Erlbaum Associates.

Grosjean, F. 1997b. "The Bilingual Individual". *Interpreting: International Journal of Research and Practice in Interpreting*, 2: 163–191.

Grosjean, F. 2001. "The Bilingual's Language Modes." In *One Mind, Two Languages: Bilingual Language Processing*. J. L. Nicol (ed.), 1–22. Malden, Mass.: Blackwell Publishers.

Gumperz, J. J. and R. Wilson. 1971. "Convergence and Creolization: A Case from the Indo-Aryan/Dravidian Border in India". In *Pidginization and Creolization of Languages*, D. Hymes (ed), 151–69. Cambridge: Cambridge University Press.

Gumperz, J. J., (ed.). 1982. *Language and Social Identity*. New York, N. Y.: Cambridge University Press.

Gutknecht, C. and L. J. Rölle. 1996. *Translating by Factors*. Albany, N. Y.: State University of New York Press.

Hall, C. 1988. "Integrating Diachronic and Processing Principles in Explaining the Suffixing Preference". In *Explaining Language Universals*, J. A. Hawkins (ed.), 321–349. Cambridge, Mass.: Blackwell.

Harris, J. 1985. *Phonological variation and change: studies in Hiberno-English*. New York: Cambridge University Press.

Hartmann, R. R. K. and F. C. Stork. 1972. *Dictionary of Language and Linguistics*. New York and Toronto: J. Wiley & Sons.

Haugen, E. 1950. "The Analysis of Linguistic Borrowing". *Language* 26: 210–231.

Haugen, E. 1953 (reprinted 1969). *The Norwegian language in America: A study in bilingual behavior*. Philadelphia: University of Pennsylvania Press/Bloomington: Indiana University Press.

Haugen, E. 1989. "The rise and fall of an immigrant language: Norwegian in America". In *Investigating obsolescence: Studies in language contraction and death*, N. C. Dorian (ed.), 61–73. New York: Cambridge University Press.

Hawkins, J. A. 1980. "On implicational and distributional universals of word order". *Journal of Linguistics* 16: 193–235.

Hawkins, J. A. 1983. *Word Order Universals*. Philadelphia, Penn.: John Benjamins.

Hawkins, J. A. (ed.). 1988. *Explaining Language Universals*. Cambridge, Mass.: Blackwell.

Hawkins, J. A. 1990. "Seeking motives for change in typological variation". In *Studies in Typology and Diachrony: Papers presented to Joseph Greenberg on the occasion of his 75th birthday*. W. Croft, K. Denning, and S. Kemmer (eds), 95–128. Amsterdam/Philadelphia: John Benjamins.

Hawkins, J. A. 1991. "Language Universals in Relation to Acquisition and Change: a Tribute to Roman Jakobson". In *New Vistas in Grammar Invariance and Variation*. L. R. Waugh and S. Rudy (eds), 473–493. John Benjamins, Amsterdam/Philadelphia.

Hawkins, J. A. 1994. *A performance theory of order and constituency*. Cambridge: Cambridge University Press.

Hawkins, J. A. and A. Cutler 1988. "Psycholinguistic Factors in Morphological Asymmetry". In *Explaining Language Universals*, J. A. Hawkins (ed.), 280–317. Cambridge, Mass.: Blackwell. 280–317.

Heath, J. 1981. "A case of intensive lexical diffusion". *Language* 57, 335–367.

Heine, B. and M. Reh. 1984. *Grammaticalization and Reanalysis in African Languages*. Chicago: University of Chicago Press.

Heine, B., U. Claudi, and F. Hünnemeyer. 1991a. *Grammaticalization: A Conceptual Framework*. Chicago: University of Chicago Press.
Heine, B., U. Claudi, and F. Hünnemeyer. 1991b. "From cognition to grammar: Evidence from African languages". In *Approaches to Grammaticalization, Volume I*. E. C. Traugott and B. Heine (eds), 149–187. Amsterdam/Philadelphia: John Benjamins.
Herring, S. 1991. "The Grammaticalization of Rhetorical Questions in Tamil". In *Approaches to Grammaticalization, Volume II*. E. C. Traugott and B. Heine (eds), 23–284. Amsterdam/Philadelphia: John Benjamins.
Hill, J. H. and K. Hill. 1986. *Speaking Mexicano: Dynamics of Syncretic Language in Central Mexico*. Tucson: University of Arizona Press.
Hill, J. H. and K. Hill. MS. Mexicano Corpus. University of Arizona.
Hill, J. H. 1988. "Ambivalent language attitudes in modern Nahuatl". In *Sociolingüistica Latinoamericana*. R. E. Hamel, Y. Lastra de Suárez, and H. Muñoz (eds), 77–99. Mexico City: Universidad Nacional Autónoma de México.
Hock, H. H. and B. D. Joseph. 1996. *Language History, Language Change, and Language Relationship: An Introduction to Historical and Comparative Linguistics*. Berlin and New York: Mouton de Gruyter.
Hoffmann, C. 1991. *An Introduction to Bilingualism*. New York, N.Y.: Longman.
Holm, J. 1988. *Pidgins and Creoles, Volume 1: Theory and Structure*. Cambridge: Cambridge University Press.
Holm, J. 1989. *Pidgins and Creoles, Volume 2: Reference Survey*. Cambridge: Cambridge University Press.
Hopper, P. J. 1987. "Emergent grammar". In *Berkeley Linguistic Society Meeting, Papers of the Thirteenth Annual Meeting*, 139–157.
Hopper, P. J. 1991. "On some principles of grammaticalization". In *Approaches to Grammaticalization, Volume I*. E. C. Traugott and B. Heine (eds), 17–36. Amsterdam/Philadelphia: John Benjamins.
Hopper, P. J. and E. C. Traugott. 1993. *Grammaticalization*. Cambridge: Cambridge University Press.
Hudson, R. A. 1980. *Sociolinguistics*. Cambridge: Cambridge University Press.
Huffines, M. L. 1989. "Case usage among the Pennsylvania German sectarians and nonsectarians". In *Investigating obsolescence: Studies in language contraction and death*, N. C. Dorian (ed.), 211–226. Cambridge: Cambridge University Press.
Huttenlocher J. and P. Smiley. 1987. "Early word meanings: The case of object names". In *Cognitive Psychology*, 19: 1987. Reprinted (1993) in *Language Acquisition: core readings*, P. Bloom (ed.), 222–247. Cambridge, Mass.: The MIT Press.
Jackendoff, R. S. 1983. *Semantics and Cognition*. Current Studies in Linguistics Series 8. Cambridge, MA: MIT Press.
Jake, J. and C. Myers-Scotton. 1998. "How to build a creole: Splitting and recombining lexical structure". Paper presented January 10, 1998 at the annual joint meeting of the Society for Pidgin and Creole Linguistics with the Linguistic Society of America at the Grand Hyatt in New York, N. Y.
Jake, J. L. 1998. "Constructing Interlanguage: Building a Composite Matrix Language", *Linguistics*, 36, 333–382.

Johanson, L. 1992. *Strukturelle Faktoren in tuerkischen Sprachkontakten.* Stuttgart, Germany: F. Steiner.
Karttunen, F. E. and J. Lockhart. 1976. *Nahuatl in the Middle Years: Language Contact Phenomena in Texts of the Colonial Period.* Berkeley: University of California Press.
Karttunen, F. 1983. *An Analytical Dictionary of Nahuatl.* Norman, Okla.: University of Oklahoma Press.
Katamba, F. 1993. *Morphology.* New York: St. Martin's Press.
Keesing, R. M. 1991. "Substrates, calquing and grammaticalization in Melanesian Pidgin". In *Approaches to Grammaticalization: Volume 1.* E. C. Traugott and B. Heine (eds), 315–342. Amsterdam/Philadelphia: John Benjamins.
Kroll, J. F. and A. M. B. de Groot. 1997. "Lexical and Conceptual Memory n the Bilingual: Mapping Form to Meaning in Two Languages". In *Tutorials in Bilingualism: Psycholinguistic Perspectives.* A. M. B. de Groot and J. F. Kroll (eds), 169–199. Mahwah, New Jersey: Lawrence Erlbaum Associates.
Labov, W. 1972. *Sociolinguistic Patterns.* Philadelphia, PA: University of Pennsylvania Press.
Lakoff, G. 1987. *Women, Fire, and Dangerous Things: What Categories Reveal about the Mind.* Chicago and London: University of Chicago Press.
Landau, B. and L. Gleitman. 1985. *Language and experience: Evidence from the blind child.* Cambridge, MA: Harvard University Press.
Landau, B. 1993. "Ontology and Perception, Object Kind and Object Naming". In *The proceedings of the twenty-fifth annual Child Language Research Forum,* E. V. Clark (ed.), 191–196. Stanford University: Center for the Study of Language and Information.
Landau, B. 1994. "Where's what and what's where: The language of objects in space". In *The Acquisition of the Lexicon,* L. Gleitman and B. Landau (eds), 259–296. Cambridge, Mass.: The MIT Press.
Langacker, R. W. 1977. "Syntactic reanalysis". In *Mechanisms of Syntactic Change,* C. Li (ed.), 57–139. Austin: University of Texas Press.
Lastra, Yolanda. 1968. *Cochabamba Quechua Syntax.* The Hague: Mouton.
Lefebvre C. and J. Lumsden. 1989. "Les langues créoles et la théorie linguistique". *The Canadian Journal of Linguistics,* 34: 249–272.
Lefebvre, C. 1986. "Relexification and creole genesis revisited". In *Substrata versus Universals in Creole Genesis,* P. Muysken and N. Smith (eds.), 279–300. Amsterdam/Philadelphia: John Benjamins.
Lefebvre, C. 1993. "The Role of Relexification and Syntactic Reanalysis in Haitian Creole: Methodological Aspects of a Research Program". In *Africanisms in Afro-American Language Varieties,* S. S. Mufwene (ed.), 254–278. Athens, Ga.: University of Georgia.
Lehmann, C. 1986. "Grammaticalization and Linguistic Typology". *General Linguistics,* 26 (1), 3–23.
Lehmann, W. P. 1992. *Historical Linguistics, An Introduction.* New York, N. Y.: Holt, Rinehart and Winston, Inc.
Levelt, W. J. M. 1989. *Speaking: From Intention to Articulation.* Cambridge, Mass.: The MIT Press.
Levelt, W. J. M. Levelt. 1992. "Accessing Words in Speech Production: Stages, processes and representations". In *Lexical Access in Speech Production,* W. J. M. Levelt (ed.), 1–22. Cambridge, MA: Blackwell.

Léon-Portilla, A. H. de. 1972. "Bibliografía lingüistica nahua". *Estudios de Cultura Náhuatl* 10: 409–441.

Li, C. 1983. "Languages in contact in Western China". *Papers in East Asian Languages* 1:31–51.

Lichtenberk, F. 1991. "On the gradualness of grammaticalization". In *Approaches to Grammaticalization, Volume 1*, E. C. Traugott and B. Heine (eds), 37–80. Amsterdam/ Philadelphia: John Benjamins.

Lipski, J. 1994. *Latin American Spanish*. London and New York: Longman, 1994.

Lumsden, J. S. 1994. Possession: Substratum semantics in Haitian Creole. *Journal of Pidgin and Creole Languages*, 9 (1): 25–50.

Lumsden, J. S. 1999. "Language Acquisition and Creolization." In *Language creation and language change: creolization, diachrony, and development*, M. DeGraff (ed.), 129–157. Cambridge, Mass.: MIT Press.

Lyons, J. 1968. *Introduction to Theoretical Linguistics*. New York, N. Y.: Cambridge University Press.

Lyons, J. 1995. *Linguistic Semantics: An introduction*. Cambridge: Cambridge University Press.

Markman, E. M. 1989. *Categorization and Naming in Children: Problems of Induction*. Cambridge, Mass.: The MIT Press.

Markman, E. M. 1993. "Constraints Children Place on Word Meanings". In *Language Acquisition: core readings*, P. Bloom (ed.), 154–173. Cambridge, Mass.: The MIT Press.

Markman, E. M. 1994. "Constraints on word meaning in early language acquisition". In L. Gleitman and B. Landau (eds), *The Acquisition of the Lexicon*, 199–227. Cambridge, Mass.: The MIT Press.

Marlsen-Wilson, W. and L. K. Tyler. 1980. "The temporal structure of spoken language understanding". *Cognition* 8: 1–71.

Marlsen-Wilson, W. 1989. "Access and integration: Projecting sound onto meaning". In *Lexical representation and process*, W. D. Marlsen-Wilson (ed.), 3–24. Cambridge, Mass.: MIT Press.

Matthews, P. H. 1991. *Morphology*. Cambridge University Press.

Mertz, E. 1989. "Sociolinguistic creativity: Cape Breton Gaelic's linguistic "tip"". In *Investigating obsolescence: Studies in language contraction and death*, N. C. Dorian (ed.), 117–137. Cambridge: Cambridge University Press.

Meyer, M. C., W. L. Sherman, and S. Deeds. 1999. *The Course of Mexican History*. New York: Oxford University Press.

Milroy, L. and L. Wei. 1995. "A social network approach to code-switching: the example of a bilingual community in Britain". In *One speaker, two languages: Cross-disciplinary perspectives on code-switching*, L. Milroy and P. Muysken (eds), 136–157. Cambridge: Cambridge University Press.

Milroy, L. and P. Muysken. 1995. "Introduction: code-switching and bilingual research". In *One speaker, two languages: Cross-disciplinary perspectives on code-switching*. L. Milroy and P. Muysken (eds), 1–14. Cambridge: Cambridge University Press.

Milroy, L. and S. Margrain. 1980. "Vernacular Language Loyalty and Social Network". *Language In Society* 9: 43–70. Cambridge, Mass.: Cambridge University.

Milroy, L. 1987. *Language and social networks* (2nd edition). Oxford: Basil Blackwell.

Mithun, M. 1984. "The evolution of noun incorporation". In *Language*, 60: 847–894.
Mithun, M. 1989. "The incipient obsolescence of polysynthesis: Cayuga in Ontario and Oklahoma". In *Investigating obsolescence: Studies in language contraction and death*, N.C. Dorian (ed.), 243–257. Cambridge: Cambridge University Press.
Molina A. de. 1571b. *Vocabulario en Lengua Castellana y Mexicana*. [México: A. de Spinos. Facsimile edition: Colección de Incunables Americanos, Siglo XVI, Vol. IV.] Madrid: Ediciones Cultura Hispánica, 1944.
Molina, A. de. 1571a. *Arte de la lengua Mexicana y Castellana*. [México: P. Ocharte. Facsimile edition: Colección de Incunables Americanos, Siglo XVI, Vol. VI.] Madrid: Ediciones Cultura Hispánica, 1945.
Mougeon, R. and E. Beniak. 1989. "Language contraction and linguistic change: The case of Welland French". In *Investigating obsolescence: Studies in language contraction and death*, N.C. Dorian (ed.), 287–312. Cambridge: Cambridge University Press.
Mufwene, S. 1986. "The Universalist and Substrate Hypotheses Complement One Another". In *Substrata versus universals in Creole languages*, P. Muysken and N. Smith (eds), 129–162. Amsterdam: John Benjamins.
Mufwene, S. 1999. "On the Language Bioprogram Hypothesis: Hints from Tazie". In *Language Creation and Language Change: Creolization, Diachrony, and Development*, M. DeGraaf (ed.), 95–127. Cambridge, Mass.: The MIT Press.
Mufwene, S. 2001. *The Ecology of Language Evolution*. Cambridge: Cambridge University Press.
Muysken, P. 1981. "Halfway between Quechua and Spanish: the case for relexification". In *Historicity and Variation in Creole Studies*, A. Valdman and A. Highfield (eds), 52–78. Ann Arbor, Michigan: Karoma.
Muysken, P. 1988. "Media Lengua and Linguistic Theory". *Canadian Journal of Linguistics*, 33 (4): 409–422.
Muysken, P. 1994. "Media Lengua". In *Mixed Languages: 15 Case Studies in Language Intertwining*, P. Bakker and M. Mous (eds), 201–211. Amsterdam: IFOTT.
Muysken, P. 1995. "Code-switching and Grammatical Theory". In *One speaker, two languages: Cross-disciplinary perspectives on code-switching*. L. Milroy and P. Muysken (eds), 177–198. Cambridge: Cambridge University Press.
Muysken, P. 1997. "Media Lengua". In *Contact Languages: A Wider Perspective*. S.G. Thomason (ed.), 365–426. New York and Amsterdam: John Benjamins.
Muysken, P. 2000. *Bilingual Speech: A Typology of Code-Mixing*. Cambridge: Cambridge University Press.
Mühlhäusler, P. 1980. "Structural Expansion and the Process of Creolization". In *Theoretical Orientations in Creole Studies*, A. Valdman and A. Highfield (eds.), 19–55. New York: Academic Press.
Mühlhäusler, P. 1990. "Tok Pisin: Model or special case". In *Melanesian Pidgin and Tok Pisin*. J.W.M. Verhaar (ed.), 171–186. Philadelphia and Amsterdam: John Benjamins.
Myers-Scotton, C. 1993a. *Duelling Languages: Grammatical Structure in Codeswitching*. New York: Oxford University Press.
Myers-Scotton, C. 1993b. *Social Motivations for Codeswitching*. New York: Oxford University Press.

Myers-Scotton, C. 1995. "A lexically based model of code-switching". In *One speaker, two languages: Cross-disciplinary perspectives on code-switching*, L. Milroy and P. Muysken (eds), 233–256. New York: Cambridge University Press.

Myers-Scotton, C. 1998. "A way to dusty death: the Matrix Language turnover hypothesis". In *Endangered Languages: Language Loss and Community Response*. L. Grenoble and L. Whaley (eds), 289–316. Cambridge: Cambridge University Press.

Myers-Scotton, C. 2001. "Explaining Aspects of Code-Switching and their Implications." In *One Mind, Two Languages: Bilingual Language Processing*. Malden, Mass.: Blackwell Publishers.

Nicol, J. L. (ed.). 2001. *One Mind, Two Languages: Bilingual Language Processing*. Malden, Mass.: Blackwell Publishers.

Paradis, M.. 1997. "The cognitive neuropsychology of bilingualism". In *Tutorials in Bilingualism: Psycholinguistic Perspectives*. A. M. B. de Groot and J. F. Kroll (eds), 331–354. Mahwah, New Jersey: Lawrence Erlbaum Associates.

Penfield, J. and J. L. Ornstein-Galicia. 1985. *Chicano English: An Ethnic Contact Dialect*. Philadelphia: John Benjamins.

Pfaff, C. W. 1979. "Constraints on language mixing". *Language*, 55 (2): 291–318.

Pinker, S. 1996. *Language Learnability and Language Development*. Cambridge, MA: Harvard University Press.

Poplack, S., and M. Meecham. 1995. "Patterns of language mixture: nominal structure on Wolof-French and Fongbe-French bilingual discourse". In *One speaker, two languages: Cross-disciplinary perspectives on code-switching*. L. Milroy and P. Muysken (eds), 199–232. Cambridge: Cambridge University Press.

Poplack, S., D. Sankoff, and C. Miller. 1988. "The social correlates and linguistic processes of lexical borrowing and assimilation". *Linguistics*, 26: 47–104.

Poplack, S. 1982. "Sometimes I'll start a sentence in Spanish y termino en español": toward a typology of code-switching. In *Spanish in the United States*, J. Amastae and L. Elías-Olivares (eds), 230–263. New York, N. Y.: Cambridge University Press.

Poulisse, N. 1997. "Language production in bilinguals". In *Tutorials in Bilingualism: Psycholinguistic Perspectives*. A. M. B. de Groot and J. F. Kroll (eds), 201–224. Mahwah, New Jersey: Lawrence Erlbaum Associates.

Pullum, Geoffrey K. and Arnold M. Zwicky. 1988. "The syntax-phonology interface". In *Linguistics: The Cambridge Survey: Volume 1: Linguistic Theory: Foundations*. F. J. Newmeyer (ed.), 281–302. New York: The Cambridge University Press.

Radford, A. 1988. *Transformational Grammar*. New York: Cambridge University Press.

Reesink, G. P. 1990. "Mother tongue and Tok Pisin". In *Melanesian Pidgin and Tok Pisin*, J. W. M. Verhaar (ed.), 189–306. Philadelphia and Amsterdam: John Benjamins.

Relinger, W. and Park, T.-Z. 1980. "Language mixing in young bilinguals". In *Journal of Child Language* 7 (2): 337–352.

Rhodes, R. 2000. Review of P. Bakker, *A Language of our own: The Genesis of Michif, the Mixed Cree-French Language of the Canadian Métis* (Oxford: Oxford University Press). *Journal of Pidgin and Creole Languages* 15 (2): 375–381.

Rickford, J. 1988. *Dimensions of a Creole Continuum*. Palo Alto, CA: Stanford University Press.

Romaine, S. 1988. *Pidgin and Creole Languages*. London: Longman.

Romaine, S. 1989. "Pidgins, Creoles, Immigrant, and Dying languages". In *Investigating obsolescence: Studies in language contraction and death*, N.C. Dorian (ed.), 369–383. Cambridge: Cambridge University Press.

Romaine, S. 1995. *Bilingualism*. 2nd Edition. [Language in Society 13.] Cambridge, Massachusetts: Blackwell.

Rosch, E. and C.B. Mervis. 1975 "Family Resemblances: Studies in the Internal Structure of Categories". *Cognitive Psychology*, 7: 573–605.

Rosch, E., C.B. Mervis, W.D. Gray, D, M. Johnson, and P. Boyes-Braem. 1976. "Basic Objects in Natural Categories". *Cognitive Psychology*, 8: 382–439.

Rosch, E. 1975. "Cognitive Reference Points". *Cognitive Psychology*, 7: 533–547.

Rosetti, A. 1945/49. "Langue mixte et mélange des langues". *Acta Linguistica*, 5: 73–79.

Sankoff, D., S. Poplack, and S. Vanniarajan. 1990. "The case of the nonce loan in Tamil". *Language Variation and Change* (2): 71–101.

Sapir, E. 1921. *Language: An Introduction to the Study of Speech*. New York, N.Y.: Harcourt Brace Jovanovich,.

Sánchez, R. 1982. "Our linguistic and social context". In *Spanish in the United States*. J. Amastae and L. Elías-Olivares (eds), 9–46. Cambridge: Cambridge University Press.

Schacter, J. 1993. "A New Account of Language Transfer". In *Language Transfer in Language Learning*. S.M. Gass and L. Selinker (eds) 32–46. Amsterdam/Philadelphia: John Benjamins.

Schreuder, R. and B. Weltens. 1993. "The Bilingual Lexicon: An Overview". In *The Bilingual Lexicon*. R. Schreuder and B. Weltens (eds), 1–10. Amsterdam/Philadelphia: John Benjamins.

Schwegler, A. Forthcoming. "Creolistics in Latin america: Past, present, and future." In *Pidgin and Creole Linguistics in the 21st century*. Glenn Gilbert (ed.). Frankfurt/New York: Peter Lang.

Selinker, L. and U. Lakshmanan. 1993. "Language Transfer and Fossilization". In *Language Transfer in Language Learning*. S.M. Gass and L. Selinker (eds), 197–216. Amsterdam/Philadelphia: John Benjamins.

Seuren, P. and H. Wekker. 1986. "Semantic Transparency as a Factor in Creole Genesis". In *Substrata versus universals in Creole genesis*, P. Muysken and N. Smith (eds), 57–70. Amsterdam/Philadelphia: John Benjamins.

Sharwood Smith, M. 1994. *Second Language Learning: Theoretical Foundations*. London and New York: Longman.

Siegel, J. 1997. "Dialectal difference and substrate reinforcement in Melanesian Pidgin". Paper presented at the annual meeting of the Society for Pidgin and Creole Linguistics, London, June 26, 1997.

Silva-Corvalán, C. 1994. *Language Contact and Change: Spanish in Los Angeles*. New York: Oxford University Press.

Singh, R. 1981. "Aspects of language borrowing: English loans in Hindi". In *Sprachkontakt und Sprachkonflikt*, P.H. Nelde (ed.), 113–116. Wiesbaden: Steiner.

Singler, J.V. 1993. "African Influence upon Afro-American Language Varieties: A Consideration of Sociohistorical Facts". In *Africanisms in Afro-American Language Varieties*, S.S. Mufwene (ed.), 235–253. Athens, Ga.: University of Georgia Press.

Slabbert, S., and C. Myers-Scotton. 1997. "The Structure of Totsitaal and Iscamtho: Code-switching and Ingroup Identity in South African Townships". *Linguistics* 35: 317–342.

Slobin, D. I. 1985. "Crosslinguistic Evidence for the Language-Making Capacity". In *The Crosslinguistic Study of Language Acquisition. Volume 2: Theoretical Issues*, D. I. Slobin (ed.), 1157–1256. Hillsdale, N. J.: Lawrence Erlbaum.

Smith, M. C. 1997. "How Do Bilinguals Access Lexical Information?" In *Tutorials in Bilingualism: Psycholinguistic Perspectives*, A. M. B. de Groot and J. F. Kroll (eds), 145–168. Mahwah, New Jersey: Lawrence Erlbaum Associates.

Spencer, A. 1991. *Morphological theory: an introduction to word structure in generative grammar*. Cambridge, MA: Blackwell Publishers.

Sullivan, T. D. 1988. *Thelma D. Sullivan's compendium of Nahuatl grammar*, W. R. Miller and K. Dakin (eds). [Translated from Spanish by Thelma D. Sullivan and Neville Stiles.] Salt Lake City: University of Utah Press.

Sweetser, E. 1988. "Grammaticalization and semantic bleaching". In *Berkeley Linguistics Society, Proceedings of the Fourteenth Annual Meeting*, 389–405.

Thomason, S. G. and T. Kaufman. 1988. *Language Contact, Creolization, and Genetic Linguistics*. Berkeley: University of California Press.

Thomason, S. G. 1997a. "Introduction". In *Contact Languages: A Wider Perspective*, S. G. Thomason (ed.), 1–8. New York and Amsterdam: John Benjamins.

Thomason, S. G. 1997b. "Mednyj Aleut". In *Contact Languages: A Wider Perspective*, S. G. Thomason (ed.), 449–468. Amsterdam/Philadelphia: John Benjamins.

Thomason, S. G. 1997c. "Ma'a (Mbugu)". In *Contact Languages: A Wider Perspective*, S. G. Thomason (ed.), 469–487. Amsterdam/Philadelphia: John Benjamins.

Thomason, S. G. 2001. *Language contact: an introduction*. Washington, D. C.: Georgetown University Press.

Traugott, E. C. and B. Heine. 1991. "Introduction". In *Approaches to Grammaticalization: Volume 1*, E. C. Traugott and B. Heine (eds), 1–13. Amsterdam/Philadelphia: John Benjamins.

Traugott, E. C. and E. König. 1991. "The semantics-pragmatics of grammaticalization revisited". In *Approaches to Grammaticalization: Volume 1*, E. C. Traugott and B. Heine (eds), 189–218. Amsterdam/Philadelphia: John Benjamins.

Traugott, E. C. 1982. "From propositional to textual and expressive meanings; some semantic-pragmatic aspects of grammaticalization". In *Perspectives on Historical Linguistics*, W. Lehmann and Y. Malkiel (eds), 245–271. Amsterdam/Philadelphia: John Benjamins.

Traugott, E. C. 1988. "Pragmatic strengthening and grammaticalization". In *Berkeley Linguistics Society, Proceedings of the Fourteenth Annual Meeting*, 406–416.

Van Hout, R. and P. Muysken. 1994. "Modeling lexical borrowability". In *Language Variation and Change*, 6 (1): 39–62.

Van Rheeden, H. 1994. "Petjo: the mixed language of the Indos in Batavia". In *Mixed Languages: 15 Case Studies in Language Intertwining*, P. Bakker and M. Mous (eds), 223–237. Amsterdam: IFOTT.

Vigil, J. D. 1980. *From Indians to Chicanos: The dynamics of Mexican American culture*. Prospect Heights, Ill.: Waveland Press.

Volterra, V. and Taeschner, R. 1978. "The acquisition and development of language by bilingual children". *Journal of Child Language* 5: 311–326.
Wang, W. S-Y and C. Lien. 1993. "Bidirectional diffusion in sound change". In *Historical linguistics: problems and perspectives*, C. Jones (ed.), 345–400. New York: Longman Publishing.
Watson, S. 1989. "Scottish and Irish Gaelic: the giant's bedfellows". In *Investigating obsolescence: Studies in language contraction and death*, N. C. Dorian (ed.), 41–59. Cambridge: Cambridge University Press.
Waxman, S. R. 1994. "The development of an appreciation of specific linkages between linguistic and conceptual organization". In *The Acquisition of the Lexicon*, L. Gleitman and B. Landau (eds), 229–257. Cambridge, Mass.: The MIT Press.
Weinreich, U. 1953 (reprinted in 1968). *Languages in Contact*. The Hague: Mouton.
West, M. 1953. *A General Service List of English Words*. London: Longman, Green and Co.
Whitney, W. D. 1881. "On Mixture in Language". *TAPA* 12: 5–26.
Woolard, K. A. 1989. "Language convergence and language death as social processes". In *Investigating obsolescence: Studies in language contraction and death*, N. C. Dorian (ed.), 355–368. Cambridge: Cambridge University Press.
Wright, R. 1992. *Stolen Continents: The Americas through Indian Eyes since 1492*. New York: Houghton Mifflin.
Zobl, H. 1993. "Prior Linguistic Knowledge and the Conservation of the Learning Procedure: Grammaticality Judgments of Unilingual and Multilingual Learners". In *Language Transfer in Language Learning*, S. Gass and L. Selinker (eds), 176–196. Amsterdam/ Philadelphia: John Benjamins.

Name index

A
Andersen 86
Andrews 133, 136, 139
Arenas 155, 156
Aronoff 61, 62, 134 n.

B
Bakker 12–15, 36, 67, 125, 180
Bavin, 9 n.
Bloomfield 54
Boretzky 175
Bybee 33, 51, 57, 60, 66–68, 71, 102–103, 112, 113, 149, 194

C
C. Lehmann 33, 34, 37 n.
Clark 72, 73, 87, 103, 109, 148
Comrie 28, 35, 37, 39, 71, 191, 192
Corder 19, 189
Croft 28, 37, 71, 75 n., 143, 191, 192, 195 n.
Cutler 20, 89

D
de Arenas 155
de Groot 10, 84, 106, 182
Degraff 19, 20
Dixon 52, 53, 73, 74, 81, 147, 149, 150

F
Friederici 99 n., 112

G
Golovko 13, 45, 176, 178
Greenberg 12, 69, 175–177, 179
Grosjean 5, 11, 20, 83, 84, 90n., 181, 186

H
Haugen 2, 8, 9, 16, 17, 22, 26, 35, 198
Hawkins 47, 58, 63, 80, 88, 90, 116, 158, 159
Heath 42, 85 n., 171, 190 n.
Heine 30, 32–34, 67, 71, 72, 75, 79, 106, 107, 113, 193
Hill 86 n., 123–125, 127–130, 132–140 144, 157, 158, 185 n., 188
Hoffmann 3 n., 10
Hopper 23, 30, 32–34, 37n., 67, 71 n., 72, 91 n., 193

J
Jackendoff 72, 80 n.
Jake 11, 168 n., 188

K
Karttunen 125, 131, 132, 134, 136, 146, 147, 150, 151, 154–157, 160, 164
Katamba 58, 61, 67, 68
Kaufman 1–4, 12, 26, 39, 85 n., 123, 173–178, 197
Kroll 31 n., 106, 183

L
Landau 72, 108, 113
Levelt 87, 89, 91 n., 101 n.
Lockhart 125, 131, 132, 134, 136, 146, 147, 150, 151, 154–157, 160, 164
Lyons 55, 56, 60, 140, 192

M
Markman 72, 73, 108 n.
Matthews 59, 192
Milroy 126, 197 n.

Molina 150–152, 156, 163
Mous 13, 15 n., 174–176
Mufwene 19, 180
Muysken 5, 6, 10, 16 n., 17, 22, 35, 36 n., 67, 114, 125 n., 126, 143, 144 n., 181, 183, 184 n.
Myers-Scotton 1, 4, 9, 11, 16, 18, 25, 44 n., 140, 143 n., 168 n., 175, 176

P
Poplack 9, 16, 44 n., 184
Poulisse 182

R
Romaine 3, 10, 36, 85, 154, 184, 197
Rosch 101, 107–109

S
Sapir 26–30, 34 n., 53, 54, 100, 102, 103, 105, 113, 192
Seuren 86

Silva-Corvalán 9, 188, 189
Singler 19

T
Thomason 1–4, 11, 12, 14 n., 26, 39, 85 n., 123–126, 172–179, 197
Traugott 23, 30, 32–34, 37n., 67, 71 n., 72, 91 n., 193

V
Van Hout 5, 6, 10, 22, 35, 36 n., 114

W
W. Lehmann 65, 172, 188 n.
Weinreich 5, 8 n., 10, 13, 16
Wekker 86

Subject index

A
abstract 23, 30–33, 71–73, 83, 87, 102–106, 109, 110, 111, 115, 119, 120, 131, 140, 145, 149–153, 163, 167, 183, 193, 194
abstract nouns 45, 52, 76, 78, 101, 106, 109, 131, 151, 163
abstracted 71–73, 101
abstraction 106, 108
abstractness 100, 101, 108, 111, 112, 131
acquisition history 10, 13, 19–21, 83, 84, 119, 183, 186, 189, 199
acquisition scenario, *see* acquisition history
activity 71–74, 77, 81, 101, 114
additions 9, 105, 167, 189, 199
adjective 5, 7, 17, 18, 23, 35, 36, 38, 43 n., 46, 47, 49, 51, 53, 60, 64, 68, 72–74, 77, 79, 80, 94, 99 n., 103, 115–117, 120, 134, 135, 139, 141, 144, 146, 148 n., 155, 156, 159, 161, 171
adposition 15, 18, 30–32, 38, 54, 61, 63–67, 72, 74, 78, 79, 100, 103, 112, 115, 161, 167, 168
adverb 38, 60 n., 72, 139
agglutinating 28, 34, 37, 38, 40, 42, 43, 45, 62, 68, 94, 95, 99, 117, 118, 130, 132, 134, 137, 141–144, 147, 156, 162, 165, 168, 171–173, 176, 178, 194–196
agreement 59, 60, 63, 65, 69, 75, 80, 94, 96, 98, 103, 104, 115, 190, 193
alternational 16, 181 n., 183, 185 n., 187
animate 47, 74–76, 78–80, 106, 114, 134, 150–153
articles 42 n., 46, 63, 66, 67, 76, 96, 104, 154

aspect 11, 32, 55, 60, 63, 69, 76, 78, 79, 98, 100, 103, 137, 139, 144, 190–192
attrition 1, 21, 129, 154, 160
auxiliaries 59, 63–67, 78
Aztecs 123

B
base language 1, 16
    see also morphosyntactic matrix
bilingual 4, 8, 182, 183
bilingual acquisition 10, 19, 83, 119, 174, 181, 186
bilingual community 10, 13, 51, 84, 145, 154, 159, 182, 185, 189, 200
bilingual lexicon 10, 21, 169, 182, 200
bilingual mixtures 11, 12, 125, 200, 124, 125, 172, 174, 180, 200
bilingual performance 8, 11, 18
bilingual phenomena 18, 83, 126, 181, 186
bilingual speakers 26, 50, 51, 86, 143, 154, 159, 189, 198, 200
bilingual speech 9
bilingualism 2, 3, 10, 14, 83, 125, 126, 157, 179, 186, 198
bilinguals 6, 9, 10, 40, 51, 85, 85, 86, 127, 128, 143, 145, 176–178, 181, 182, 186, 189
bilinguals compound (Type B) 10
bilinguals coordinate (Type A) 10
bilinguals subordinate (Type C) 10
borrowability 5, 22, 26, 29, 34–40, 42, 43, 46, 63, 65, 70, 71, 82–84, 89, 99, 112–121, 143, 162, 163, 167, 169, 179, 173, 174
borrowing hierarchy 141, 146
    see also hierarchy of borrowability

borrowing scale 39
bound morphemes 13, 25, 38, 58

C

calques 8, 109
category value 89, 111, 137, 144,
  146–148, 156, 157, 169, 173,
  190–197
  see also inflectional categories
chronology of borrowing 154
  see also relative timing of
  borrowed elements
cline 22, 23, 27, 31–34, 37, 49, 71, 112,
  131, 132, 142, 161, 165
cline of grammaticality 29–32, 66, 67,
  78,
cline of grammaticalization, *see* cline of
  grammaticality
cline of lexicality 32
clitic 30, 33, 42 n., 66, 100, 194
  enclitics 66
  proclitics 66
closed-class 25, 61, 66
code-switching 1, 9, 10, 15–16, 44, 45,
  125–128, 130, 169, 181–187, 189,
  199, 200
  inter-sentential 16, 26
  intra-sentential 16, 21, 26
compatibility 15, 25, 41, 40, 41, 117,
  118, 127, 130, 165, 169, 173, 176,
  177, 190, 194, 195, 200
complementizer *que* 140, 159
complexity 29, 32, 36, 58, 92, 113–115,
  114, 115, 120, 132, 142, 161,
  171–173
composite matrix 187–189
compounding 112
concept types 81, 146–149
conceptual 87, 106, 108, 140, 163, 182,
  183, 195, 196
concrete 23, 26, 27, 29, 30, 33, 37, 45,
  51, 52, 54, 71–73, 75, 76, 78–81,
  85, 87, 93, 95, 100–102, 104–106,
  108–112, 114, 116, 119, 120, 131,
  145, 149, 150–152, 163, 167, 183

concrete nouns 45, 52, 72, 75, 76, 80,
  85, 93, 95, 102, 108, 114, 183
concreteness 100, 101, 104, 109–111,
  114, 119, 120, 145, 149, 151, 154,
  163, 167, 170, 171, 173
conjunctions 63, 64, 79, 107, 112, 139,
  140, 142, 159, 161, 167, 170, 198
connectives 63, 64, 100, 105, 139
contact 1–4, 8, 10–13, 15, 19, 21, 22,
  24–26, 35, 40, 42, 43, 46–50, 53,
  67, 83, 110, 117, 123–126, 130,
  132, 134, 141, 142, 144, 157, 159,
  160, 162, 165, 168–174, 176,
  178–181, 183, 187–190, 193,
  197–200
contact language 1, 11, 83, 124
contact phenomena 1, 10, 11, 15, 21, 24,
  25, 83, 117, 126, 168, 169, 180,
  181, 183, 189, 190, 199, 200
contact situation 11, 20, 40, 49, 117,
  141, 157, 159, 160, 165, 168, 171,
  187, 188, 190
contact-induced language change 1
content 9, 23, 25–27, 29, 30–34, 53, 54,
  57–62, 65–68
content item 5, 6, 10, 14, 15, 20, 29,
  34–39, 41, 43, 45–47, 53, 57, 58,
  59–62, 66–68, 73, 76, 81, 84,
  87–92, 94, 99, 103, 104, 112, 113,
  115, 116–120, 124, 130, 139–143,
  146, 147, 154, 156, 161, 162, 164,
  165, 166–168, 170–173, 195
content morpheme 5
content word, *see* content item
continua of forms 98, 113
continua of meanings 105, 113
convergence 1, 8, 24, 178, 186–188
co-occurrence 47, 98, 115, 124, 158,
  159, 186, 187, 198
coordinating conjunctions 64, 140, 159
creole 1, 7, 19–21, 123, 197, 200
creolization 6, 189,

D

demonstratives 59, 63

Subject index

derivational affixes 42 n., 60 n., 66–70, 143, 144
determiner 38, 62, 63, 65, 80, 101, 103–105, 112, 134 n., 139, 192
diminution of form 30, 32, 82, 92
dominant group 4
dominant language 2, 4, 35, 20, 21, 70, 123, 160, 172, 185–187, 190, 198
donor 2–6, 8, 9, 13, 14, 17–20, 24, 36, 39–42, 49–51, 67, 70, 81–86, 109, 110, 117, 118–120, 130, 141, 145, 160, 163, 165, 167, 170–173, 182, 184, 186, 195, 198

E
effects of borrowing 12, 16, 29, 49, 123, 124, 131, 154, 158, 159, 161, 187, 198
equivalence 5, 7, 17, 18, 31, 50, 52, 195
ethnic identity/status 21, 157, 158, 168, 175, 177, 197
ethnic language 21, 86 n., 127
ethnic marker 110 n.
exceptions 168, 173, 174
extension of meaning 72, 107,
extensive borrowing 3, 11, 16, 154, 173, 186, 187, 200

F
family trees 123, 172, 179
  see also genetic classification
genetic and non-genetic origins
FMIC 93, 104, 119, 120, 130, 144–149, 151, 166–170, 172
form class 5, 17, 18, 23, 30, 35, 36, 40, 42, 43, 49, 52–56, 70, 81, 82, 142, 146
formal characteristics 5, 18, 41, 57, 87, 166
formal properties 30, 88
form-meaning interpretation characteristic, *see* FMIC
form-meaning sets 83–88, 91, 94, 95, 127, 134, 136, 140–148, 150, 154, 159–163, 165–167, 170–173, 182–184, 186, 188, 189, 194, 199
free-standing 5, 13, 14, 18, 20, 25, 29, 30, 38, 39, 54, 56, 136, 139, 159, 193
frequency 5–7, 35, 36, 39, 43, 45, 67, 80, 86, 91, 100, 102, 109, 110, 120, 134, 137, 139, 142, 143, 151, 163, 186, 189
function item 14, 49, 99, 100, 141, 142, 147, 157, 159, 198
function word 3, 6, 14, 18, 20, 25, 26, 31, 34, 36–39, 43, 46, 53, 54, 57, 62, 65, 66, 70, 78–80, 85, 88, 89, 93, 94, 103, 104, 118, 120, 124, 136, 139, 140–142, 147, 148, 154–156, 158, 161, 162, 165, 167, 170, 171, 195, 198
fusional 28, 33, 34, 37–40, 42, 43, 45, 57, 60–62, 75, 87, 94–96, 98, 99, 103, 104, 117, 118, 120, 127, 131, 132, 137, 141–144, 146, 148, 161, 162, 165, 166, 171–173, 176, 194–197

G
gender 5, 11, 55, 59, 60, 63, 65, 69, 75, 76, 80, 94, 102, 103, 102, 104, 105, 115, 134, 157, 176, 177, 190–192, 196
general 87, 100, 101, 103–105, 107, 108, 110, 115, 119, 120, 131, 140 n., 145 n., 146, 151–154, 160, 167, 194
generality 61, 82, 100, 104, 108, 111, 112, 145
genetic and non-genetic origins 1, 123, 125
genetic classification 12, 124, 125
  see also family trees
grammatical affix 24, 30, 41, 53, 57, 59–61, 95
grammatical category 7, 11, 29, 33, 36, 37, 46, 59, 63, 65, 80, 81, 102, 104, 134
  see also inflectional category

grammatical concept, *see* grammatical meaning
grammatical items 28, 35, 37
grammatical meaning 7, 19, 27–33, 39, 53, 63, 195
grammatical morpheme 5, 13, 18, 38, 41, 176
grammatical prepositions 112, 147
grammaticality 29–35
grammaticalization 22, 23, 25–27, 29, 30, 32–35, 37, 38, 58, 61, 67, 69, 71, 72, 74–76, 78, 81, 82, 89, 92, 94, 99–102, 104–106, 109, 111, 112, 119, 120, 124, 131, 132, 142, 145, 161, 162, 164, 165, 171, 172, 188, 191, 193, 194, 198

H
hierarchy of borrowability 22, 26, 34, 35, 41, 117, 118, 142, 168
hierarchy of inflectional concepts 71
hierarchy of morpheme types 37, 38, 42, 43, 45, 142
homonymy 91, 93, 94
hyperonym 100, 108, 109, 146, 151, 153, 163, 167, 171
hyponym 100, 108, 109, 146, 151, 153, 163, 167, 171

I
imageable 101, 104, 147, 163
importation 2, 8, 11, 17, 49
inanimate 47, 74–76, 79, 106, 134, 150–152
incompatibility 15, 22, 40, 41, 49, 117, 118, 130, 148, 165, 169, 195
index of fusion 28, 43, 45, 132, 171–173
index of synthesis 28, 45, 62, 64, 124, 132, 159, 171–173
indigenous 14, 19, 20, 23, 24, 123, 128, 157, 158
inflectional affix 3, 25, 28, 29, 35–37, 39, 42, 43, 46, 53, 55, 57–59, 62, 66, 67–70, 74, 75, 81, 84, 85, 92–94, 99, 102, 104, 105, 120, 121, 123,
141, 142, 143, 146, 147, 149, 167, 170, 171, 190
inflectional categories 5n., 33, 38, 57, 61, 62, 67–70, 78, 82, 85, 89, 93, 94, 102–104, 109–113, 120, 137, 146–149, 157, 164, 168, 169, 173, 185, 190–196
see also category value
inheritance 192
inherited 12, 14, 192, 193
insertional 16, 181 n., 183, 185n.
integration 2, 6, 8, 9, 18, 21, 44, 81, 84, 86, 155, 161, 176, 182, 184, 185, 187
interferences 3, 10
interlanguages 1, 188
isolating-analytical 28, 34, 40, 45, 103, 118, 148, 154, 171–174, 178, 179, 195

L
language acquisition 1, 18, 19, 23, 27, 46, 73, 108, 113, 125, 143, 163, 181, 199
language attrition 1
language borrowing 4, 7, 9
language contact 8, 10, 15, 24, 25, 67, 117, 126, 144, 157, 168, 169, 174, 180, 181, 183, 189, 190, 197, 199, 200
language intertwining 11, 14
language mixing 1, 14, 19, 83, 123, 125, 126, 158, 180, 182, 183, 189
language mode 181, 182, 199
langue mélange 13
langue mixte 13, 14
legítimo mexicano 127
lexical access 10, 21, 90 n., 102 n.
lexical borrowing 1, 3, 8, 25, 49, 51, 81, 184, 186, 189, 198
lexical concepts 28, 33, 53
lexical donor see donor
lexical gaps 4, 161
lexical interference 10, 16

Subject index   249

lexical items 3, 6, 11–13, 19, 25, 26, 32, 36, 39, 68, 124, 130, 175–177, 179, 182, 187
lexical meaning 7, 26, 28, 29–33, 60, 68
lexical morphemes 13
lexical structuring 29, 31, 36
lexical system 102, 110
lexicality 30–33
lexicon 5, 6, 8, 10–12, 14, 16, 17, 21, 28, 29, 50, 52, 53, 56, 70, 105, 109, 110, 115, 124, 131, 132, 145, 162, 169, 174, 176, 178, 182, 184, 198, 200
linguistic environment 3, 83, 119, 149
linguistic factors 1, 5, 6, 10
loan translations 8, 83
loanblends 8, 109
loanshifts 8
loanwords 8, 9, 16, 17, 70, 160, 170, 188

M
Ma'a 11, 125, 126, 174–176, 178–180
mapping 31, 39, 76, 87, 90, 92–96, 95, 96, 98, 100, 101, 111–113, 119, 120, 162, 173, 194
material content see content
matrix 1–3, 11–14, 16–18, 20–22, 36, 39, 43, 45, 83, 84, 117, 130–132, 143, 144, 154, 159, 161, 162, 169, 174, 175, 177, 179, 181, 182, 183, 185–189, 193–195, 198, 200
see also morphosyntactic matrix
Media Lengua 11, 14, 18, 125, 126, 143, 144 n., 174, 179, 190
Mednyj (Copper Island) Aleut 11, 15 n., 45, 125, 175–177, 179, 180
mestizos 157
metaphorical abstraction 71, 106
metaphorical categories 73
metaphorical extension 72, 114
metaphorical processes 72
Mexicano 6, 9, 18, 23, 24, 43, 86, 123–137, 139–144, 149, 150, 154, 156–169, 172, 182, 185, 187, 188, 190, 195–198, 200

Michif 14, 15 n., 42 n., 43 n., 51, 67, 125, 126, 176, 178, 179
mixed language 1, 11–17, 20, 39, 42, 125, 126, 159, 162, 179, 180, 186, 189
mixing 1, 13–15, 19, 21, 83, 84, 123, 125–127, 157, 158, 178–180, 182, 183, 186, 189
modality 29, 63, 69, 84, 103, 111, 137
mood 29, 63, 69, 96, 103, 104, 137, 138, 192
morpheme types 5, 11, 15, 18, 22, 23, 33, 34, 38, 40–44, 49, 53–57, 61, 62, 70, 73, 78, 88, 117, 120, 142, 143, 156, 165, 168, 184
morphological integrity 42, 45, 49, 53, 117
morphological properties 27, 52
morphological structure 22, 25, 41, 44, 45, 49, 161
morphosyntactic matrix 2, 7, 14, 16, 22, 117, 128, 132, 144, 161, 162, 174, 175, 181, 183, 186–188, 189, 193
see also matrix
morphosyntactic system 11, 45, 88, 99, 102, 130, 143, 188

N
nativized forms 125 n.
new varieties 21, 200
nonce borrowings 9, 10, 16
noun 5, 7, 15, 22, 23, 35–37, 43, 45–47, 51, 52, 54, 55, 59, 60, 62, 64, 65, 67, 68, 73–80, 85, 93–96, 99, 101, 102, 106, 108, 111, 113, 114, 116, 117, 120, 123, 131, 134, 135, 141, 146, 149–152, 155, 156, 158, 161, 163, 166, 171, 172, 190, 192, 196
noun-to-affix cline 32, 37 n.
number 5, 11, 27, 49, 54, 55, 60, 62, 63, 65, 69, 74, 75, 80, 81, 96, 98, 100, 102–105, 111, 115, 134, 137, 138, 144, 156, 157, 173, 177, 190–193, 196
numerals 63

O

object (entities) 8, 29, 51, 52, 59, 60, 64, 65. 71–76, 78, 80, 81, 84, 87, 88, 101, 105–109, 114, 115, 134, 137, 139, 148, 163, 192
object (grammatical) 26, 64, 103, 115, 137, 139
obligatory 5, 59, 66, 67, 85, 92–94, 99, 100, 102, 103, 112, 119, 120, 131, 147, 148, 162, 167, 168, 173, 193
One-to-One Principle 86
ontological categories 71, 73, 80 n.
opacity 89, 90, 93, 94, 104, 119
opaque, *see* opacity
open-class 30
optional 99, 120, 131, 146, 147, 162

P

PCC, *see* Principle of Categorial Compatibility
PCI, *see* Principle of Categorial Incompatibility
perceptual properties 106, 163, 167, 183
perceptual salience 23, 26, 43, 58, 65, 89, 106, 108
performance 1, 8, 11, 18, 19, 21, 50, 114
phonemes 2, 17, 55, 90, 91, 98
phonological form 23, 58, 67, 100, 112
phonological processes 2, 33, 91 n.
phonological properties 54, 84, 91–94
pidgin 1, 6, 7, 19, 21, 123, 200
pidginization 6, 189, 200
polysemic extension 101
polysemy 91, 93, 94
possessives 54, 63, 100
postposition 64, 107, 136, 158, 159, 193
prestige 4, 86, 160, 197 n.
Principle of Categorial Compatibility 194–196
Principle of Categorial Incompatibility 169, 194–196
Principle of System Compatibility 15, 40–42, 50, 117, 119, 130, 143, 144, 165, 169, 187, 190, 194

Principle of System Incompatibility 15, 40–42, 44, 49, 50, 117, 118, 120, 121, 130, 131, 143, 156, 161, 165, 166, 168–170, 173, 187, 190, 194
proficiency 3, 6, 7, 10, 43, 70, 85, 117, 144, 145, 159, 165, 181–183, 185–187, 189
progenitor 13, 14, 123, 125, 132
pronoun 26, 46, 54, 63–67, 72, 74–76, 89, 104, 105, 112, 135, 139, 177
PSC, *see* Principle of System Compatibility
PSI, *see* Principle of System Incompatibility

Q

qualitative distinction 13
quality 20, 32, 71, 72, 79, 80, 101, 115, 150
quantifier 29, 63
quantitative measure 13

R

reanalysis 3, 5, 39, 44, 45, 49, 50, 53, 67, 81, 86, 125, 177, 178, 196, 234, 236
recessive 2, 4, 86, 160, 187, 190
recipient 2–6, 8, 9, 11, 13, 16, 18, 24, 39, 41, 42, 44, 45, 49–53, 70, 81–86, 99, 105, 109, 110, 114, 117, 118, 120, 132, 141, 160, 161, 163, 165, 171, 172, 182, 184–186, 190, 194, 195, 198
register 6, 24, 85, 129, 157, 166, 175, 176
relational 18, 27, 29, 33, 39, 53, 54, 61, 71, 75, 99, 100, 103, 136, 147–149, 159
relative pronouns 63, 64
relative timing of borrowed elements 46
   see also chronology of borrowing
relevance 6, 43, 46, 89, 109
relexification 9, 12, 17, 39, 47, 48, 125, 160, 177, 199
root 5, 6, 25, 29, 32, 34, 36–38, 40, 42, 43, 45, 52–54, 56, 60, 62, 66, 68, 69, 76, 77, 88, 89, 94, 95, 99, 111,

120, 118, 135–141, 143, 147, 159, 162, 165, 166, 170

S

salience 23, 26, 37 n., 38, 39, 43, 45, 46, 58, 64, 65, 67, 70, 84, 88, 89, 99, 100, 105 n.
salient, *see* salience
second/subsequent language acquisition 1, 19, 20, 125, 143, 163, 188
segmentability 28, 37, 70, 92–95, 99 n., 111, 119, 120, 166, 173, 194
segmentable, *see* segmentability
selection 9, 59, 61, 92, 93, 98–100, 111–115, 119, 120, 131, 145–147, 162, 166–168, 173
semantic bleaching 23, 30, 37 n., 71, 100
semantic characteristics 8, 15, 18, 30, 45, 46, 59, 62, 63, 71, 73, 100, 114, 131, 140, 147–149, 184, 190
semantic complexity 32, 36, 113–115, 121, 132, 142, 161
semantic extension 8, 83
semantic subtypes 51, 52, 55, 68, 73–81, 87, 102, 104, 105, 109–112, 114, 117, 119, 120, 131, 146, 148, 149, 151, 167
semantic transparency 6, 17, 23, 26, 37 n., 38, 39, 43, 46, 70, 84, 86, 87, 89–96, 98–100, 104, 110, 116, 119, 163, 176
semantic types 6, 23, 49–53, 60, 65, 69, 70, 72–74, 77, 78, 80, 81, 87, 102, 104, 107, 109–111, 117, 119, 131, 141, 146, 148, 149, 152, 164, 167, 168, 173, 195
sequential acquisition, *see* acquisition history
shape (phonetic) 9, 17, 90, 92–94, 98, 99, 107, 111, 119, 120, 145, 146, 162, 166, 173
shape (physical) 79, 106, 108
shift 4, 20, 21, 48, 86 n., 154, 160, 187, 199

simultaneous acquisition, *see* acquisition history
SLA, *see* second/subsequent language acquisition
social factors 1, 4, 49, 171
social identity 127, 157, 158, 177
social status 6, 176, 178
societal bilingualism 186
space 61, 71, 72, 74, 78, 103, 106, 123, 130, 148, 149, 183
Spanish 3, 5, 6, 9, 11, 17, 18, 21, 23, 24, 28, 30, 33, 36, 43, 49, 55, 58–60, 62–67, 75, 86, 89, 92, 94–96, 98, 99, 112, 123, 124, 125–135, 137, 139–144, 146, 147, 149–151, 150, 151, 154–163, 166–168, 172, 177, 180, 187–190, 192, 193, 196, 198, 199
specific 87, 101, 105, 107–109, 111 n., 113, 116, 120, 131, 145–147, 163, 164, 167
specificity 100, 104, 107, 108, 110, 111, 119, 120, 131, 145, 148, 151–154, 163, 167, 170, 171, 173
speech borrowing 4, 9
states and properties 74–80, 150–153
structural borrowing 3, 8, 12 n., 16, 131, 157, 186–188, 198, 200
subordinating conjunctions 64, 79, 140, 159
substitutions 9, 17, 189, 199
substrate 1, 7, 18–21, 200
syncretic 127
syntactic complexity 36, 115, 120, 132, 161, 171–173
synthetic types 104, 173

T

taxonomies 61, 72, 101, 108–110
tense 11, 27, 32, 33, 55, 58–60, 62, 63, 69, 75, 76, 78, 79, 89, 94–96, 98, 100, 102–105, 111, 137, 139, 144, 177, 190–193, 196
time 52, 54, 61, 71, 72, 78, 79, 103, 148, 191, 193 n.,199

transfer 1, 18–21, 50, 84, 184, 187, 188, 190, 199
see also interference
transparent, *see* semantic transparency
typology 22, 37, 40, 42, 43, 54, 124, 128, 164, 168, 169, 171, 172, 174

U
uniqueness of form 90–93, 111, 119, 145, 163
uniqueness of meaning 90–93, 145, 163
uniqueness point 90
unsegmentable, *see* segmentability
Uto-Aztecan 123, 132, 139

V
valence 103
verb 5, 7, 9, 17, 18, 22, 23, 32, 35, 36, 43, 46, 47, 55, 59–61, 63–68, 73, 74, 76–80, 93, 95, 96, 98–100, 102, 103, 105, 111–115, 114, 116, 117, 120, 132, 137, 139, 141, 144, 146, 155, 156, 161, 171, 177, 190, 191, 196

verb-to-affix cline 32, 33
voice 63, 69, 103

W
word 3, 5–10, 15, 16, 18, 22, 23, 25–28, 30–32, 34, 36–38, 41, 43, 45, 46, 49, 50–62, 65–77, 80, 81, 87–89, 92, 94, 98, 99, 107, 109, 111, 113, 115, 114–118, 120, 128, 129, 136, 139, 140, 142, 143, 145, 147, 150, 151, 152, 151, 152, 154, 155, 157–159, 162, 167, 176, 178, 183–185, 187, 194, 198
word class 15, 18, 50–53, 55, 56, 58–60, 69, 71, 77, 80, 81, 89, 107, 113, 115, 116, 139, 147, 184
Wutun 178, 179

In the STUDIES IN LANGUAGE COMPANION SERIES (SLCS) the following volumes have been published thus far or are scheduled for publication:

1. ABRAHAM, Werner (ed.): *Valence, Semantic Case, and Grammatical Relations. Workshop studies prepared for the 12th Conference of Linguistics, Vienna, August 29th to September 3rd, 1977.* Amsterdam, 1978.
2. ANWAR, Mohamed Sami: *BE and Equational Sentences in Egyptian Colloquial Arabic.* Amsterdam, 1979.
3. MALKIEL, Yakov: *From Particular to General Linguistics. Selected Essays 1965-1978.* With an introd. by the author + indices. Amsterdam, 1983.
4. LLOYD, Albert L.: *Anatomy of the Verb: The Gothic Verb as a Model for a Unified Theory of Aspect, Actional Types, and Verbal Velocity.* Amsterdam, 1979.
5. HAIMAN, John: *Hua: A Papuan Language of the Eastern Highlands of New Guinea.* Amsterdam, 1980.
6. VAGO, Robert (ed.): *Issues in Vowel Harmony. Proceedings of the CUNY Linguistics Conference on Vowel Harmony (May 14, 1977).* Amsterdam, 1980.
7. PARRET, H., J. VERSCHUEREN, M. SBISÀ (eds): *Possibilities and Limitations of Pragmatics. Proceedings of the Conference on Pragmatics, Urbino, July 8-14, 1979.* Amsterdam, 1981.
8. BARTH, E.M. & J.L. MARTENS (eds): *Argumentation: Approaches to Theory Formation. Containing the Contributions to the Groningen Conference on the Theory of Argumentation,* Groningen, October 1978. Amsterdam, 1982.
9. LANG, Ewald: *The Semantics of Coordination.* Amsterdam, 1984.(English transl. by John Pheby from the German orig. edition *"Semantik der koordinativen Verknüpfung"*, Berlin, 1977.)
10. DRESSLER, Wolfgang U., Willi MAYERTHALER, Oswald PANAGL & Wolfgang U. WURZEL: *Leitmotifs in Natural Morphology.* Amsterdam, 1987.
11. PANHUIS, Dirk G.J.: *The Communicative Perspective in the Sentence: A Study of Latin Word Order.* Amsterdam, 1982.
12. PINKSTER, Harm (ed.): *Latin Linguistics and Linguistic Theory. Proceedings of the 1st Intern. Coll. on Latin Linguistics, Amsterdam, April 1981.* Amsterdam, 1983.
13. REESINK, G.: *Structures and their Functions in Usan.* Amsterdam, 1987.
14. BENSON, Morton, Evelyn BENSON & Robert ILSON: *Lexicographic Description of English.* Amsterdam, 1986.
15. JUSTICE, David: *The Semantics of Form in Arabic, in the mirror of European languages.* Amsterdam, 1987.
16. CONTE, M.E., J.S. PETÖFI, and E. SÖZER (eds): *Text and Discourse Connectedness.* Amsterdam/Philadelphia, 1989.
17. CALBOLI, Gualtiero (ed.): *Subordination and other Topics in Latin. Proceedings of the Third Colloquium on Latin Linguistics, Bologna, 1-5 April 1985.* Amsterdam/Philadelphia, 1989.
18. WIERZBICKA, Anna: *The Semantics of Grammar.* Amsterdam/Philadelphia, 1988.
19. BLUST, Robert A.: *Austronesian Root Theory. An Essay on the Limits of Morphology.* Amsterdam/Philadelphia, 1988.
20. VERHAAR, John W.M. (ed.): *Melanesian Pidgin and Tok Pisin. Proceedings of the First International Conference on Pidgins and Creoles on Melanesia.* Amsterdam/Philadelphia, 1990.

21. COLEMAN, Robert (ed.): *New Studies in Latin Linguistics. Proceedings of the 4th International Colloquium on Latin Linguistics*, Cambridge, April 1987. Amsterdam/Philadelphia, 1991.
22. McGREGOR, William: *A Functional Grammar of Gooniyandi*. Amsterdam/Philadelphia, 1990.
23. COMRIE, Bernard and Maria POLINSKY (eds): *Causatives and Transitivity*. Amsterdam/Philadelphia, 1993.
24. BHAT, D.N.S. *The Adjectival Category. Criteria for differentiation and identification.* Amsterdam/Philadelphia, 1994.
25. GODDARD, Cliff and Anna WIERZBICKA (eds): *Semantics and Lexical Universals. Theory and empirical findings.* Amsterdam/Philadelphia, 1994.
26. LIMA, Susan D., Roberta L. CORRIGAN and Gregory K. IVERSON (eds): *The Reality of Linguistic Rules.* Amsterdam/Philadelphia, 1994.
27. ABRAHAM, Werner, T. GIVÓN and Sandra A. THOMPSON (eds): *Discourse Grammar and Typology.* Amsterdam/Philadelphia, 1995.
28. HERMAN, József: *Linguistic Studies on Latin: Selected papers from the 6th international colloquium on Latin linguistics, Budapest, 2-27 March, 1991.* Amsterdam/Philadelphia, 1994.
29. ENGBERG-PEDERSEN, Elisabeth et al. (eds): *Content, Expression and Structure. Studies in Danish functional grammar.* Amsterdam/Philadelphia, 1996.
30. HUFFMAN, Alan: *The Categories of Grammar. French lui and le.* Amsterdam/Philadelphia, 1997.
31. WANNER, Leo (ed.): *Lexical Functions in Lexicography and Natural Language Processing.* Amsterdam/Philadelphia, 1996.
32. FRAJZYNGIER, Zygmunt: *Grammaticalization of the Complex Sentence. A case study in Chadic.* Amsterdam/Philadelphia, 1996.
33. VELAZQUEZ-CASTILLO, Maura: *The Grammar of Possession. Inalienability, incorporation and possessor ascension in Guaraní.* Amsterdam/Philadelphia, 1996.
34. HATAV, Galia: *The Semantics of Aspect and Modality. Evidence from English and Biblical Hebrew.* Amsterdam/Philadelphia, 1997.
35. MATSUMOTO, Yoshiko: *Noun-Modifying Constructions in Japanese. A frame semantic approach.* Amsterdam/Philadelphia, 1997.
36. KAMIO, Akio (ed.): *Directions in Functional Linguistics.* Amsterdam/Philadelphia, 1997.
37. HARVEY, Mark and Nicholas REID (eds): *Nominal Classification in Aboriginal Australia.* Amsterdam/Philadelphia, 1997.
38. HACKING, Jane F.: *Coding the Hypothetical. A Comparative Typology of Conditionals in Russian and Macedonian.* Amsterdam/Philadelphia, 1998.
39. WANNER, Leo (ed.): *Recent Trends in Meaning-Text Theory.* Amsterdam/Philadelphia, 1997.
40. BIRNER, Betty and Gregory WARD: *Information Status and Noncanonical Word Order in English.* Amsterdam/Philadelphia, 1998.
41. DARNELL, Michael, Edith MORAVSCIK, Michael NOONAN, Frederick NEWMEYER and Kathleen WHEATLY (eds): *Functionalism and Formalism in Linguistics. Volume I: General papers.* Amsterdam/Philadelphia, 1999.

42. DARNELL, Michael, Edith MORAVSCIK, Michael NOONAN, Frederick NEWMEYER and Kathleen WHEATLY (eds): *Functionalism and Formalism in Linguistics. Volume II: Case studies.* Amsterdam/Philadelphia, 1999.
43. OLBERTZ, Hella, Kees HENGEVELD and Jesús Sánchez GARCÍA (eds): *The Structure of the Lexicon in Functional Grammar.* Amsterdam/Philadelphia, 1998.
44. HANNAY, Mike and A. Machtelt BOLKESTEIN (eds): *Functional Grammar and Verbal Interaction.* 1998.
45. COLLINS, Peter and David LEE (eds): *The Clause in English. In honour of Rodney Huddleston.* 1999.
46. YAMAMOTO, Mutsumi: *Animacy and Reference. A cognitive approach to corpus linguistics.* 1999.
47. BRINTON, Laurel J. and Minoji AKIMOTO (eds): *ollocational and Idiomatic Aspects of Composite Predicates in the History of English.* 1999.
48. MANNEY, Linda Joyce: *Middle Voice in Modern Greek. Meaning and function of an inflectional category.* 2000.
49. BHAT, D.N.S.: *The Prominence of Tense, Aspect and Mood.* 1999.
50. ABRAHAM, Werner and Leonid KULIKOV (eds): *Transitivity, Causativity, and TAM. In honour of Vladimir Nedjalkov.* 1999.
51. ZIEGELER, Debra: *Hypothetical Modality. Grammaticalisation in an L2 dialect.* 2000.
52. TORRES CACOULLOS, Rena: *Grammaticization, Synchronic Variation, and Language Contact.A study of Spanish progressive -ndo constructions.* 2000.
53. FISCHER, Olga, Anette ROSENBACH and Dieter STEIN (eds.): *Pathways of Change. Grammaticalization in English.* 2000.
54. DAHL, Östen and Maria KOPTJEVSKAJA-TAMM (eds.): *Circum-Baltic Languages. Volume 1: Past and Present.* 2001.
55. DAHL, Östen and Maria KOPTJEVSKAJA-TAMM (eds.): *Circum-Baltic Languages. Volume 2: Grammar and Typology.* 2001.
56. FAARLUND, Jan Terje (ed.): *Grammatical Relations in Change.* 2001.
57. MEL'ČUK, Igor: *Communicative Organization in Natural Language. The semantic-communicative structure of sentences.* 2001.
58. MAYLOR, Brian Roger: *Lexical Template Morphology. Change of state and the verbal prefixes in German.* 2002.
59. SHI, Yuzhi: *The Establishment of Modern Chinese Grammar. The formation of the resultative construction and its effects.* 2002.
60. GODDARD, Cliff and Anna WIERZBICKA (eds.): *Meaning and Universal Grammar. Theory and empirical findings. Volume 1.* 2002.
61. GODDARD, Cliff and Anna WIERZBICKA (eds.): *Meaning and Universal Grammar. Theory and empirical findings. Volume 2.* 2002.
62. FIELD, Fredric W.: *Linguistic Borrowing in Bilingual Contexts.* 2002.
63. BUTLER, Chris: *Structure and Function – A Guide to Three Major Structural-Functional Theories. Volume 1: Approaches to the simplex clause.* n.y.p.
64. BUTLER, Chris: *Structure and Function – A Guide to Three Major Structural-Functional Theories. Volume 2: From clause to discourse and beyond.* n.y.p.
65. MATSUMOTO, Kazuko: *Intonation Units in Japanese Conversation. Syntactic, informational and functional structures.* n.y.p.